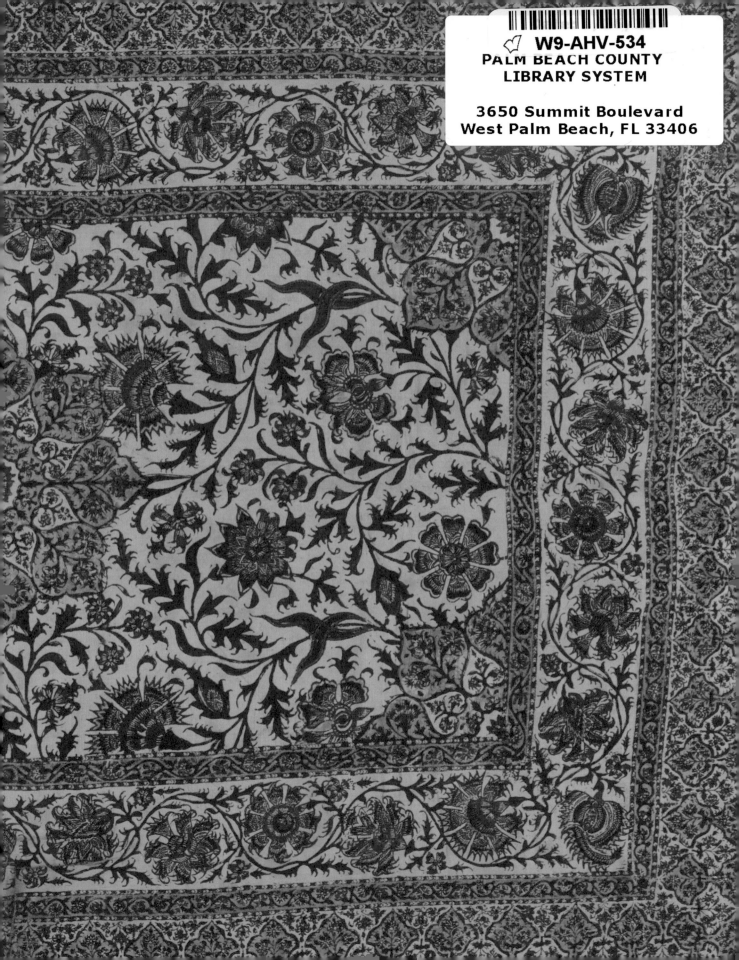

Yogurt

&

Whey

Yogurt

&

Whey

Recipes of an
Iranian Immigrant Life

HOMA DASHTAKI

W. W. NORTON & COMPANY
Celebrating a Century of Independent Publishing

This book is dedicated to all the immigrants who are, with humility, grace, and a relentless sense of humor, constantly explaining themselves to others.

And to my daughters, in whose strong and beautiful hands I place the responsibility, joy, and privilege of carrying on our traditions. Don't fuck it up.

Contents

Introduction

My Story

Although as a teenager I was particularly averse to helping out in the kitchen, cooking and food have since become the most useful tools in helping me make sense of my identity, my Iranian history, and my sense of belonging in America. I am Zoroastrian, the ancient culture and religion of the Persian Empire. My family is from a cluster of Zoroastrian villages in the province of Yazd, a desert region located in the center of modern-day Iran. My dad is from the village of Mobarakeh, and my mom is from the village of Ali-Abad. Though I spent most of my childhood in Tehran, our villages in Yazd were always home. The village of Mobarakeh, where we still have a home, is composed of a few dozen mud and straw houses. Each house has an open-air garden in the middle that children play in and herbs and trees grow in. On summer nights, to escape the heat, we'd climb up to the roof with our thin mattresses and sleep between the rolling bumps molded in the rooftop. As the sun set, the air finally cooled, but the mud rooftops still radiated heat. Without streetlights, there was nothing to see but the stars; without traffic, nothing to hear but the nearby bubbling spring. We woke to the sounds of villagers starting their days, sometimes calling across from their

rooftops, asking to borrow a shovel or inviting themselves over for dinner. There was no sleeping in. It was impossible to ignore the blazing sun and the flies buzzing about our ears and noses, desperately searching for moisture.

Mobarakeh is home to families of farmers. Each family has its own plot of land, and a centralized irrigation system brings well water to each plot from a big pool that channels out like veins from a heart. It is one man's job to switch the flow from one channel to another, the water meandering from farm to farm in equal allotments of time. Everyone plans their days and weeks around when the water comes. As kids, my cousins, sister, and I would chase the water through the village so we could play in the wake of its mud. Politics and war had not found their way to Mobarakeh.

As with all politics, the circumstances of the 1979 Iranian revolution are nuanced. The beginning of the revolution is marked by the Ayatollah's return to Tehran from exile on January 31, 1979: the day I was born. While I was too young to understand the politics unfolding around me as I grew up, I do remember the air surrounding Tehran as cautious and electric.

As quickly as the revolution caught fire in 1980, Iran entered into an eight-year war with Iraq. Sirens became part of my daily soundtrack. I walked to school with my dad, observing which buildings had turned into rubble the night before. But even in times of war and revolution, life goes on. We went to school and to work, attended birthdays and weddings; babies were born, and grandparents were laid to rest. We cooked and we ate.

Mobarakeh was where we went to feel safe from politics and war. It was a place to be at home despite the ostracism that affected non-Muslim minorities. It had become mandatory to wear hijab and abstain from makeup and alcohol. You risked arrest for playing music. Moving ahead in school or work required a knowledge of the Quran, which we minorities did not have.

When we drove south from Tehran to Mobarakeh, we left early in the morning. We cracked sunflower seeds between our teeth and sang along to popular Iranian songs in Farsi and to Zoroastrian tunes in our dialect of Dari. We brought sandwiches and tea and a whole watermelon and stopped for a roadside picnic lunch. After ten hours of driving, we arrived to family welcoming us with a dinner of stew, rice, herbs, and yogurt.

Zoroastrian living, in the deserts of Yazd, is dictated by the crops, the weather, the availability of water, and how many sheep can be sold or slaughtered. These factors informed our cuisine, and the festivals and celebrations that mark our calendar.

Nothing was wasted because there was no central trash pickup; whatever we discarded we discarded right in our own backyard. Because we were always staring down our own garbage, we took care not to waste anything that could serve a purpose. Plastic was hoarded for various tasks—from thatching roof leaks to makeshift Tupperware. Every drop of food was used, which led to delicious dishes and rich soups. Necessity dictated storing, fermenting, and preserving foods to last beyond the season it was harvested in.

Our day-to-day life was broken up by various harvest festivals, where we would cook for each other, give thanks, and gossip. The pomegranate harvest in October left the deepest imprint on me. When the pomegranates were ripe, we would go out to the orchards to pick the fruit, making two piles with the harvest—one pile of whole intact pomegranates, the other containing pomegranates with tears in their skins. Intact fruit stored well into the winter in their leathery encasings; where the skin was torn and exposed the pomegranate seeds to the air, the fruit had to be immediately eaten or juiced.

There were piles of fruit to clean and open, a collective haul from everyone's farms. Men and women worked together. While we performed the repetitive task of seeding

each pomegranate, we chatted. The piles of fruit transformed into piles of seeds, and all of those seeds went into a hand mill to be pressed out for juice. Pomegranate juice has a distinctive taste when you drink it immediately after pressing; even fifteen minutes of rest makes a difference in the flavor.

After lunch, when the sun made it too hot to work in the fields or to cook, we napped, rousing at four o'clock in the afternoon for a cup of hot tea, dates, dried mulberries or dried apricots—or even cake. As the sun set, we returned to work, preparing a wood fire and slowly cooking the pomegranate juice down into a paste well into the night.

The day after, I was always abuzz with energy and a sense of communion, knowing everyone had a portion of the same pomegranate paste we'd made together stowed away in their cupboards for the year to come. And the dishes we would cook with it! We'd spike stews with it as you might with tomato paste. The greatest of these dishes is Fesenjān, made with ground beef and walnuts (page 134).

Since my summers in Mobarakeh in the 1980s and '90s, the villages have emptied, the fields have dried, and harvests are unpredictable. Those days informed my understanding of community and, all of a sudden, that same community dispersed from our homeland to survive. Our family left for the United States, in search of peace and opportunities. At the peak of the Persian Empire, there were forty million Zoroastrians in the world. Currently, there are only 15,000 to 25,000 Zoroastrians remaining in Iran. I have always been sadly aware of our dwindling number.

My family moved to Southern California, where an enclave of Zoroastrians had flocked together. We enrolled in school and rented an apartment. My mom found a secretarial job; my dad secured a landscaping gig. I tried to assimilate to the lunchroom culture by enthusiastically embracing Ding Dongs and chocolate milk. At home, rice, stew, and yogurt remained the foundations of our meals. We snacked on homemade savory moosir yogurt with potato chips (page 91), and dried apricots, and soaked walnuts. My family's homemade foods were my comfort foods, but I worried that they put distance between me and the friends I wanted. I was ashamed that we made yogurt at home.

The second American holiday we adopted, after Valentine's Day, was Thanksgiving. It felt familiar—family and cornucopias of seasonal produce and giving thanks. My father, the primary cook in our house, staunchly held on to our Iranian roots and refused to cook American foods. My mother was more open to American culture, so she searched for recipes to make that holiday meal memorable. But her preparation betrayed her origins. Our first Thanksgiving turkey turned out green rather than the golden brown of TV and magazine spreads. She had instinctively chopped up all the herbs traditional to our Iranian dishes—cilantro, tareh, parsley, and tarragon—mixed them with butter, and encrusted that bird with a coat of chlorophyll. Today, I'd kill for that recipe. But back then, I thought I'd die of embarrassment and tried to block out our family's failure.

When we returned to Iran every summer, I felt at home in the food, language, sense of humor, and mannerisms of my family and friends, but I also felt alienated from the other girls I grew up with because we no longer had common ambitions and opportunities for our futures. I reassured myself that this was proof I was properly assimilating to America. But I couldn't shake the feeling there was something wrong with me. I didn't have any other examples of immigrant girls who were straddling both worlds.

In my early teens back in the States, I took on more cooking obligations around the house while my parents worked. I used food to play around with my sense of identity. I baked apple pie almost weekly because it was something I had seen on TV. I perfected making crust from scratch. I wanted so badly to change my culture, to feel some sense of connection, to belong. I cooked pasta and other dishes from *The Frugal Gourmet*. I was confused by my love for *Yan Can Cook*. I scanned the pages of *Better Homes and Gardens* for what "real Americans" ate. Once I made my family shrimp scampi in the microwave; I was proud for being cool and modern. My parents were appalled at how dry the meal turned out, and how small the portions were. We ended up having rice and yogurt that night.

When a meal went bad; yogurt was the default that saved the day. When we were low on money, yogurt was always there for comfort, which I would need down the line.

At nine years of age, just a year after moving to the States, I decided I'd become a lawyer. I loved the idea of writing contracts—of putting your black-and-white expectations on paper—and the respect that attorneys seemed to receive. In the legal field, my naive impression was that you were judged on intellect and accomplishment.

I chased every extra-credit point and did every extracurricular activity I could find in order to boost my résumé and chances to making that dream a reality. I studied literature and languages at UCLA and went to Cornell Law School on a scholarship. After graduation I landed a coveted six-figure-salary job, the kind that opened doors and changed lives. I clocked in hundred-hour weeks at a top-five law firm. I didn't love the actual work, but I loved being a lawyer. I loved the wardrobe and the intensity. I loved the money and the privilege that I had been so hungry to taste.

I was no longer living in the "consume what you need" mindset that I grew up with as a child—but rather "consume everything you can." And somehow this quest to continue growing and accumulating wealth and power and education and prestige started to become a goal in and of itself. This felt virtuous at the time. Grow to grow. Succeed to succeed. I embraced all of my unbridled ambition as a way to show I had truly made it in America.

At times when it didn't feel good or natural to be a corporate lawyer in Manhattan or to achieve just for achievement's sake, I would accuse myself of being ungrateful and force myself to stay on the path. I did this as a way to cope with the guilt of having opportunities my friends back in Iran didn't have, thinking (falsely) that many would kill to have the opportunity that lay before me. I thought I had to keep on this path to prove to Americans that I belonged in America.

Then, when the economy tanked in 2008, I was laid off. And while my hardcore personality pushed me to get back to work, back on the fast track, something else in me was reluctant to continue being an attorney. I couldn't recapture the mad drive that had propelled my life until that point. Every success, both in my life and in my career, seemed superficial. I was thirty-one and, for the first time, I stepped off the track. And all I felt was relief.

My first stop in the journey to eat-pray-love myself was in early autumn 2009. I went to work on an avocado farm in San Diego. Turns out avocado season in that area is in February, so I spent three months chain-smoking and watching movies as I let the gravity of the shift sink in. I moved on from the farm to other seemingly random activities. I painted. I taught yoga. I put on a dance production for the Fringe Festival. I exercised new parts of my brain and body. I held on so tightly to all the shape-shifting in hopes that I would soon find someplace to land.

In the winter of 2010, I headed to Iran for four months, where I filmed the Zoroastrians who lived in our villages of Yazd in hopes of making a documentary. It was mostly older folks who had remained in town, the youth having gone abroad or to the bigger cities for jobs. I met grandparents who were lonely and sad; I met folks my parents' age who were content and comfortable. I also met brilliantly innovative people who had maintained our cultural traditions of farming or innovated within the ethos that had guided us for centuries. One woman, the mayor of her town, told me how she converted a swimming pool into a fish farm so that her fellow villagers could get fresh fish (in the desert!). Those four months felt like a cathartic homecoming: I wasn't split between Iran and America, but I made sense as the combination of the two cultures.

Shortly after I returned from Iran, my father's brother, Amu Mehraban, died suddenly. Amu Mehraban was the uncle who had sponsored our green cards to the States. He'd been a force of nature, so charismatic that he'd been invited to moonlight as a minister in a Baptist church in North Carolina. A dark sadness fell over our home. My father was retired and I was unemployed, both depressed and very bored in the suburbs of Southern California. Two generations, two immigrants, and no clear path forward.

My family had always made yogurt from scratch. I had thought we made it at home only because we were cheap and didn't trust store-bought products, but I realized we also did it because it was comforting. Yogurt forces you to slow down. It takes a long time for the milk to boil—and an even longer time for the milk to cool. And in that time, everything feels better.

Making yogurt for the farmers' markets felt like the perfect choice to get us out of our rut. It was an opportunity to spend purposeful time together, to make something by hand, put it on sale, and operate in a low-pressure environment. It felt like a safe space to connect with my dad and with my heritage.

The time between my uncle's passing and our first sale snapped something very primal into place for me: this activity felt like home. And so it grew. We got permission to work in the kitchen of an Egyptian restaurant, Kerostena's, located in a strip mall near my parents' home. They allowed us to come in at nine o'clock in the evening and work through the night, packing out before morning. I had secured a booth at the Huntington Beach farmers' market in January 2011 and, suddenly, we were in business. We named our company The White Moustache, after my dad's large, white handlebar moustache.

All those hours spent boiling the milk, cooling it down, and straining the yogurt allowed my father and me to have endless cups of tea and conversations. I got to know him as an individual with stories and opinions and tastes. Amid discussion of flavors, he'd share long-forgotten stories of his sandwich shop back in Tehran. This sandwich shop defined my dad for most of my childhood. It was where he went to work every day after he dropped me off at school, and where we would get mortadella sandwiches and soda in glass bottles on Fridays as a treat. I've always been close with my father, but as we talked about the past, I found out so many additional little kernels of his life story. I came to learn that this shop was where he first worked when he came to the big city of Tehran from his small village of Mobarakeh. I learned that he was born in a barn, because it was December and the barn was the warmest room in the house. I learned that he used to throw discus for the town of Yazd and that he bullied the neighbor's son to do his home-work for him. I could feel his years of experience infusing themselves into each batch of yogurt we made, and I just wanted to sit around and drink tea and chat all day.

We show up with four gallons of plain yogurt on our first day at the farmers' market in Huntington Beach. We made twelve dollars— the sweetest twelve dollars I had ever made. I felt, for the first time, that I'd *earned* my pay. I was hooked.

Before long, we built a small, magnetic community. Hatem Nicola, the owner of Kerostena's, was a source of support and encouragement. And incredible kibbeh. Members of our Zoro-astrian community stitched the cloths we used to strain our yogurt. My cousin Ava helped at the farmers' markets. My mom's brother, Dayee Kaikhosrow, begrudgingly helped chop nuts and had an opinion (or seven) about how to make pre-serves. Yogurt was the excuse for this togetherness, the result of longing to connect and rebuild some semblance of communal village activities around food that we'd been yearning for ever since we left Iran.

There is poetic irony that making yogurt would be the way that I would finally gain a sense of belonging in America. Yogurt has been the thread that runs through my attempts at creating community, of being in touch with my ancestors. Yogurt is equally ancient and modern. The creation of yogurt was actually an accident. People did not have the proper means to store their milk, so it fermented and turned into yogurt. The Smithsonian discovered yogurt whey deposits left behind in dirty clay dishes from at least eight thousand years ago (definitely my relatives, given my track record with wash-ing dishes).

People continued to make and eat yogurt because it was a natural way to make milk last longer. Yogurt cultures preserve and, arguably, enhance the nutritious benefits of fresh milk. Such a simple method to preserve something so special. By the time I learned it, my parents and grandparents had been making it for generations using very basic techniques. The way I make yogurt, and even the way I *eat* yogurt, is based on their teachings.

❖ ❖ ❖

From our stall at the Huntington Beach farmers' market, we were invited to three more farmers' markets. And then we were accepted to the Laguna Hills farmers' market, which, in Orange County, California, means you have arrived.

Our first morning at this prestigious market in March 2011, a woman called from the California Department of Agriculture. She said I was illegally selling yogurt and I needed to shut down. I thought I was being pranked.

"If you don't shut down immediately," she said, "I will come and shut you down and have you arrested—with a possibility of one year of prison time and a fine of $10,000."

"I have a permit from the city and the county and the farmers' market. I think you're mistaken. I'm not the kind of business you want to be shutting down. What we make is totally safe. I can prove it," I said.

"You're dealing with dairy. That's enough. You're not the first. I shut down a Vietnamese family just a few weeks ago, and a Mexican family a month ago," she said.

I couldn't process what she was saying. All the intoxicating hope shrank instantly into loss. We loaded up the car and drove off. My sister describes my sobbing on that ride home as an animal wail, visceral and so sad. In this little yogurt business, raking in a little more than $300 a week, I had found belonging. I had found myself. The thought of losing that, especially to some bureaucratic bullshit, was unbearable.

After a solid day of quality moping, I dusted off my legal skills. Every drop of the eight gallons per week that we were making was my life, and my life was being threatened. So I fought.

I fought not just for myself, but also for the Mexican and Vietnamese families that had also been shut down. I had the privilege of my education and the fire of my freshly resolved identity crisis to fuel this fight. California state laws' implications for food businesses were clear: if you can't start big and stay big, you don't belong. It dawned on me that because of these types of regulations, no one in the United States was really making yogurt! Virtually all yogurt made in America is handled by machines. The milk is heated in a vat, then gets hosed into an incubation chamber before being strained via centrifuge. In most cases, the yogurt is incubated right in the individual plastic cups in which it is sold, along with thickeners and stabilizers. This is standard, in order to ease oversight by federal and state regulators. The White Moustache's yogurt was (and is) cultured, set, strained, and whisked by hand in separate, tiny batches before being parceled out into its individual glass containers for sale. We handle it every step of the way, checking for smoothness and thickness, examining its glossy sheen. What sets our yogurt apart was exactly what the law was designed to quash.

The following two years were a torrent of advocacy, legal work, and bureaucratic fighting. We submitted pH lab results and obtained pro bono counsel. We went to Sacramento and met with politicians. We teamed up with assemblyman Mike Gatto of our district to work on a cottage food bill. I wrote a plea to *The Economist* to save my eight-gallon-a-week yogurt business. They ran an earnest article in response, and got us a call from Kate Brown, the secretary of state of Oregon (and later governor), inviting us to move our operation to Portland. But, ultimately, even that most liberal and food-friendly of cities couldn't get on board. In most jurisdictions in the country, the only legal way to make yogurt to be sold is in a machine; no human hands should touch the product at any point to protect against unnamed pathogens. It is a rule from the 1970s that has been adopted by all fifty states.

As 2013 neared, I was broke, and broken. I felt heartsick that I hadn't made a single batch of yogurt since I began fighting to save the business. I had finally found something that made me make sense in America, something that I could contribute, and here was America shutting me out again. After two years of what felt like screaming in the wind, I had no viable plan to make my business work.

On a whim, I called up an old friend, Betsy Devine, who owns Salvatore BKLYN, makers of artisan ricotta. I asked if we could make one batch of yogurt in her space in Brooklyn as a final attempt to breathe life back into The White Moustache before I moved on. Betsy said yes, and my family and I hopped on a plane to New York. We made a batch during a blizzard in January 2013. I divvied up the batch and took it to four of the top grocery stores in New York City. After tasting our product, they all put in an order. "When can we get it?" "Two weeks! No problem!" Our dreams of making yogurt for a living were revived in New York City, where the laws were the same as in California, but the attitude was more open to accommodating the process. Regulators in New York State understood the importance of small artisanal products to the local economy and were willing to work with our process, to spend the time with us so we didn't have to compromise our traditions but could still satisfy their public health concerns. And so, The White Moustache and I abandoned our fight in California and officially immigrated to New York, starting a miraculous new chapter for our product and advocacy efforts.

A Political Whey Forward

Making yogurt using old-world techniques is a quiet but powerful act. It is an uncompromising exercise in using all parts of what the environment and climate give us. It pays homage to one of the most sacred ingredients we get from nature: milk. Our products are handmade and labor intensive. The White Moustache's business model is by design and intention not a volume business (and thus sometimes confusing to potential investors). The goal isn't to learn how to mass-produce, but to profit by staying small and connected to the product and our sources and our customers. And my heritage. This is our quiet political statement.

Merely existing is not the end of our advocacy efforts. We recognize that the value in our company is not just in the dollars that we provide our staff, but in the staff themselves. We also came to realize we could no longer continue to ignore the fact that yogurt companies' main byproduct—yogurt whey—was damaging to the environment.

Whey is the liquid reserve left after one strains yogurt. It is a glorious, nutritious, and hard-earned liquid form of yogurt. To my amazement when I started selling yogurt, I learned that almost all commercial yogurt makers throw away this incredibly versatile and nutritious liquid. I made it my mission to change this.

Initially it wasn't a problem, because making only eight gallons of yogurt yielded enough whey for our family to consume ourselves. But as The White Moustache started making more yogurt commercially, from twenty gallons to eighty-five gallons per day, we found ourselves swimming in whey. There is no market for whey in America, and whey, still being dairy, eventually goes bad. So we had to dispose of what we couldn't consume. But throwing out all that whey—which we had always thought of as perfectly good food—felt wrong.

And we were part of a much bigger food waste problem. Currently, most yogurt manufacturers pay to have their whey carted away. Some pay farmers to take it as animal feed. Pigs, cows, and chickens love it, but there's only so much they can consume. These manufacturers pay additionally for wastewater treatment companies equipped with anaerobic digesters to haul away their whey and convert it into biogas (usually methane), which can be converted into energy—a good use, I admit, but the process is expensive. University research departments are looking for other ways to use whey by separating out the protein, lactose, acid, and water for use in industrial food manufacturing, but these technologies are still in the early phases and, again, the process is expensive.

A 2013 article in *Modern Farmer* magazine by Justin Elliott, "Whey Too Much: Greek Yogurt's Dark Side," was one of the first media sources to call attention to the yogurt industry's open secret. The story—and several subsequent ones in other outlets—reveals how whey, if dumped directly and untreated into waterways, can destroy life therein. The bacteria already present in the water devour the lactose in the whey, which depletes the oxygen. With no oxygen, all the fish die. A high and unnecessary price to pay for thick, creamy yogurt.

Because The White Moustache is a small, handmade-yogurt company, we are closer to our product and feel the loss of the whey more personally. In our view, it's as nonsensical to throw out gallons of liquid yogurt whey as it would be to toss out gallons of solid yogurt. These two yin-yang products are equally nutritious. If you lived in a world where everyone knew what to do with egg yolks but always threw out the egg whites, wouldn't you share your knowledge and teach everyone about meringue?

And so, in August 2014, after only a year and a half in business, we made a conscious and intentionally un-savvy business move to cap our yogurt production until we had created a market for our whey. We were not going to make more yogurt and end up with more whey on our hands than we could use.

While it might be seen as a counterintuitive business decision to focus on selling an unfamiliar ingredient like yogurt whey, we see it as a long-term, ambitious strategy. Even if we make a ton of yogurt, it doesn't feel like a true success if we're creating all this waste. We consider our celebration of yogurt whey to be the greatest contribution that The White Moustache can make to the food system.

When we made yogurt at home, my family just drank the whey left over after straining. We considered whey to be hydrating, light, and an aid in digestion. My dad would have a sip, pass it to my mom, she would drink it and make a face, then I'd get it and take a gulp and pour some in the dog's water bowl before my sister would grab the glass, sip it, and give any remaining dribbles to a plant in the yard.

We thought that's how we would present it to consumers: Drink whey! There was no blueprint—there are no packaged whey drinks back in Iran or elsewhere in the world that I knew of to use as inspiration or reference. There is no widespread reference to using whey in cooking because home cooks have only a little bit of whey at their disposal. Commercial yogurt makers throw out the product or sell it to be dehydrated, making sure it never reached the mainstream the way yogurt had.

We put our whey in one-liter bottles and slapped on a label that said "Whey!" We went to stores that carried The White Moustache and asked the buyers to drink it. These bottles hit the shelves. We priced them fairly as a byproduct. The bottles shone bright with their natural neon-yellow hue, full of the probiotics, calcium, and riboflavin (a B-vitamin) that gives the whey its brilliant color. And then we waited. And waited.

No one knew what to do with the whey or which section of the store to put it in. Was it a juice? A kefir? Even stores that were fully behind the idea of a food product that reduced waste were unsure of how to communicate this to their customers.

And so, the customers did not come. Fearlessly honest New Yorkers were not shy about letting us know what they thought: "It's weird" and "The color is strange" and "We don't know what to do with it." We scrambled to make it more familiar, by adding descriptions of what whey was, how it tasted, and what to do with it, but the bottles of whey just didn't sell.

But where we failed in our attempts to explain whey's uses directly to retail customers, we found a curious and receptive audience with chefs, restaurateurs, and bartenders. They dazzled us with their creative applications. Chefs are trained to play with ingredients, to come up with new flavor and texture combinations, and to be acutely aware of the bottom line, finding uses for scraps and leftovers rather than throwing them away. Whey fit the bill perfectly, and so my traditional, old-world yogurt-making technique with its modern, new-world child (whey) was suddenly being tested, coddled, and heralded by talented chefs.

Holding fast to our yogurt-making technique and Zoroastrian values while celebrating the inspired innovation coming out of our New York City community felt like a symphony orchestra breaking out into a Britney Spears cover: fun, light, unexpected. That's how it feels to cook with yogurt whey.

Curbing our growth when we have a wait-list of stores that want the yogurt was a stubborn choice for a small company like ours to make. And yet, that commitment to slow down and look at all aspects of the business allowed us to grow and innovate in meaningful ways—ways that include setting aside the time to write this very book, a journey you are now a part of.

Watching The White Moustache succeed given all the obstacles and challenges we've faced has helped redefine my notions of success and failure. As the business grows, we're building a community of chefs, scientists, and home cooks who are inspired by yogurt and the process of making it. The recipes I've included in this book expand the range of what's possible with both yogurt and its incredible byproduct, whey. I hope this book inspires you to experiment and discover the magic for yourself.

My Zoroastrianism

Zoroastrianism is both my religion and my culture. It is woven like a bright ribbon into the fabric of my identity and worldview. I consider myself an avid practitioner of our ancient celebrations and our spiritual faith. Because the number of Iranian Zoroastrians is so small and many of our traditions are fading, I feel a great deal of responsibility to my community who read this book. It has taken me seven years of trying to write this book to understand that words on a page can never capture the depth of our Zoroastrian cultural heritage or the heaviness associated with being born into our circumstances.

Zoroastrianism is the first monotheistic religion in the world, dating back to the fifth century BCE. The tenets are simple and beautiful: Good Thoughts, Good Words, and Good Deeds. It teaches that each individual has the power to determine good and evil for themselves. Zoroastrianism encourages every person to make their own decisions, knowing that there is a path of righteousness and truth that is worth following for its own sake. And that deep down in each of us there is a goodness that guides the impact of our words, thoughts, and deeds on other people, animals, and the environment. Everything is of consequence.

When you think about Zoroastrianism as a whole, it is thriving. There are over 2 million people of all backgrounds who practice the Zoroastrian faith, which gives me a lot of hope that the religion will continue for generations to come. But when I think of the Iranian Zoroastrian community within the Iran that I was born into, I sense that I am mourning the end of a culture even as I celebrate it and watch other interpretations of it live on.

The religion dominated the Persian Empire with a peak of 40 million followers until Islam took over in the seventh century AD. Around 650 AD, a group of Zoroastrians left for India and evolved into a community and culture of their own known as Parsi Zoroastrians. They have since adopted their own language, food, dress, ceremonies, etc. The population that remained within Iran has declined steadily since. There are currently only 15,000 to 20,000 Zoroastrians left throughout Iran, mainly in the villages of Yazd and the suburbs of Tehran. And approximately 50,000 Iranians Zoroastrians, like myself, who have recently immigrated within the last generation or so, since the Iran-Iraq war in the 1980s. It is these Iranian Zoroastrians, both that celebrate our communal holidays in Iran and now here in the diaspora, that I identify with and celebrate our shared history.

Our minimalist religion is peppered with elaborate celebrations, ceremonies, and holidays, which are dictated by the sun, moon, and harvests of the seasons. Tirgān is our festival for water, held at the heart of summer, when we splash water on everyone to symbolize the coming of the rains. In the fall celebration of Mehragan, the community gathers to celebrate the harvest that will get them through the winter and pays respect to the land that gives them food and sustenance. In the winter, we celebrate Shabeh-Cheleh (Yalda), the longest night of the year, by staying up all night with poetry, music, wine, fruits, and nuts. The spring equinox is our New Year (NoRooz, "New Day"), when tradition dictates a meal of white fish and herb rice. In between these holidays are gahambars—harvest festivals that occur once every two months. Every family decides which of the six gahambars to hold in their home. The morning of a gahambar, we wake up, put on clean clothes, and go to the first house where the priest would do prayers around a sofreh, a spread of symbolic foods and candles. The host family serves whatever is within their means—as little as a piece of freshly baked bread or as generous as a meat stew. As you leave a gahambar meal, women grab the corners of their skirts and men their handkerchiefs, creating little slings for the host to toss in handfuls of lork, dried fruit, and nuts that were prayed over. Then everyone heads to the next house. The gahambar that my family historically hosts in the village of Mobarakeh is held in July. Since immigrating to the United States, we would regularly go back and uphold these celebrations in my dad's adobe home. Since becoming busy with our modern Western lives, it is now just my parents who have been going back almost every single summer to keep this tradition alive.

As I wonder what my role will be in the future of this community, both in Iran and in America, I think a lot about how my ancestors endured many tribulations in order to hand this religion down to me, wrapped in the comfort of our very own language, food, ceremonies, funeral rites, music, towns, clothing, and prayers. I try to share many of these in these pages.

And now being a part of the diaspora myself as an immigrant, I feel frozen in time and culture. To hold onto the culture you feel in your bones, while at the same time assimilating to survive in a foreign land, is an exhausting contradiction. I have barely maintained the use of our dari dialect; I eat see-rogh every few years instead of every few months; there are only a handful of weddings I go to where it is appropriate to yell, "Habiroh!" I feel the heartbreaking reality of being part of these traditions that are slowly disappearing—and of my role in that disappearance—as sometimes the maintenance of them seems contrived instead of being an effortless part of our daily existence.

I sometimes feel guilty and responsible for this. I did not marry a Zoroastrian, although my hot agnostic husband supports raising our beautify baby daughters as Zoroastrians. But as we predominantly speak English in our house, I shoulder the responsibility of teaching these traditions to my daughters in a bubble, when their peers and classmates will not be participating, where the community is fragmented across the country and across the world. The toughest part of being an immigrant, for me, is that in order to not merely survive but thrive in my new home, I have to acknowledge the constant dynamic tug between loss and gain, between erasure and reclamation. This book is a way to connect and capture all that I can about this experience, from a childhood staple of aash to a delightful slice of lemon meringue pie.

My elders all remind me that we must fight rigidity and be open to change—as they have done to survive. I think they are right, of course, and I hold onto that. But writing this book for what I assume will be mostly a non-Zoroastrian audience, I have tried to preserve as many recipes in here as possible—even if the only ones who use them will be my own children.

How to Use This Book

This book connects my family, our food, and our business across place and time. It covers the recipes of our life back in Iran, American dishes we have learned to adapt into our own, and innovative recipes we created using whey. The language of yogurt is woven throughout.

TRADITIONAL RECIPES

Traditional Zoroastrian recipes respect the seasons. As I mentioned earlier, in winter we would eat a lot of mixed nuts (lork or ajeel) and stew (often Aash-e-Reshteh, page 101) for the festival of Yalda, and in spring, I looked forward to the white fish and herb rice on NoRooz. Many of the foods are simple yet take time to make. The food and our ceremonies, holidays, and rituals are all connected. These recipes are like love letters to the bounty of the earth.

You'll notice that many of these recipes (particularly those that open the Soups and Stews chapter) have an uncommonly high yield. Whether fancy or not, they are traditionally prepared in great quantities in a community setting and then are enjoyed in a community setting. The time we invest in cooking is time to gossip, tease, and support one another. Our cooking, and our attempts to keep this culture alive, demands patience, perseverance, and company. To remain authentic to the preparation of these dishes, I have kept the yields high and encourage you to prepare them with your own feasts in mind.

I learned most of these recipes through oral tradition or through observation. Once I learned how to make them by "feel," they seeped deep into my bones. In writing down our recipes, I found myself struggling to be methodical. I wanted to give a lot of control to the reader: Add cilantro to taste. Butter to taste. Cardamom to taste. Coming up with ingredient measurements was challenging; these recipes have always been based on what's available. It makes no sense to me to have to say "2 cups chopped onions." When grocery shopping, we buy onions in *onion* quantity, not cup quantity. If there are three eggplants that are on the verge of going off, I can teach you to add the correct proportions of turmeric, tomatoes, and onions to help salvage those eggplants and turn them into something nourishing. I encourage you to try these recipes that may be unfamiliar, and I'm confident that once you cook them once, twice, maybe three times, you too will feel them in your bones.

WHEY RECIPES

The recipes in this book that incorporate whey are not based in any tradition or familiarity but born out of a commitment to preventing food waste. At The White Moustache, we work to make the greatest yogurt we can, and we value and cherish the whey that is a natural byproduct. A community of family, friends, chefs, customers, critics, and fans helped us figure out what to do with it.

While many of these whey recipes are variations on classics, they were all created by The White Moustache team and our growing culinary community. The style of these recipes will likely be the most familiar to contemporary cookbook users as they are modern creations. I'm excited to introduce you to an ingredient that has been around for a long time but that has not found a following yet. Consider yourself a pioneer. Build on the recipes we have gathered here to further explore an incredibly old food whose potential as an ingredient has remained largely untapped.

My Pantry

These are the ingredients that I cook with most often and that you will see throughout this book. Most, if not all, are available at well-stocked Middle Eastern stores.

BARBERRIES: Barberries (zereshk) are small dried berries, generally fried and used in Persian rice to add a pop of tart flavor. They are nonperishable and relatively easy to find online and in Middle Eastern grocery stores.

BREAD: Use bread to sop up condiments or dips and to cleanse your palate between bites. Some favorites you will find are lavash, pita, barbari, and sangak.

Noon-e-khoshk is a traditional Yazdi dried bread that we have been known to smuggle back to the States by the suitcase because it's so flavorful and good. It is made from wheat flour, flavored with cumin or rye, cooked into flatbreads in a clay oven, and then left in a hot, dry room until it is completely dry. This results in what is essentially an enormous cracker (18 to 20 inches in diameter) that you break into pieces and eat with soup all year long.

DRIED LIMES (ALSO CALLED OMANI LIMES): Dried limes are a staple in Iranian soups and stews to add a bright and concentrated citrus flavor. For the dishes in this book, make sure to choose the ones with brown skins and not black skins, which are more bitter. I use them whole (see Dizi, page 105, and Ghormeh Sabzi, page 132), but you can also pulverize them in a food processor and sprinkle them into any dish or sauce that needs an extra citrusy kick. Find them in Persian markets. My trusted brand for these is Sadaf. They're shelf-stable and will last for many years.

DRIED MINT: Dried mint packs a more concentrated punch than fresh mint. The dried mint I call for is of the spearmint variety, not peppermint. Dried peppermint is used for more sweet preparations, whereas spearmint lends itself better to savory soups and stews, such as Persian Egg Drop Soup (page 107) or Yogurt Stew (Aash-e-Maast, page 97). You can find dried mint at most grocery stores.

To dry your own, wash whole mint sprigs and drain in a colander. Arrange the sprigs in single layer over a tea towel and allow to air-dry for several days at room temperature.

Once completely dried, crumble the leaves and compost the stems. Dried mint may be stored in an airtight container for months without losing much of its flavor.

FRESH HERBS (SABZI KHORDAN): A few of my recipes call for fresh herbs that may be a challenge to find (you won't be able to order them online, as they don't hold up well in the mail). If your nearby Middle Eastern or Indian grocery doesn't have them, order some seeds and start growing them.

In addition to the familiar parsley, mint, cilantro, and basil, it's worth seeking out fresh fenugreek (shambalileh), tareh (sometimes referred to in stores as Persian leeks), tarragon (talkhoon), and cress (shahi).

How you prepare the herbs depends on whether you are cooking them or eating them raw. For cooking, you can leave the hardy stalks and stems on, as they will cook into a soft mush. For eating raw, you can strip off the tougher stalks and set them aside to cook with later.

The recipes that call for herbs to cook with (Ghormeh Sabzi, page 132, and Aash-e-Reshteh, page 101), as well as those that call for herbs to serve raw alongside a dish (Dizi, page 105, and Kabab Koobideh, page 128), require a three-step washing method. Washing fresh herbs is very important as they tend to grow in bunches close to the ground and collect and retain the earth when they are plucked.

Next, dry the herbs: Spread a single layer onto a large, clean tablecloth or towel. The herbs should not be stacked on top of each other; you want them to air-dry.

To store your clean herbs, wrap in a cheesecloth in the fridge. They will stay fresh for up to three days.

KASHK AND KASHK SAUCE: Kashk are soured, dried yogurt balls that last for years. Kashk sauce is the rehydrated form of kashk. I include my recipes for Kashk (page 54) and Kashk Sauce (page 57) so you can make them at home. If you are not

---

To Wash Herbs

Fill a sink or large tub with cool water, dump in the herbs, and tussle them through your fingers with a little vigor, shaking them loose from each other and letting any dirt settle to the bottom of the tub. Soak for 5 minutes, then skim the herbs off the top (they will float) and put them in a colander. Empty out the tub or sink and rinse out any visible dirt. Repeat this process three times.

making your own kashk, I suggest buying it in its rehydrated form, as sauce. You can find it sold in jars in the refrigerated section, where it is sometimes (incorrectly) labeled "whey sauce."

MEAT: I gravitate toward the meat recipes I grew up with, which call for such cuts as beef tongue and lamb neck. In the United States, these cuts may be less sought-after and therefore harder to find, but I assure you they exist. If you don't see the meat you need to make the Fried Tongue Sandwich with Labneh (page 157) or the Dizi (page 105), ask your butcher to help. She may have some in the back of the shop and may even agree to a significant discount if you ask.

MOOSIR: Moosir is an ingredient lost in translation. It is sometimes referred to in the West as a shallot—and, sadly, many packaged versions carry this misleading translation. In actuality, moosir is not from the allium family at all. Botanically, it is the bulb of the grape hyacinth flower (*Leopoldia comosa*). It is usually packaged in its dehydrated form in slices and must be rehydrated to release its flavor. It is deeply savory, earthy, and pungent, and there is no substitute. Moosir features most prominently in Maast-o-Moosir (page 64), a classic Iranian condiment.

POMEGRANATE MOLASSES: Pomegranate molasses (sometimes sold as pomegranate syrup) is simply concentrated pomegranate juice. It can be added to stews or to sauces the same way you might use tomato paste, or to replace balsamic vinegar in dressings and drizzles. Though it's now more readily found in supermarkets, I recommend making your own pomegranate molasses at home. This allows you to control the viscosity, tang/sweetness, and even color.

To make, simply pour pure pomegranate juice into a pot and simmer until it is reduced to roughly 80 percent of its volume, depending on how viscous you would like it. I recommend making it this way first and getting a feel for its resulting tang and color. Next time, before boiling the juice, you can add some sugar to sweeten it and a roughly cut cooked beet if you'd like a richer purple color. Either way, stir continuously as it simmers to prevent burning. Let cool overnight at room temperature, remove any beet chunks (if you used them), and transfer the molasses to an airtight bottle. It will keep at room temperature for at least six months.

RICE: Mastering Iranian cuisine starts with the right kind of rice. Parboiled white rice is not going to work. Neither is Texmati rice, for that matter. Head to an Indian or Middle Eastern grocery to seek out long-grain basmati rice. Its fragrance, flavor, and texture really are extraordinary.

ROSE WATER: Rose water is used in Iranian sweets and drinks to add a welcoming floral note. It is distilled from rose petals, and though it has a strong fragrance, it is used primarily for flavor. Look for pure rose water that does not contain rose oil or alcohol, as they will make your food taste perfumy and bitter. Cortas and Sadaf are brands I recommend.

SAFFRON: Saffron, the stamen of the crocus flower, is an aromatic addition to many Iranian meals. The flower blooms for just a few weeks and the stamens must be picked by hand. Though it is expensive, only a few threads of good-quality saffron are needed to flavor a dish. Crush the threads with a mortar and pestle, then steep them in a little hot water for 15 to 20 minutes right before use so they achieve the full expression of their flavor and color (as in Persian Rice, page 124). Conventional supermarket brands are generally not potent enough to be worth their while, so I would splurge on true Iranian saffron from a reputable Iranian grocer. A little bit of the good stuff will go an extremely long way.

SALT: In most recipes, I use kosher salt, so consider this the default. However, every old aunty I know makes rice with rock salt, so I do too, and I encourage you to do so in those recipes as well. Rock salt dissolves in water, has very large grains, and is sometimes called ice cream salt. Morton's makes a version that is available in most grocery stores. Finally, I opt for sea salt when making pickles.

SOUR GRAPE JUICE: This is the juice of a very sour green grape (ghooreh). The ghooreh is typically picked and juiced when it is still raw so it is particularly tart. This juice is used to flavor soups, stews, and vegetable side dishes. You can also add a splash of it to salad dressings or even a cocktail for a fun little pucker.

SUMAC: This ground powder is made from crushing the red berries of the sumac plant. I sprinkle it on top of rice and kababs to add a bright lemony taste and love the dramatic color it imparts to a bowl of Maast-o-Moosir (page 64) or Maast-o-Khiyar, (Cucumber Yogurt, page 66). Sumac is available in many mainstream grocery stores.

WHEY: Every recipe that calls for whey in this book refers to yogurt whey—the liquid obtained by straining yogurt, a technique I lay out on page 50. If you are not making your own whey, or need gallons of whey, you'll need to learn how to track down yogurt whey. It may be closer than you think (see Need Even More Whey? on page 51). Also, please note that cheese whey and yogurt whey are not the same substance; they have different flavors and pH levels and behave differently in recipes. Cheese whey is therefore not an acceptable substitute for yogurt whey in any of my recipes. (See Acid Whey versus Sweet Whey, on the opposite page.)

YOGURT: All yogurt called for in these recipes is homemade plain cow's whole milk yogurt (The White Moustache Yogurt and Whey, page 47). I always indicate whether a recipe requires strained yogurt instead. Each recipe will specify one of the following: either plain whole milk yogurt or strained (Greek-style) whole milk yogurt. (See Strained versus Unstrained Yogurt, page 44.)

ZIZIPHORA: Ziziphora (kakooti), a medicinal herb, is often used to make a beverage known as Doogh (page 235), either in combination with or in place of dried mint, and it shares some similarities of flavor with that more common herb. Grown in the mountains of Iran, it is nearly impossible to find in the United States, but no discussion of Iranian herbs would be complete without mentioning it. Lore holds that kakooti has cancer-fighting properties as well as scientifically documented digestive benefits. Yogurt with kakooti is a potent, delicious combination.

Acid Whey versus Sweet Whey

Acid whey—yogurt whey—is a product of the yogurt-making process, and has the same acidity level as the yogurt it comes from. So, technically, if you're going to call it acid whey, you should call it acid yogurt as well. Yogurt and yogurt whey are about as acidic as orange or tomato juice and far less acidic than most soft drinks, energy drinks, or even kombucha. Any whey derived from straining yogurt contains the same probiotics, and many of the same nutrients, as the yogurt itself, minus all the fat, which remains in the solid part.

Yogurt whey is only acidic compared to its milder-sounding counterpart, sweet whey. Sweet whey—lower in acid and higher in protein—is a byproduct of some kinds of cheesemaking. Sweet whey can taste sour when cheesemakers salt their curds before straining them. Sweet whey is also the key ingredient in many brands of protein powder. Sweet whey has not been tested as an acceptable substitute for yogurt whey in the recipes in this cookbook.

At the Table: The Accoutrements of an Iranian Meal

I've devoted a portion of the Condiments chapter to recipes for the accompaniments present on the Iranian table at every meal. They add a kick and brightness to nearly every dish. Think of using condiments as a chance to "choose your own adventure" with every bite, doctoring each individual morsel or spoonful to your liking. Here is a list of the usual accoutrements of an Iranian meal:

YOGURT: A bowl of yogurt is always on the table as a way to add a tangy kick to the food, and also to encourage a variety of texture, taste, and temperature in each bite. The yogurt is mostly likely homemade, usually plain, but may also be dressed up with moosir, cucumbers, rose petals, walnuts, or dried mint.

FRESH HERBS (SABZI, AKA GREENS): There is always a heaping platter of fresh herbs, including basil, mint, green onions, cilantro, tareh, cress, fenugreek, and parsley, along with a bunch of radishes and usually some water-soaked walnuts. To eat, simply imagine the flavor you want to add to your next bite—take a spoonful of food into your mouth and grab your herbs to go with it.

FETA: Feta cheese adds a creamy, salty addition to the meal. Feta is usually grabbed with the herbs, rolled in a piece of bread, and eaten throughout, like a break from your entrée. Walnuts, radishes, and green onions make a welcome appearance in these bites, too.

BREAD: Either lavash—a light flatbread—or barbari—a thick, fluffy flatbread topped with nigella seeds—is on hand to soak up stew or dip into yogurt. It is at the table even when there is also rice—there is no such thing as too many carbs on the Iranian table.

TORSHI: Vegetables of all kinds are pickled and add a colorful acidic kick to all meals. Some of my favorites are Torshi Makhloot (Mixed Iranian Pickle, page 72) and Torshi Sír (Black Garlic Pickle, page 73). Even plant parts that would normally go to waste can get the torshi treatment. I've been known to pickle cauliflower stems, cilantro stems, you name it!

FRIED GARNISHES: Additional garnishes accompany two Iranian recipes in this book,

Aash-e-Reshteh (page 101) and Eggplant and Kashk (page 86). Typical on these two dishes, in addition to a drizzle of kashk, is copious amounts of fried garlic, fried onions, and fried mint oil. I beg you to have fun with this family of garnishes. The bright white color of the kashk makes a beautiful mosaic, peppered with the caramel sheen of the onions and the emerald hue of the mint oil. These garnishes are a unique way to communicate warmth and beauty to your guests.

HOT AND COLD FOODS

Many Iranians have adopted the teaching that there is a duality in foods: some foods have hot properties and some have cold properties. There are similar teachings in China—the yin and yang of foods—and also in Ayurvedic principles, associated with present-day India. Using these ancient teachings, you can balance the body's disposition and functions through food.

Hot foods include meat, carrots, mint, and honey; some cold foods are fish, yogurt, and pomegranates; and tea and onions are considered neutral. If you have a "hot" disposition, you should eat cold foods to balance yourself out. If it is summertime, counterintuitively, you should try to avoid having foods that are too cold, as that is a contradiction. When you have a cold, there will be a million differing opinions on what types of food to eat, depending on the season and so on. If you are pregnant, you are encouraged to not eat too many hot foods, which are thought to increase the risk of miscarriage. If you are depressed or down, do not have too many cold foods, as they will further slow you down. We are taught by our parents, who were taught by their parents. Questions often go out the window over time—you just "know" and learn not to question your elders.*

The idea of balance is key in Iranian cooking. This is why you see a lot of hot and cold dishes paired. This is why yogurt (a cold food) and various herbs and walnuts (hot) are always at the table so that each person may balance out their meal. It's also why yogurt and fish—two cold foods—are thought to make you stupid if eaten together. Taste and completely unprovable anecdotes aside, we are cognizant that food becomes a part of our anatomy, and affects our body, mind, and spirit.

---

* The FDA has not reviewed any of these claims. This is not legal medical advice. I don't even think it counts as scientific advice, to be quite sure. But all this information has been reviewed by my aunt, and frankly there hasn't been a toothache or a tummy ache that she hasn't accurately navigated me through. Just waiting on the FDA to catch up to her level of wisdom.

WHAT TO SAY: NOOSHEH-JAAN

There's a phrase we say before eating: "Noosheh-Jaan." The translation—according to my favorite Los Angeles restaurant's commercial on Iranian television—is "May your soul enjoy it." The ultimate goal is to care for your guests, be they new acquaintances, dear friends, family, or enemies. No meal, and no person at the table, is taken for granted.

HOW TO SAY IT: THE ART OF TAHROF

Tahrof is the Iranian art of saying yes when you mean no and saying no when you mean yes. It is a delicate dance of etiquette that has no equivalent in English but is the epitome of good manners. To the unacquainted, it will be extremely frustrating. Even some Iranians who adopt American customs and go back to Iran can get it wrong. Tahrof is like a fine-tuned flirtation between host and guest, a little dance of give and take, to get to the bottom of one's desires. Iranians pride themselves on their generosity and hospitality, and probably also their tolerance of discomfort and high threshold for pain—especially when it comes to being a good host or guest. We will feed you until you cry mercy or roll out the door.

Let's say there is only one slice of watermelon but there are two people. I, the host, offer you the slice of watermelon and, according to tahrof, you should refuse. Even if you have just walked in from a five-mile hike through the desert and your lips are falling off from dehydration: in a display of gracious manners, you decline. I will split the slice of melon and hand you half. You still refuse; I'll offer again. Finally, you take it not because you want it, but because you want to make me happy by not refusing me.

This can be maddening. Your host would think it rude that you don't take what is being offered. Your being vegetarian has absolutely no bearing on the host offering you a piece of lamb continuously over the course of a meal; maybe you will change your mind on the fifth offer. It's torturous, but effective. If more diplomats understood this nuance, we would get much further in politics.

FILLING THE VOID: FOR MISSING GUESTS

If a family member is missing, we will all say: "Jayeh [insert name of missing person] sabz." Translation: "The place of [person who is missing] is green." Further translation: "May we keep [person who is missing]'s place open for him or her." Furthest translation: "Man, I wish my cousin was here."

Naming Conventions

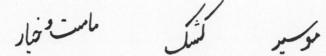

Given that I have written this book in English, I use English words wherever possible. For example, chai-e simply means "tea" and so I call it tea, as I feel little is lost here and I'm sensitive to exoticizing certain recipes. However, sometimes the translations do lose the essence of the word. For example, noon-khoshk directly translates to "dried bread," but it's not just any sort of dried bread and I'd be worried it would be confused for a crouton.

Other times, there is no appropriate translation at all for an ingredient of a dish and so I have chosen to refer to them only in the Iranian language—with no translation. I want you to learn that moosir and kashk are ingredients with no American equivalent. They are what they are, and if I were to offer an imprecise translation just to make them more familiar or accessible, something crucial would be lost.

Similarly, I have thought a lot about when and where I use "Persian" versus "Iranian." For the most part here, I have proceeded on instinct, and I hope you will trust me as you come along.

FOUNDATIONAL

RECIPES

Do not surrender your grief so quickly
Let it cut more deeply
Let it ferment and season you
As few human or divine ingredients can

Something is missing in my heart tonight
That has made my eyes so soft
And my voice so tender
And my need of God so absolutely clear.

—**HAFIZ**

Informed by my ancestors,
my simple yogurt-making technique
combines milk and probiotics with time and
patience. I invite you to make the yogurt once, then
make it again. And then again, each time discovering
the magic that is not just yogurt but also yogurt whey.
It is my hope that you'll fall in love with yogurt
and take comfort in it as I have.

An Introduction to Yogurt

Yogurt is the magic that happens when you have the perfect combination of living ingredients and the right temperatures to make them thrive. It is an exquisitely simple process that takes my breath away with each and every batch.

MILK

Milk, believe it or not, was at one time considered a byproduct. Nomads kept goats, sheep, and cows to provide meat, leather, wool, manure, and labor. When livestock's offspring were born, they would nurse from their mothers, and then move on to grazing. But the mothers continued to lactate, resulting in extra milk. With this rich milk, humans began incorporating nutrient-dense cheese, yogurt, and milk into their diets from around 8000 BC.

Modern dairy farms, particularly in the United States, have varied approaches to milk production, and thus sourcing good milk is crucial to having good yogurt. Labels such as local, organic, grass-fed, and raw lead to much confusion and political deliberation, and the debate rages on about the health benefits of low-fat or nonfat milk versus whole.

UNHOMOGENIZED MILK: The best milk possible, in my opinion, is unhomogenized whole milk that comes from a small dairy. Homogenization is a mechanical process that breaks apart the fat globules under thousands of pounds of pressure, leaving the fat suspended and the milk more consistent throughout. I prefer unhomogenized milk because it's the way the milk came out of the cow and has not been mechanically altered. It also makes for a creamier yogurt because you haven't manipulated the fat globules. When you make yogurt with unhomogenized milk, a layer of fatty, creamy yogurt will rise to the top of your batch. Simply mix it well before eating it. If, however, you can find only homogenized milk, don't worry—your yogurt will still turn out delicious!

RAW MILK VERSUS PASTEURIZED MILK: I prefer raw milk because the yogurt-making process requires you to boil the milk anyway and, ideally, that would be the only time in the milk's life that it is heated. You don't want to overwork the milk or its sugars too much, in part to maintain its distinct flavor. However, because raw milk can be hard to find, and there are strict rules around it depending on where you live, using pasteurized milk is fine.

AVOID ULTRA-PASTEURIZED MILK: If the best you can find is supermarket "organic" milk, be sure it's not ultra-pasteurized. Ultra-high-temperature (UHT) pasteurized milk is essentially dead and, in my experience, won't make successful yogurt. That means you also want to steer clear of any milk sold outside of a refrigerator section. This applies primarily to those living outside of the United States, where shelf-stable UHT milk in boxes is much more common.

WHOLE VERSUS 2 PERCENT MILK: As I said earlier, I want my milk as close as possible to the way the cow made it, so my yogurt recipe uses whole milk. Most whole milk has only about 4 percent fat content. If you do choose reduced-fat milk, there will be differences in the taste and texture of the yogurt. When you boil reduced-fat milk, the sugars normally found in the cream of whole milk will not be there to enhance the creamy-sweet taste or texture. As a result, yogurt from reduced-fat milk will be more tart, even sour, and the consistency will be stretchier, like a very wet dough.

COW'S MILK: Nondairy milk and yogurts have proliferated of late—almond, soy, coconut, oat, and so on—but this book's focus is on yogurt and whey made from cow's milk. The milk of goats, sheep, and even camels all make delicious yogurt with different textures, fat contents, flavors, and health benefits, but they require slight variations in cooking time and technique.

PROBIOTICS

In yogurt-making, probiotics are bacteria that feed on lactose, sugars found in milk, and create lactic acid. These probiotics turn milk into yogurt, preserving the milk so it can last much longer. Like yeast, probiotics are alive! But unlike yeast, which dies when you bake a loaf of bread, probiotics stay alive in your yogurt and continue thriving in the billions!

Probiotics have been held up as the cure for everything from digestive problems to

autism. I am not a scientist and can't substantiate these claims on a molecular level. Everyone's body has a different balance. These are matters only you and your health care providers can take on at the individual level.

To produce yogurt on a commercial scale in the United States, you are legally required to use powdered probiotics. When you make yogurt at home, you can and should use already-made yogurt as a starter culture or "mother"—either plain yogurt you get from the store or your own previous batch. Why? Because it's thriftier than purchasing commercial probiotics when your previous batch is already alive and thriving. If you have a nice batch, it can continue to perpetuate itself over time with just a bit of care. Each batch requires only a few tablespoons of starter culture. When using a store-bought yogurt as your starter, make sure the only ingredients in the yogurt are milk and probiotics. If you live in a city where The White Moustache is available, such as New York and Los Angeles at the time of this writing, our yogurt is jam-packed with billions of probiotics that make for a potent starter. We use seven different strains of probiotic bacteria.

STRAINED VERSUS UNSTRAINED YOGURT

Commercially marketed "Greek" or "strained" yogurt refers to yogurt that is thicker because the liquid whey has been removed. Many cultures strain their yogurt, not only the Greeks—indeed, Chobani, a well-known American brand, was founded by a Turkish man. To call strained yogurt "Greek yogurt" is a convenient shorthand that we at The White Moustache also resort to for our line of strained yogurt simply because the Greeks beat us to the market. We do call our unstrained yogurt "Persian" yogurt even though we also recognize that many cultures do not strain their yogurt either.*

The vast majority of recipes in this book call for yogurt that has not been strained. I refer to this in the ingredients list throughout as "plain whole milk yogurt." On those few occasions when a recipe benefits from the thicker consistency of strained yogurt, I call instead for "strained (Greek-style) whole milk yogurt."

---

* Missed opportunity here to make a joke about Persian-Greek cultural rivalry.

STABILIZERS, THICKENERS, AND PRESERVATIVES—AND WHY WE DON'T USE THEM

If the ingredients label on your store-bought plain yogurt lists powders, stabilizers, thickeners (such as powdered milk, starches, gelatin, or vegetable gum) or anything other than milk and probiotics, it is being artificially thickened. There is no need to use these additives to get the consistency you desire. The probiotic cultures themselves act as the stabilizing, thickening, and preservative agents in the yogurt. Naturally. By manipulating the temperature and length of time for which these cultures incubate in the yogurt, you can manipulate the thickness and the sourness; keep your yogurt a little warmer and incubate it for longer if you fancy a nice tangy pop of flavor.

You can further achieve the thickness you desire simply by mastering the straining process. The chemical and artificial stabilizers, thickeners, and preservatives many commercial yogurt companies use mimic and speed up what probiotics and straining are perfectly capable of doing on their own (with a little help from us, and a lot of patience), but they are unnecessary and a poor substitute for the real thing. Plus, once you have strained yogurt to your desired consistency, you're left with a bonus: pure whey. It has endless uses, as you'll discover through the course of this book.

TEMPERATURE

The temperature at which you add the yogurt culture to the milk is crucial. The milk must cool down gradually, gently coddling the probiotics into action. If the probiotics in the milk stay too warm for too long, there will be a cooked, musky taste to your yogurt and the whey will start separating too soon. For this reason, I do not recommend using an automatic yogurt maker or a thermos or even an Instant Pot to make yogurt. These high-tech heat retention devices are not ideal for understanding and getting the process right. Instead, you want to develop a feel for the ideal temperature that brings your probiotics to life, essentially giving birth to each batch of yogurt you make. You will become more attuned to all aspects of creating the perfect environment for the probiotics to thrive: the temperature and drafts of your home, the consistency and behavior of your milk, the ceramic or glass bowls you use to incubate the yogurt. Temperature now transforms from a technical factor to a living ingredient.

TIME

Your wellbeing, your mood, and your patience will inform each and every batch of yogurt. So much of the process is about waiting, and about making the time to be fully present with the milk as it warms and cools. Embrace the reality that this process cannot be rushed. There is a meditative quality to making yogurt, and it goes back to the sublime beauty that we humans are so privileged to take something so simple and sacred—the milk from a mother cow—and combine it with millions of living bacteria to create a product that can be eaten by our loved ones. So, let a piece of yourself, as Hafiz says, "ferment" right into each batch.

STRAINING CLOTHS

You can use a clean cloth, muslin, or a flour-sack towel for straining the yogurt. I refer to these generically throughout the book as "straining cloths." The finer the weave on your straining cloth, the clearer the whey will be. Grocery store cheesecloth has too open a weave and you will lose a lot of the solids, resulting in a cloudy whey. If it's all you have you can certainly use it, but I suggest doubling or tripling the layers. This will keep your whey pristine and all the solids in the cloth.

STORING YOGURT AND WHEY

Loosely cover your bowl of yogurt with a plate or plastic wrap before you refrigerate it. Refrigerate whey in a covered container, too. It is best to use both yogurt and whey within one month of when you make them. After that, you can cook with them or freeze them. Defrosted yogurt has a very inconsistent texture, so I do not recommend using it for anything other than marinades or baking. Whey, on the other hand, defrosts to its same original creamy and clear consistency and can be used interchangeably with fresh whey. See page 51 for how to combine batches of whey to build your inventory over time.

THE WHITE MOUSTACHE
YOGURT AND WHEY

MAKES 1 GALLON OF YOGURT

Plan ahead! This recipe occurs in stages over the course of 3 days (mostly inactive time).

This yogurt-making technique is the one I learned to make as a child and the one I make at home today. It has informed how I make yogurt at The White Moustache, how I run my business, how I run my life. It has helped me find my place in this world.

I feel like I'm sharing a secret family recipe with you—although it's thousands of years old and it belongs to all of us. As you make yogurt following this ancient and beautiful method, my ancestors and I will be right there with you, every step of the way. I have nothing bigger to offer.

EQUIPMENT

Large pot—make sure there is at least 3 inches of headroom after you've poured in your gallon of milk

Mixing spoon

2 large blankets, ideally flannel

Small kitchen towel

Large ceramic bowl—at least 1 gallon capacity

Teacup

Cover for the ceramic bowl—not a tight-fitting lid, but just a plate or tray that covers the entire mouth of the bowl

---

DAY 1: Start this process in the evening, 3½ hours before you go to bed.

1 gallon whole milk

3 tablespoons plain whole milk yogurt, as your starter

Play music you listen to when you feel like you are totally in love—with your family, a wonderful moment, a partner, a time in your life.

Pour the milk into the pot and bring it to a boil over medium heat,

CONTINUES ⚘

stirring almost continuously to avoid getting a crust on the bottom. That crust will eventually burn, and that burn will take hours to clean out and quite possibly leave you with a permanent pot tattoo.

Pay close attention: the instant the milk starts to erupt, turn off the heat and remove the pot from the burner. Stir the milk, allowing it to start cooling. Meanwhile, lay the blankets on top of each other on a kitchen countertop or other flat surface in a warm place free of any drafts. Put the kitchen towel right in the middle of the blankets and place the ceramic bowl on top. When the milk is no longer scalding-hot, pour it into the ceramic bowl and let it cool.

The milk will take 35 to 45 minutes to cool, depending on the ambient temperature of your home, the time of year, your altitude, and where your milk came from. The variables go on, but you can walk away at this point. Don't go far. Call a friend, enjoy the music, meditate—just don't forget about the milk.

At around the 35-minute mark, take your starter out of the fridge and let it warm up to room temperature on the counter.

Dip your pinkie finger into the bowl of milk. If you can hold your pinkie in the milk for 3 seconds, your milk is ready to culture. This is not a masochistic test, but an intuitive one, so trust yourself. (Pinkie fingers are a tried-and-true test in many cultures and surprisingly do not differ greatly in their sensitivity from person to person. My pinkie is small and dainty, and my dad's is fat as a sausage, yet we both have the same feeling with respect to timing and milk temperatures.)

At 35 minutes, the milk will most likely still be too hot. But you will start to gain an idea of how milk loses its heat, and what a gradual process it is (milk holds heat *very* well). You're looking for warm, not hot. If the milk is still too hot—if you want to jerk your pinkie out immediately—come back and test again every minute or two. Do *not* go on to the next step until you can pass the "pinkie test"—remember, you'll be adding live cultures to your yogurt, and they need to survive. If the milk is too hot, it will kill the cultures and the yogurt won't set. If it's too cold, they will not activate enough.

When you can comfortably keep your pinkie in the milk for 3 seconds, scoop some milk into your teacup and add the yogurt starter. Stir to break it all up and "activate" the probiotics. This is similar to activating yeast in warm water.

Dump that cup of diluted mother culture into the ceramic bowl. Give it one strong stir and then leave it. The cultures will disperse themselves.

Set whatever cover you're using on top of the bowl—remember, you do *not* want a tight-fitting lid.

Wrap the blankets up and over the covered bowl, making a cocoon with no room for drafts. This will help your yogurt stay warm overnight and keep the milk's temperature from dropping too quickly, which can lead to thin, flaccid yogurt.

Do the dishes, brush your teeth, go to bed.

DAY 2: First thing in the morning

The yogurt will get as much sleep as you do. It is fine. Telling you how much time to incubate yogurt is like telling you how long to sleep. I recommend 8 or 9 hours. Yogurt is just as alive as you are. Wake up, brush your teeth, unwrap the yogurt, feel the side of the ceramic bowl, and marvel at how it is still warm. Marvel further at the millions of gorgeous probiotics you have nurtured into life.

Uncover and take a whiff of the newly fermented milk. It will smell earthy and creamy. Visually, it will vary in appearance from batch to batch. As a living food, this is normal. Sometimes it will look like a still lake. Other times, it will look like the surface of the moon, especially if your milk frothed when you poured it into the bowl. Either way, once fully incubated, it will look set (you'll know when you see it what that means) and there will be a ring of whey at the edges of your bowl.

Put the lid back on the bowl and put it in the fridge. Go about your day.

DAY 3

It will take about 20 hours for the yogurt to reach the temperature of the refrigerator. Waiting a day is an important part of the process, as the yogurt will continue to set as it chills. It will always be alive and working.

Your yogurt is now optimal to strain or eat.

HOW TO STRAIN YOGURT

Every batch of yogurt, whether it's made in a ceramic bowl at home or in a stainless steel vat in a factory, starts out relatively runny. The only natural way to achieve the thick, creamy, won't-fall-off-an-upside-down-spoon kind of texture is to strain the yogurt of its whey. If you're doing it the slow way, this means pouring the yogurt into a straining cloth and letting gravity do the work. The liquid whey comes through drop by drop. The more whey you strain out, the thicker the yogurt.

For a 1-gallon batch, it can take anywhere from 4 to 8 hours to achieve a Greek yogurt texture and 36 to 48 hours to get Labneh (see page 53), depending on the particular batch of yogurt, the time of year, the weather, and Mercury's position in the heavens (kidding, sort of . . .). Conventional yogurt factories "strain" using machinery that employs centrifugal force to fling the whey out of the yogurt, or they mechanically press it out. The straining method I outline below is intentionally slow, because letting gravity do the work, over time, results in a pure, clear whey. I don't just want really creamy yogurt—I want really creamy yogurt and perfect whey. Both the yogurt and the whey are valuable, and delicious, and are crucial ingredients in the recipes that follow in this book.

Line a colander or large strainer with a straining cloth (see page 46) and place the colander in a large bowl so that it is suspended 2 to 3 inches from the bottom. If necessary, use an inverted shot glass for added lift and support. Pour your yogurt into the colander, then fold the edges of the cloth over the surface of the yogurt. You can place the bowl and colander in the refrigerator at this point, though I am personally comfortable leaving mine at room temperature.

When you have a consistency you want, plop the yogurt out of the cheesecloth into a clean bowl. Loosely cover the bowl, so you leave some room for the yogurt to breathe. For reference, straining 1 gallon of yogurt generally yields 4 to 5 cups of liquid whey. Transfer the whey to a jar, cover tightly, and store in the refrigerator for up to 1 month.

Need Even More Whey?

I want you to make yogurt so you can have whey. Many of the recipes in this book call for no more whey than what you'd get if you made a 1-gallon batch of yogurt at home and then strained it.

But, if you need a large quantity of whey, such as the amounts called for in recipes like Juiciest-Ever Whey-Brined Roast Turkey with Life-Changing Gravy (page 147) and Cauliflower Whey Soup (page 118), I call upon you to get creative. Is there a yogurt company in your city? Is there a yogurt vendor at your farmers' market? Email them and ask them if you can buy some whey. Chances are, they'll say yes. If you're willing to make the trip to them, they might even give it to you for free. The White Moustache welcomes these calls from home cooks and restaurant chefs alike. Bonus points if you bring your own jar, growler, or bucket.

NOTE: If a business is legally allowed to sell yogurt, it is legally allowed to sell whey. Technically, whey is still yogurt in the same way that egg whites are still eggs. Most companies don't sell whey simply because there's not yet consumer demand for it. Together, we can all change this.

DISCLAIMER NUMBER ONE: Please be patient with small businesses. They probably don't have a dedicated customer service department.

DISCLAIMER NUMBER TWO: If you are contacting a large company or a yogurt maker that uses mechanical means of separating their yogurt, the resulting whey maybe somewhat cloudy, with more trace amounts of yogurt in it. If you are concerned about how cloudy your commercial whey is, go ahead and strain it, and you will be all set. Whey generally lasts for a full month in a covered container in the refrigerator, and you can combine multiple batches over the course of that month in a single container and even freeze it for future use.

Variations on the Theme:
Labneh, Kashk, and Gharagooroot

Once you make yogurt, you have yogurt and whey, but with a little added straining time or additional heat, you can have three new products: labneh, kashk, and gharagooroot. All three are derived from either yogurt or whey. Labneh is the creamy yogurt cheese you get from straining yogurt for a full day, or ideally longer. Kashk is a dried salted yogurt ball that can be rehydrated into a sauce. The process of making kashk produces its own whey. When kashk whey is caramelized, this creates gharagooroot; it is used to spike sauces and stews.

LABNEH

My family is not very outdoorsy. The only reason we go on a hike is for the picnic food. Where the French have a baguette, Brie, tomatoes, and a bottle of wine, we Iranians have sangak, labneh, cucumbers, and tomatoes with a cup of hot tea.

Labneh is a spreadable yogurt "cheese," the consistency of mascarpone or cream cheese. Spread it on crackers or use as a dip, or whip it into a thick icing or dessert topping. Its texture depends on how long you strain it.

To make labneh, follow the straining instructions for yogurt (page 50), and continue to leave the yogurt to strain for at least 24 hours, and up to 72 hours; the longer you strain, the thicker the labneh will be and the more whey will collect. After straining, mix the labneh well to smooth out the texture.

You can enjoy labneh on its own, or it can be spiced with a teaspoon of ground sumac, za'atar, or nigella seeds. I include recipes for The White Moustache's popular labneh flavors in the Condiments chapter (page 60).

Plain labneh will last up to 6 weeks in an airtight container in the refrigerator.

KASHK

MAKES ABOUT 2 DOZEN MARBLE-SIZE BALLS

*Plan ahead! You'll need 5 to 7 days (mostly inactive time)
for the yogurt to sour and then dry.*

If culturing milk to make yogurt or labneh is a way to make milk last longer, kashk is the way to make it immortal. Kashk is yogurt that has been soured, salted, cooked, and then strained of all liquid, rolled into balls, and left in the sun to dry. Kashk has a strong tradition in cuisines from Egypt, Israel, Iran, Lebanon, and elsewhere.

For the best flavor and most authentic results, always let your yogurt sour at room temperature for 2 days before you begin this process. In my experience, most store-bought yogurts do not sour at room temperature because they have too many chemicals or have undergone too much processing. Seek out an all-natural yogurt that contains only milk and probiotics and has been made in small batches. Or, my true preference, start off with homemade yogurt to make your kashk. Consider doubling or quadrupling this recipe as making kashk is a lot of work and making more requires almost no additional effort.

Once made and fully dried, kashk may be kept for years. When ready to use, rehydrate it to a saucy consistency as described in the recipe for Kashk Sauce (page 57).

Use the liquid whey left over from making kashk to make Gharagooroot, or Black Whey (page 58). Kashk and gharagooroot are used in similar ways: to add a moderate tang in the case of kashk, or to add a stronger, more intensely acidic tang in the case of gharagooroot. They may be added to soups, stews, and meats. The hardcore Iranians in my life also enjoy them straight.

FUN SIDE NOTE FOR THOSE FASCINATED BY THE DIGESTIVE-RELATED MAGICAL QUALITIES OF YOGURT: Whereas yogurt and whey make you more, er, regular in a rocket-fuel sort of way, kashk is actually a home remedy for diarrhea. Simply suck on the kash for best results.

Put your homemade or completely natural small-batch yogurt in a bowl or container and cover loosely. (Do not use an airtight lid.) Leave it out at room temperature until it smells ripe and sour, about 2 days. Stir your yogurt once a day, but try to minimally handle it. You will know when it is ready because it will smell sour and the yogurt around the edges of the bowl may even start to bubble up. You may think it has gone off, but it has basically just ripened for making a perfect earthy kashk. (If you see mold, however, you've left it out too long.)

In a large saucepan over low heat, combine the soured yogurt, whey (or water), and salt, stirring to dissolve the salt. Slowly bring to a simmer. Don't get an itchy trigger finger on that stove dial. The goal is not only to heat up the mixture but to coax the solids and the liquid to separate from each other without letting too much liquid evaporate in the process. It takes time.

For the first hour, you'll stir occasionally so the solids don't settle on the bottom and burn, but not much will happen. Then, soon after the 1-hour mark, you'll see a teeny bit of foam around the edges and, in one or two places, the solids will begin to separate and a little window of clear liquid will appear in the middle of the milky white expanse. Soon after, the entire surface of the liquid will start slowly rolling and percolating, the solids drifting like a sky full of clouds. Once this happens, continue cooking for 10 minutes longer, stirring gently but frequently to prevent the bottom layer from burning. If you agitate it too much, you may reincorporate the solids into the liquid—this is the opposite of what you're after, which is the total separation of these two components. It will look remarkably like baby spit-up.*

Turn off the heat. Line a strainer or colander with a straining cloth and place over a bowl. Pour the contents of the saucepan into the cloth-lined strainer. Let strain for 2 hours at room temperature, until the liquid whey accumulates in the bowl and the thicker solids (which will look like creamy white clay) remain in the cloth. You will use the

1 quart plain whole milk yogurt

1 quart yogurt whey or water, at room temperature

1 tablespoon kosher salt

---

* I'm deeply apologetic about this visual; I tried my hardest to come up with something more palatable, as kashk really does deserve it. It is truly so delicious, will knock your socks off, and is different from anything else you have tried. Please stay with me.

CONTINUES

solids in the next step. Use the whey to begin making Gharagooroot (page 58) immediately, or else store it in a covered jar in the refrigerator.

Transfer the solids from the cloth to a clean bowl. Using a fork, break up the solids and work them together, moving around the bowl, to create a more even consistency. Have a large baking dish or platter nearby. Grab a tablespoon-size mound of the kashk and using your hands, roll the solids into a 1-inch ball, pressing firmly to compact the solids together. Place the ball in your baking dish. Repeat until you have used all the solids. (You should have 20 to 24 balls.)

If you live in a dry climate, like Iran or Southern California or Libya, place the baking dish outside in the sun until the balls are completely dry, 3 to 5 days. If you prefer to do this indoors, pick a windowsill or any spot with direct sunlight. It will take slightly longer indoors as there is less air circulation, and longer in a humid climate than a dry climate. If you live in a humid climate or are uncertain, a surefire way to assist in drying your kashk is to do a lot of baking around this time and just put the tray of kashk balls in the turned-off oven to dry them out.

As the kashk dries out, the balls will shrink. It's a joy to watch them become more and more concentrated before your eyes. Once they transform to half their original size and look like solid, spherical marbles, they will be completely dried. The kashk will continue to become harder and more compact over time, so if in any doubt, just leave them out longer.

While there's no risk in overdrying, there is a risk in underdrying, as microbes can find shelter in the moist center of the balls. To make sure they're sufficiently dry, check one by pounding it open with a hammer or meat mallet. Touch the center to make sure it's dry. Once dried, transfer the kashk to an airtight container and refrigerate until you're ready to use them . . . or forever. Whichever comes first.

KASHK SAUCE

MAKES 1 CUP

Plan ahead! You'll need 12 hours for the dried kashk balls to soak.

Though it is made *from* yogurt, kashk sauce tastes nothing *like* yogurt. Instead, it has an earthy, salty flavor, created through the slow process of simmering, reducing, and dehydrating yogurt over the course of several days, then rehydrating it to an ultra-concentrated but once again fluid form. It is traditionally drizzled over soups and stews, such as Aash-e-Reshteh (page 101) or atop Eggplant and Kashk (page 86), to complement other strong flavors.

If you don't want to make your own kashk sauce, you can buy it in most Iranian or Middle Eastern grocers. Whether homemade or store-bought, each batch (and each brand) will have a varying degree of saltiness and sourness. Taste it and adjust your recipes accordingly.

1 batch dried kashk balls (20 to 24, from recipe on page 54)

1 cup hot water

Put the kashk in a bowl, add the hot water, and set aside, lightly covered, at room temperature to soak overnight.

The next day, the kashk will be moist throughout, and you should be able to break it up without much effort. Crumble it into a blender and add half the soaking water. Blend until smooth, adding a little more soaking water as necessary to achieve a consistency similar to chocolate sauce. There will be quite a few lumps at the beginning; be patient and let the water reinvigorate and smooth out the dried yogurt clumps, resting between blends to give the kashk some time to absorb the water and soften up. (The common error here is adding too much liquid.)

Use immediately or store in an airtight container in the refrigerator for about 1 month.

GHARAGOOROOT (BLACK WHEY)

Gharagooroot is the yin to kashk's yang. Kashk uses all the solids; gharagooroot uses all the liquid whey. Kashk is a hard ball; gharagooroot is smooth and silky, the consistency of fudge. There isn't a drop of waste here. As with kashk, the cooking process for making gharagooroot is tedious, but the results are worthwhile and last a long time.

On its own, gharagooroot tastes pungent and toasty. Adding it to soups, stews, and sauces gives them not just a mysteriously deep tang but a darker hue. It's a go-to trick when you want people to raise their eyebrows in delight and wonder what your secret ingredient is.

My cousin Farshad chips away at his gharagooroot daily and proudly offers it to guests to nibble on. He once used it to plug up a hole in his gas tank back in Tehran when he couldn't make it to the mechanic shop (which he thinks enhances its desirability, lest you be confused about that). He also believes the lore that it cures fertility and virility issues—for what it's worth he does have two of the most perfect children in our family tree. My family eats gharagooroot straight. At the risk of being disowned, I have to admit that I prefer it in soups and sauces, where I treat it like a bouillon cube—intense, salty, and concentrated.

NOTE: The whey reserved from making kashk has been boiled and salted, and this is what you need for gharagooroot. Do not substitute the simpler form of whey you get from straining yogurt.

3 ½ cups whey reserved from
making Kashk (page 54)

2 teaspoons cornstarch dissolved
in 2 tablespoons cold water

Choose a pan or pot you don't love too much—I recommend stainless steel or a nonstick frying pan, with a large diameter to maximize surface area—and pour in the whey. Place over high heat and bring to a boil. Be very careful as this can still boil over—it is still milk, after all. Once it has come to a boil, reduce the heat to medium, or medium-high if you can, and simmer until it reduces by three-quarters, 35 to 40 minutes. Stir constantly as it gets thicker as it will start wanting to burn.

Scrape in the dissolved cornstarch. Reduce the heat to medium, cover, and cook, stirring occasionally and then re-covering, until the whey has the consistency of warm fudge and the color turns coppery, about 10 minutes.

Remove from the heat. Transfer the sludge to a thick, heat-resistant glass or ceramic jar or bowl—thin glass may crack under the heat—and let it cool to room temperature until it solidifies. (Make sure to label "Not Fudge.")

Store, covered, in the refrigerator. Gharagooroot, like kashk, will last forever.

Condiments

.Con
dim
ents

I insist you eat Iranian food with a spoon.
Do it for the condiments.

Now before you start thinking of condiments as a squeeze of this or a dab of that, we Iranians think of condiments very differently. Yogurt is a condiment, as is labneh, as are pickles. We eat these in significant quantities at every meal. We need these tangy flavors in large amounts because the rest of our food can be very mild and even rich. Condiments contribute contrasting tartness, tang, and texture. Imagine a simple bite of buttery rice followed immediately by a bright pickled carrot.

My family and I eat condiments as if they were sides, scooping some up with every mouthful of food. We place them on the table in separate bowls so each person can dress up their plate however they wish and add a pop of flavor, acid, punch, or brightness to each bite. Here's the standard playbook approach I recommend: Scoop up some rice and some stew with your spoon. Dip one side of the spoon into yogurt—that becomes your canvas. Pile on the sidekicks—a small scoop of Torshi Makhloot (Mixed Iranian Pickle, page 72) to balance out the flavors, or pick up a whole clove of Torshi Sír (Black Garlic Pickle, page 73) with your hands (don't worry, it's not rude) and crunch into it as you are chewing. You are creating a custom-blended taste experience in your mouth.

While technically condiments are "optional," I highly recommend you treat them as the star and build your meal around them. It's not so different from picking out a pair of fabulous shoes first and then working your way to a full outfit.

MAAST-O-MOOSIR
(SAVORY LEOPOLDIA YOGURT)

MAKES 1 QUART

*Plan ahead! You'll need at least 4 hours for the moosir to soak
and 1 day in the fridge for the flavors to meld before serving.*

In Iran savory yogurt is at every table and every gathering. Yogurt
(maast) with Leopoldia bulbs (moosir) is given to finicky kids and
homesick adults alike. It soothes upset tummies and lonely hearts.
If I were to introduce you to maast-o-moosir for the first time, I
would dollop it on a plate of rice with a few cracks of fresh pepper.

Savory yogurt is still not common here in the United States.
Even for some of our more adventurous White Moustache customers, a delightful sense of surprise lights up their eyes with the
first taste.

The most common way you will see maast-o-moosir is in a large
bowl served as part of a meal. My family goes through at least a
gallon of it a week. The simplest way to have maast-o-moosir is
with Persian Rice (page 124). I've even adopted it as a staple in
my American diet with pizza (in place of ranch), drizzled over an
omelet, as a salad dressing, or as a dip with crudités. One of my personal comfort foods, and a common Iranian snack, is potato chips
doused with maast-o-moosir (page 91).

Whether to use strained or unstrained yogurt here depends
entirely on how you enjoy eating it, what you are eating it with, and,
most importantly, what sort of mood you are in.

Try to make maast-o-moosir at least a day in advance to allow
the flavors to meld. Over time, both the salt and the moosir really
announce themselves.

My Pantry (pages 29–33)

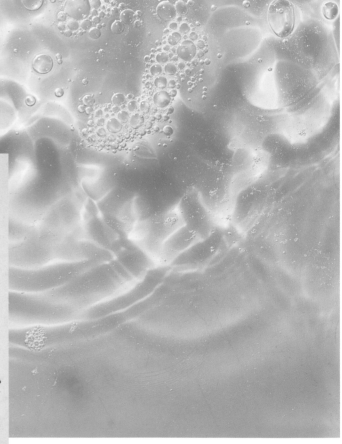

CLOCKWISE FROM TOP LEFT:
Fresh yogurt (see page 47); Gharagooroot
(page 58); Kashk Sauce (page 57); The
White Moustache Yogurt (page 47)

**FACING PAGE, CLOCKWISE FROM
TOP LEFT:** Strained yogurt (page 50);
Labneh (page 53); Whey (page 32);
Kashk (page 54)

Persian Rice (page 124) served with Maast-o-Moosir (page 64)

FACING PAGE FROM TOP:
Noon-e-khosk (page 29); sabzi khordan (page 30)

Juiciest-Ever Whey-Brined Roast Turkey (page 147)

FACING PAGE, CLOCKWISE FROM TOP LEFT:
Whey-Fermented Sauerkraut (page 78); (Radish) Pickles with
Raw Whey (page 74); Persian Cucumber Ice Pops (page 214);
Fluffy Whey Biscuits (page 176)

Plain yogurt whey for inspired concoctions (see page 47)

6 large or 9 medium
  slices dried moosir

1 quart plain whole milk yogurt

1 teaspoon kosher salt,
  plus more to taste

Put the moosir in a small dish and cover with warm water. Let soak for at least 4 hours, until plump and pliable. Drain off and discard the water. Finely mince the moosir.

Put the yogurt in a medium bowl and stir in the salt. Taste and add more salt if you like. You are aiming for a dip or sauce that packs a punch as it will brighten whatever it accompanies. When you're satisfied with the saltiness, add the chopped moosir. Cover and refrigerate for at least 24 hours to intensify the flavors before serving. Store in an airtight container in the refrigerator for up to 1 month.

NOTE: The moosir used in this recipe is sold sliced and dried. It can be found at Middle Eastern markets (see My Pantry, page 31).

MAAST-O-KHIYAR (CUCUMBER YOGURT)

MAKES ABOUT 2 CUPS

Like Maast-o-Moosir (page 64), maast-o-khiyar is both universal and personal: universal because it goes so well with so many dishes and personal because I honestly make it differently every time I make it.

When I eat maast-o-khiyar, I fill at least a quarter of my plate with it. I'm not demure about it and want some with every bite. That said, sometimes I eat it on its own as a snack or with bread. There are no rules.

You'll notice I'm listing a lot of ingredients as optional. At its most basic, maast-o-khiyar requires just yogurt, cucumbers, salt, and pepper—but you can make it much more elaborate if you'd like to. If I am in the mood, it brings me pure joy to decorate the top in intricate patterns using dried rosebuds and dried mint and finely crushed walnuts.

The consistency of yogurt you use—unstrained or strained or a combination of the two—is entirely up to you. (I prefer a saucier consistency.) Double or quadruple the recipe if you like!

1 cup plain whole milk yogurt

2 Persian cucumbers, diced or grated (about ¾ cup)

¼ cup toasted walnuts, chopped, plus more for garnish (optional)

¼ cup raisins, chopped (optional)

1 green onion, finely sliced (optional)

1 tablespoon dried rose petals, crushed, plus more for garnish (optional)

1 tablespoon dried mint (optional)

1 tablespoon dried dill (optional)

Kosher salt and freshly ground black pepper

Combine the yogurt, cucumber, and any of the optional ingredients in a bowl. Season generously with salt and pepper to taste. Decorate with additional walnuts and/or rose petals as desired in a meticulous, ideally over-the-top manner or in a haphazard, avant-garde show of confidence.

SHANKLEESH LABNEH

MAKES 1 QUART

This Lebanese-inspired spread is a versatile, spicy condiment that can be served at any meal. It's ideal as a sandwich spread, as an addition to a meze platter, or served with vegetables and crackers. More often than not, I use it to dress up leftovers I'd otherwise neglect.

Its flavor comes from Aleppo pepper, that slightly oily, brick-red, earthy spice with a subtle heat, and za'atar, a spice blend that usually contains sesame seeds, dried sumac, dried thyme, and dried oregano. (You can find za'atar in most spice aisles or make your own. I use 3 parts toasted sesame seeds, 2 parts dried sumac, 2 parts dried thyme, and 1 part dried oregano.)

4 cups plain, unsalted Labneh (page 53), at room temperature

1½ teaspoons Aleppo pepper, or more to taste

1 teaspoon za'atar

2 teaspoons kosher salt, or more to taste

Put the labneh in a medium bowl. Mix in the Aleppo pepper until its red tint is evenly distributed and no white patches or streaks remain. Stir in the za'atar. (While you can add more Aleppo pepper if you'd like more heat, resist the temptation to add more za'atar. One teaspoon of za'atar doesn't sound like much, but adding more will make the labneh bitter.) Sprinkle in the salt and mix. Taste, and add a little more salt if you like, keeping in mind that the salt flavor will bloom and intensify over time.

Serve right away, or store in an airtight container in the refrigerator for up to 1 month.

KURDISH LABNEH

MAKES ABOUT 2 CUPS

*Plan ahead! Allow 1 week to brine the garlic shoots
(they may be made up to 3 months ahead).*

This recipe came to me the way many of my recipes do: by word of mouth. I had just launched The White Moustache in Brooklyn and was experimenting with making labneh, perfecting its texture and taste. I spread the word within the Zoroastrian community to see if anyone had any favorite ways of using it. My uncle's coworker at a chemical factory in California told my uncle about a combination of labneh and brined green garlic shoots, which they saved from the harvest at the beginning of spring. He'd rarely tasted these flavors outside of the Kurdish regions of Iran. Moved by his nostalgia, I was inspired to create this Kurdish labneh recipe from the memories of a man whose name I never knew. It has since become a beloved addition to The White Moustache line.

First, to brine the garlic shoots, pour the water into a jar and stir in the salt until dissolved. Wash the garlic shoots, chop off the tiny bulbs (these can be pickled separately), and finely slice the tender green shoots into tiny medallions. Add the chopped shoots to the brine, cover, and refrigerate for 1 week. These brined shoots will last for at least 3 months and can be used in omelets, on salads, or as a garnish to many other dishes.

To prepare the labneh, use a slotted spoon to remove ¼ cup garlic shoots from the brine. Spread them on a tray lined with paper towels to air-dry for 30 minutes, then mix them into the labneh. (Removing excess water is key as otherwise it would make the labneh watery and compromise its shelf life.)

Serve right away, or store in an airtight container in the refrigerator for up to 1 month.

NOTE: While not commonly used in American cooking, green garlic shoots add an intense, herbal garlicky flavor. Look for these tender, bud-tipped green shoots with delicate white bulbs in Asian markets or at farmers' markets in the springtime.

1 quart tepid water

¼ cup kosher salt

1 bunch green garlic shoots

2 cups plain, unsalted Labneh
  (page 53), at room temperature

Pickling with Whey

Like making yogurt, pickling is—at its most basic—a way to make perishable foods last longer. Traditionally, my family made pickles using vinegar, but I've since discovered that whey is like a turbo-charge to the fermentation process. You can of course ferment without a starter, relying on the naturally occurring bacteria on the surface of the food, as many people do. But even a spoonful of bacteria-rich whey speeds things along. In addition to a faster fermentation, I've found that making pickles with whey allows me to use much less salt. Not only do you get a vibrant pickle, but the resulting brine is more conducive to salad dressings and sauces.

If you have a bit of whey to spare, I highly recommend making a very basic pickle (Pickles with Raw Whey, page 74). Looking to other cultures* for additional inspiration, I've included my adaptations of making kimchi and sauerkraut with whey at the end of this chapter.

Below are some preliminary tips that I hope will guide you on the road to creating many successful whey-based pickles! Fair warning that this can be a very addictive undertaking, but I encourage you to have fun with it as we are all one more environmental crisis away from being doomsday preppers anyway.

SANITIZE YOUR JARS: Before packing your pickles into jars, you want to make sure not to have any competing bacteria in this host vessel. I boil the jars and lids to sanitize them, then lay them on a clean, dry towel to air-dry completely. You can also leave the jars in a 230°F oven for 10 to 15 minutes.

USE FILTERED WATER: These fermentation recipes all call for filtered water. Tap water often contains chlorine, which kills bacteria and prevents your fermentation from getting started. If you don't have access to filtered water, you can leave a jar of tap water at room temperature for 24 hours to allow the chlorine to evaporate or put your tap water through a charcoal filter if you have one.

USE SEA SALT: While I use kosher salt in the rest of my recipes, I prefer unrefined sea salt when pickling because it contains naturally occurring minerals. (You can still use kosher salt if you prefer.) The one kind of salt I will warn you against is table salt—it is often iodized and could kill off the bacteria you need for fermentation.

---

* Pun obviously intended. (And I'm here all week, folks!)

VARY YOUR VEGGIES: You can basically pickle any vegetable you like, which is where the process becomes so much fun. The main advice here is that they have to be raw and as fresh as possible. And consider pickling things that you would otherwise discard—such as the tough stems of herbs—as a way of adding an interesting crunch to your foods.

SAY YES TO ADD-INS: I also encourage you to play around with the add-ins in these recipes. Add some fresh dill and chiles to your pickles, fresh ginger to your Beet Kvass (page 242), caraway to your Whey-Fermented Sauerkraut (page 78).

UNDERSTAND LACTO-FERMENTATION: While "lacto" shares obvious linguistic similarities with "lactose" (naturally occurring milk sugars), lacto-fermentation refers to the process whereby bacteria eat sugars (either in dairy or in vegetables) and create lactic acid. It doesn't actually involve dairy or lactose. It is an anaerobic process, meaning it takes place without any oxygen. To keep oxygen from interfering with the process (and the top layer of the pickle from getting moldy), it's important to keep the vegetables covered with liquid.

BE ADAPTABLE REGARDING TIME AND TEMPERATURE: The fermentation process is ongoing. In most of these recipes, we start the process at room temperature for a specified time range and then move it to the fridge to slow down the process. The time range you need will vary based on the temperature of your home, the origin of your vegetables, and the mineral content of your water. I give a range of fermentation times in these recipes; you may find that you need to let your recipes ferment for a longer or shorter time depending on how sour, fizzy, or funky you like your pickles. In a hot kitchen at the height of summer, you can have results in as little as two days, whereas it can take a week or more to get the same level of fermentation in the middle of a northeast winter.

Once the pickles reach your desired level of sour, place them in the refrigerator. Remember that while the refrigeration slows down the fermentation process, it does not stop it, so you will be building on the kick-start we got in those first few days.

BURP YOUR JARS: Burping refers to the process of opening the lid to your jar and releasing the built-up gases. You can invest in a pickling pipe or other airlock that acts like a vented lid and releases the gases automatically without the risk of introducing any oxygen into your jar. To manually accomplish this, when you pass by your pickle jars, you can just burp them and then go about your day. It's like saying hello. Every day. Oh hello pickle, I see you have been working overnight, let me unscrew the top and relieve some of your stress. Now carry on. Have a nice day, see you tomorrow.

WHAT TO DO IF YOU ENCOUNTER YEAST OR MOLD: A white fuzzy film on the top of the ferment is most likely a kind of yeast. It's not harmful, but you should skim it off because it can affect the flavor of what's in the jar.

Fermentation projects can grow mold if the raw vegetables are exposed to air or if the salt content is too low. If it has molded, you can add it to your compost bin. Don't be discouraged! This is a process that, like baking bread and making yogurt, takes time, finesse, and knowledge of your environment. With some stubborn determination, you will grow to understand the art of pickling and fermentation—and the variety of things you can make by repurposing scraps of vegetables is endless.

HOW YOU'LL KNOW WHEN YOUR PICKLES ARE READY: There is a bit of intuition that you will develop as you get more comfortable and familiar with pickling. Your biggest hint will be how much gas or fizzing is released each time you burp the jar—as it becomes less, you are getting closer to moving it to the fridge. My advice for beginners is to trust your gut (ha ha) and move the jar to the fridge the minute you feel the pickles are ready. I would rather have you err on taking the jar to the fridge too early than too late. If it's too early, you may not reach peak fermentation, but the fermentation process will continue in the fridge, and you don't risk the vegetables getting too soft on you (by waiting too long to move the jar to the fridge). You will always get a tasty pickle. Over time, based on the vegetable and your own palate, you will start to develop preferences for how long you want to keep the jars out. I have surprised myself by wanting my cherry tomatoes to have a very fizzy pop to them, so I leave them out a bit longer than others. The biggest risk (which is not all that big) is that you might miss out on a peak fermentation—meaning a combination of the exact right texture (crunch!) and flavor. It's kind of like figuring out what year is the best to drink that 1982 bottle of merlot someone gifted you.

SCALE UP: The recipes that follow all scale well. Once you get a feel for the proportions, you can go rogue based on what you have on hand and double or quadruple these recipes easily.

TORSHI MAKHLOOT
(MIXED IRANIAN PICKLE)

MAKES ABOUT 2 ½ CUPS

Plan ahead! This pickle takes 2 to 4 days for fermentation.

This recipe for mixed pickles is a whey-infused version of an Iranian classic that is normally made with a confetti of different vegetables, herbs, and vinegar. It's incredibly versatile as you can use up any and all vegetable scraps you have in your fridge. Just make sure the scraps are still firm, as firm vegetables make the best pickles. (Soft or wilted vegetables are better turned into soup.) In recipes throughout this book, I suggest keeping a container of left-over vegetables for a soup or for a pickle—*this* is the ideal pickle for those leftovers, as the confetti of different vegetables can be eaten as a relish or condiment with almost any Iranian meal or on any sandwich. I regularly use carrots, cauliflower, cucumber, and garlic in varying quantities, but don't be limited by this list. You can even double or triple the recipe, using several or larger jars.

ADD-INS: Consider adding bay leaves, mustard seeds, nigella seeds, and/or green chiles. This mixed pickle can also handle any chopped fresh herbs you have on hand, such as mint, cilantro, savory, tarragon, and/or parsley.

3 cups assorted vegetables scraps, cut into small dice like vegetable confetti

1 teaspoon ground turmeric

1 teaspoon sea salt

1 cup yogurt whey, or more as needed

Boil a quart-size jar and lid to sanitize them.

Put the vegetables in a medium bowl. Stir in the turmeric and salt until well combined. Transfer the vegetable mixture to the jar and pour in enough whey to fill to the top. Secure the lid. Give the jar a good shake. Leave at room temperature for 2 to 4 days—2 days in the height of summer, closer to 4 days in the dead of winter—and shake the jar occasionally to give the turmeric a chance to infuse evenly. If you have an airlock or fermentation lid, that will be foolproof, but you can also unscrew the lid to burp the jar once a day to release the pressure, then screw it back on. You will know it is ready when it has started fizzing. At that point, move the jar to the refrigerator. Use within 2 months.

TORSHI SÍR (BLACK GARLIC PICKLE)

Plan ahead! This pickles needs at least 5 weeks for fermentation.

MAKES 1 CUP

There is a fermented garlic pickle that people back in Iran leave for 10, 15, even 20 years before it is perfectly aged. Whole heads of garlic are submerged in vinegar and, after a decade or two, they are black in color and buttery in texture. At that point they don't taste vinegary—they don't even have the pungent taste of garlic. They are sweet and spreadable, mellowed out by time. Since even my patience has its limits, I've created a quicker variation with whey.

I love these pickles so much, I can eat a whole head of garlic in one sitting. I eat them like I'd eat a plate of olives, just one after another. And I keep them around throughout the meal, eating them as a garnish or palate cleanser, or rolling up a few cloves with lavash along with walnuts and herbs.

Pick a jar that will hold all the garlic tightly packed. I like an 8-ounce canning jar. Boil the jar and its lid to sanitize them.

Pack the garlic cloves snugly into the jar, leaving ½ inch of headspace for extra liquid, so the garlic will remain submerged during the process.

In a small bowl, combine the salt and whey and stir until the salt is dissolved. Pour the whey into the jar. Screw on the lid and leave at room temperature for 2 weeks. Burp the jar every day or so (see page 70). Transfer the jar to the fridge and leave for at least 3 additional weeks. As time goes by, you may notice that the garlic starts to absorb the whey. Keep it completely covered with whey, adding more whenever needed.

The pickle is ready when the garlic is extremely soft, essentially "cooked" by its brine. (Test a clove and give it a taste. When it's ready, it will not only feel soft but taste mature, like it has bloomed and become more "garlicky" without being spicy.)

Store the finished pickle in the refrigerator for up to 1 year.

NOTE: There's no need to peel the garlic cloves. The skins will slip off much more easily after they've been pickled. Indeed, part of the fun of eating them is to pop the soft flesh out of its casing with your teeth.

2 heads garlic, unpeeled, separated into individual cloves

1 teaspoon kosher salt

¼ to ½ cup yogurt whey, plus more as needed

PICKLES WITH RAW WHEY

MAKES 1 CUP

Use this versatile brine to kick-start your pickles and pack them with probiotics. I love it for cucumbers, radishes, red onions, carrots, cauliflower, even tomatoes—basically anything you want to pickle. I've offered some additional suggestions as well as prep tips in the recipe.

When making the brine, it is important to get the balance of salt and whey right. Too little salt will result in mushy pickles and too much salt will result in sulfurous-smelling brine. When optimally balanced, you'll be amazed at how easy it is to make. The recipe and proportions below are for about 1 cup of vegetables to pickle in an 8-ounce jar.

Reserve the brine from the pickling process to make the Bloody Mary, Two Wheys (page 259) or to add to any salad dressing.

BASIC WHEY BRINE

¾ teaspoon kosher salt

½ cup filtered water

2 tablespoons whey

Boil an 8-ounce jar and its lid to sterilize them.

Put all your add-ins in the jar first, then pack the vegetables tightly into the jar.

Combine the salt, filtered water, and whey in a small bowl to create the brine. Mix thoroughly to dissolve the salt. Pour the brine into the jar; add more water as necessary to cover the vegetables completely. Screw the lid on tightly.

Leave the jar at room temperature for 2 to 4 days (see Pickling with Whey, page 69). After the first day, check the jar lid for bulging and unscrew to release gases if necessary, then retighten it. The next day, burp the jar again. And again on the third day, and maybe taste a pickle. Repeat daily until the pickles have reached your ideal level of sourness.

Transfer to the refrigerator and use within 2 months.

ADD-INS: Raid your fridge or pantry for inspiration, including the herbs and spices suggested below. I'm someone who tosses a few garlic cloves into every jar.

Garlic cloves, peeled (at least 3 per jar)

Dill fronds or dill flowers

Whole mustard seeds (about 1 teaspoon)

Peppercorns (about 1 teaspoon)

Star anise (about 1 teaspoon)

Bay leaves (1 per jar)

Serrano chile, sliced (to taste—a small amount will go a *long* way)

Jalapeño, sliced (to taste—note that jalapeños can be a pickle in and of themselves)

VEGETABLE SUGGESTIONS: To ensure your pickles turn out satisfyingly crisp, it helps to start with fresh, firm produce. Get creative and experiment! You want to use enough vegetables to pack your jar tightly so they will remain submerged once you add the brine and will not float to the top.

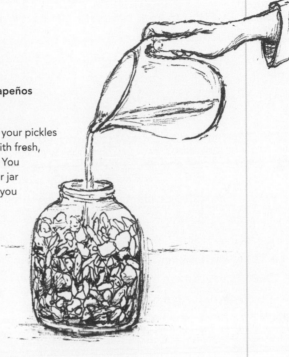

Radishes: Trim both ends. Either keep whole or thinly slice.

Cucumber: I like to use Kirby or gherkin cucumbers. Trim about ⅛ inch off the blossom end (the end opposite the stem where there's often a small rough patch). This small blossom contains an enzyme that might make your pickles mushy. Cut cucumbers in slim disks or spears, or leave whole.

Cauliflower: Cut the florets into bite-size pieces. Dice the stalk into small cubes.

Carrots: Cut large carrots into thin disks or spears.

Tomatoes: Keep small cherry tomatoes whole to enjoy a fizzy little pop of flavor after pickling!

Red onions: Slice in half, then slice again into thin half-moons.

WHEY-FERMENTED KIMCHI

MAKES ABOUT 2 QUARTS

Plan ahead! Allow 3 days to ferment.

Jumong was a Korean TV drama about the founder of the ancient kingdom of Goguryeo. The Iranian government dubbed this series in Farsi and broadcast it over state-controlled airwaves. The entire nation was glued to their televisions after dinner. In my family, we were all gripped, watching the story of a young man building a dynasty and drawn into a very complicated, soap-opera-level love story.

Cab drivers, neighbors, store clerks—everyone—had an opinion about what would happen next and whether Jumong would ever find lasting love with Soseono. Teenagers had posters of the Korean actors on their walls. Students learned everything they could about Korean food, music, language. The photos of the show's stars started appearing on everything from backpacks to serving trays. They were true celebrities in Iran.

Like the Iranian government's wise decision to introduce its population to a beloved Korean drama, I've found this recipe to be the surprise hit of this chapter. My adopted version of whey-fermented kimchi is bright and alive and enhances everything from eggs to rice. You might even want to hang a poster of it in your room.

NOTE: Gochugaru (Korean chile powder) is available in most Asian markets.

1 large head napa cabbage, leaves rinsed, dried, and roughly chopped

1 bunch green onions, thinly sliced

½ cup grated carrot (about 1 medium carrot)

½ cup grated daikon radish (about ⅓ medium daikon)

¼ cup yogurt whey

2 teaspoons fine sea salt

1 tablespoon minced garlic (about 3 large cloves)

1 tablespoon grated ginger (no need to peel)

1 tablespoon fish sauce

¼ cup gochugaru (see Note)

Boil two 1-quart jars and their lids to sterilize them.

In a large bowl, combine the cabbage, green onions, carrot, daikon, whey, and salt. Mix, knead, and squeeze with your hands until the vegetables release their juices, at least 5 minutes.

Add the garlic, ginger, fish sauce, and gochugaru and work them into the vegetable mixture. Using a wooden spoon, pack the kimchi into the jars. Make sure some of the liquid released by your kneading sits above the kimchi so none of the solids are exposed to the air. Seal the jars tightly and let sit at room temperature for 3 days, burping them daily. (As the third day approaches, put your ear to the jar and listen: you can actually *hear* your kimchi fermenting!)

Move the jars to the refrigerator. At this point your kimchi is ready to eat, but the flavor will continue to improve. It will keep in the refrigerator for at least 6 months.

WHEY-FERMENTED SAUERKRAUT

MAKES 1 QUART

Plan ahead! Sauerkraut requires 1 to 4 weeks for fermentation.

Many conventional sauerkraut recipes call for you to beat and mash and knead your cabbage. In this version, you can save some effort by simply mixing the salt and whey into the shredded cabbage and letting it sit for 20 minutes. During this time, the salt will do the work of drawing the liquid out of the cabbage. Once the process is underway, come back and knead the cabbage with your hands for a couple of minutes, just until it's limp and pliable.

Pack your kraut into a crock with an airlock if you own one; otherwise, clean glass canning jars with tight-sealing lids work fine.

This recipe can easily be scaled up or even modified. Simply follow the basic method but add red cabbage, shredded beets, carrots, fennel, or green onions. Tossing in fresh ginger, caraway seeds, curry powder, chiles, or garlic will spice things up if you're feeling a little Extra.

Boil a clean, wide-mouth quart jar and its lid to sterilize it.

Peel one outer leaf off the cabbage and set it aside. Split the cabbage head into quarters and cut out the core. Use a sharp knife or the shredding blade of a food processor to finely shred the cabbage quarters.

Put the shredded cabbage in a large mixing bowl and add the whey and salt. Toss with your hands to combine. Let sit for 20 minutes to allow the salt to draw moisture out of the cabbage.

Knead and squeeze the cabbage with clean hands for up to 5 minutes, until the cabbage is very limp.

Pack the cabbage tightly into your jar. Pour in enough filtered water to completely cover the cabbage. Trim the reserved cabbage leaf to the diameter of the jar and press it down onto the surface of the shredded cabbage mixture. Top it with an inverted shot glass or any other clean object that will fit into the jar to push down the mixture and keep the cabbage submerged. Screw the lid on the jar and set on a plate in case it leaks.

Leave the jar at room temperature. After 3 days, begin checking it by unscrewing the jar daily to release gases and then retightening. Taste the sauerkraut after 1 week to check its level of fermentation. Is it sour enough? If not, continue checking every few days. You can let it ferment for up to 4 weeks. Once it has reached your desired sourness, store it in the refrigerator. Use within 6 months.

1 small head green cabbage

¼ cup yogurt whey

2 teaspoons fine sea salt

Filtered water

SNACKS

& SIDES

In Iran, most meals are served family-style.

There's no traditional appetizer course, and bringing out a progression of dishes just isn't common. Instead, the table becomes a palette of dishes, holding everything at once. We help ourselves to what we want, crafting not only the ideal plate, but even the ideal bite. Serving sizes are therefore difficult to guess. Each of the side dishes is intended to be part of a meal, but how many they'll serve depends completely on how many sides you'll be offering. I encourage you to approach serving sizes with an open mind and (Iranian!) flexibility.

Chips and Yogurt (page 91) truly is a stand-alone snack (the best snack, I would argue), and the remaining dishes in this chapter may all appear next to one another on the table without any one dish holding more prominence than the others. That said, Spinach Boorani (page 84) and Eggplant and Kashk (page 86) may be served in larger quantities or entirely on their own as a small meal. This chapter's community contribution, the Eggplant Salad (page 89) from the Israeli couple behind New York Shuk, is just as much a salad as a side.

Perhaps a better chapter name would be Yogurt 2.0, as each of these dishes illustrates yogurt's ability to freshen the plate. Yogurt on the table—either in its plainest, least adorned form or thoughtfully paired with a slew of decorative and flavorful garnishes—makes whatever else you're enjoying taste not just better, but livelier.

SPINACH BOORANI

MAKES 8 CUPS; SERVES 8 AS A SIDE OR 4 AS AN ENTRÉE

*Plan ahead! After cooking the spinach, you'll need to let it cool
for at least 30 minutes before combining it with the yogurt.*

This dish can be the centerpiece of a meal when surrounded by
sliced tomatoes, walnuts, and pita. Or it can make an appearance
with other sides in a meze-style meal without an entrée in sight.
Eggplant also makes a nice pairing, either the Eggplant and Kashk
(page 86) or the New York Shuk Eggplant Salad (page 89). I've also
served it at every single post-Thanksgiving dinner I've ever had as
it adds some much-needed greens to leftover bites of Juiciest-Ever
Whey-Brined Roast Turkey with Life-Changing Gravy (page 147),
Leftover Turkey and Dumplings (page 151), or Whey Cornbread
(page 177). In truth, I've eaten it countless times as a meal on its
own because it's so easy.

You can prepare boorani up to three days in advance, making it
a low-effort, make-ahead contribution to a potluck. (It tastes even
better after the flavors have a chance to overcome their shyness.)

Whichever direction you take it, serve boorani at room temperature with a basket of pita alongside.

NOTE: When shopping, reach for bunches of mature spinach rather than
the bagged baby variety. The heartier, more fibrous leaves add more texture,
though they'll soften considerably as you wilt them down. Added bonus:
Their flavor is more pronounced, too.

2 tablespoons unsalted butter

2 tablespoons extra-virgin olive oil

1 large yellow onion,
 finely chopped

5 garlic cloves, minced

Kosher salt and freshly
 ground black pepper

3 pounds mature or savoy spinach
 (it will feel like too much,
 I know), rinsed and dried

2 cups strained (Greek-style)
 yogurt

Za'atar, for garnish

Pita, cut into wedges, for serving

Start with the widest sauté pan or pot in your arsenal; you want to maintain a lot of contact with the heated surface area. Melt the butter in the olive oil over medium heat. Add the onion, garlic, and a generous pinch or two of salt and pepper and cook, stirring frequently, until the onion is caramelized and browned, 15 to 20 minutes.

Add the spinach to the pot in large handfuls, allowing it to wilt slightly before adding more. Continue this process, stirring over moderate heat, until all the spinach fits in the pot, about 20 minutes. The spinach will drastically reduce in volume and be very tender. (This may seem like a long time, but you're dealing with a lot of leaves here. Your patience will pay off.) Transfer to a medium serving bowl, season with salt and pepper to taste, and let cool completely, at least 30 minutes.

Add the yogurt and mix well. Taste and season with more salt and pepper, if you like. Sprinkle some za'atar on top and serve with pita.

EGGPLANT AND KASHK

SERVES 4 IRANIANS OR 8 AMERICANS

Plan ahead! If you are starting off with dried kashk, you will need 12 hours to rehydrate them overnight. You can do this up to 1 month ahead and store the kashk sauce in the refrigerator.

If you don't like them, eggplants will haunt you in Iranian cuisine. If you do like them, they will delight you! Iranians do things with eggplant that will make you never look at an eggplant the same way again. Basically eggplant has been our Iron Chef ingredient for centuries, and we *nailed it*.

This dish celebrates the perfect marriage of eggplant and kashk. If you don't already have any kashk sauce on hand, you will need to rehydrate the dried kashk overnight, so you can make it saucy enough to mix in with the eggplant and to drizzle on top upon serving. The garnishes bring in a variety of necessary textures and flavors and make this dish equally good warm or at room temperature. Serve with lavash or pita. It's as versatile and crowd-pleasing as they come.

NOTE: Since we are roasting large whole eggplant (instead of frying) to get an added smoky flavor, try to source young eggplant in order to avoid bitterness. At the market, look for eggplant that is shiny.

EGGPLANT AND KASHK

3 large purple eggplants (about 3 pounds)

½ cup olive oil

3 large yellow onions, cut into thin half-moons

1 head garlic, individual cloves peeled and minced

1 tablespoon ground turmeric

2 tablespoons dried mint

Kosher salt and freshly ground black pepper

1 cup Kashk Sauce (page 57 or store-bought)

GARNISH

2 tablespoons olive oil

1 tablespoon dried mint

MAKE THE EGGPLANT AND KASHK: Preheat the oven to 425°F. Line a rimmed baking sheet with parchment paper.

Use a sharp knife to score the eggplants' skins top to bottom, at 2-inch intervals, and place on the prepared baking sheet. Roast until the skin is crisp and charred (this adds a lovely smoky flavor) and the flesh has separated some from the skin, 45 minutes to 1 hour, flipping halfway through. The flesh should be very soft when pressed. Remove from the oven and let cool.

Heat the olive oil in a large skillet over medium-high heat. Add the onions and cook, stirring often, until browned, 15 to 20 minutes. Remove one-third of the fried onions and set aside for garnish. Add the garlic and turmeric and cook until browned, about 5 minutes. (Watch carefully, as garlic can quickly go from brown to burnt.) Add the mint, season with salt and pepper to taste, and remove from the heat within 1 minute as mint burns quickly.

Once the eggplants are cool enough to handle, pull off and discard the charred skin and stem. Chop or mash the flesh very fine.

Add the eggplant to the skillet with the onions and garlic. Return to medium heat, mashing the eggplant into the onions and garlic with a spatula or the flat side of a wooden spoon. Cook for 2 to 3 minutes, stirring, to incorporate the flavors. Remove from the heat and stir in half the kashk sauce. Taste, adding more salt and pepper as necessary.

MAKE THE FRIED ONION AND MINT OIL GARNISH: Put the reserved fried onions and any oil that has accumulated in a small saucepan or skillet. Fry over medium-high heat till they are almost crispy, 5 to 10 minutes depending on your preference. Transfer the onions to a small bowl. Add the olive oil to the same pan. When the oil is hot, fry the dried mint for just a few seconds (it burns very quickly). It will release an earthy smell almost immediately. Transfer the mint and its now-dark-green oil to another small heat-resistant bowl.

BRING IT ALL TOGETHER: Spoon the eggplant mixture into a serving dish, drizzle liberally with the remaining kashk sauce, and garnish with the crispy onions and mint oil.

WHEY-CREAMY MASHED CAULIFLOWER

SERVES 4

Cauliflower has become the darling of The White Moustache test kitchen. When combined with whey, not only does the cauliflower sing, it puts on a one-woman chorus line. It is such a simple canvas, one you can enhance with roasted garlic, caramelized onions, chopped parsley, or even kimchi. Enjoy on its own or serve with grilled meats or vegetables.

And while I chose to highlight cauliflower, this treatment works with any vegetable you can puree, especially potatoes and sweet potatoes. Whey-mashed vegetables are particularly suited to offer a bright, lightly acidic contrast to the heavier foods on the table.

NOTE: I don't use the cauliflower leaves and stems in this recipe, but I never throw them away. You can pickle them (see Pickling with Whey on page 69) or tuck them in the "soup bin" in your refrigerator to use in an end-of-the-week, clean-out-the-fridge soup.

1 head cauliflower (about 2 pounds), leaves and stems removed, florets chopped to golf ball size

½ to ¾ cup yogurt whey

Kosher salt and freshly ground black pepper

Bring a large pot of generously salted water to a boil over high heat. Add the cauliflower. Boil until the florets are tender but not mushy, about 10 minutes. Drain.

Transfer the cauliflower to the bowl of a food processor or high-powered blender. Add ½ cup of the whey and puree until smooth, not grainy. Add up to ¼ cup more whey, little by little, if you prefer a looser consistency. Season to taste with salt and pepper. Serve warm.

NEW YORK SHUK
EGGPLANT SALAD

SERVES 4 TO 6

Plan ahead! You'll need to let the saffron yogurt infuse for 12 hours.

The White Moustache built a business on the need to preserve the flavors of our homeland, and we're hardly alone in that respect. New York Shuk, a harissa company owned by Israeli couple Ron and Leetal Azari in the Bedford-Stuyvesant neighborhood of Brooklyn, did the same. We've bonded over many meals together, discussing our journeys to America and the roadblocks we've faced as entrepreneurs.

Before The White Moustache was faced with the challenges of selling whey, we had a hard time finding an access point for our savory Maast-o-Moosir yogurt (page 64). Ron and Leetal had a similar challenge with their harissa, a spicy chile paste prevalent in North African cuisine, and used across the Middle East. The irony is how common our respective products are in our own homes and in our cooking, and how difficult it has been to translate that to American customers.

This dish—which, in Israeli culinary tradition, is a salad as much as a side—was born out of a dinner I co-hosted with Ron and Leetal for the Jewish holiday Shavuot, which centers around dairy. It has three parts: an overnight-infused saffron yogurt, roasted eggplant, and harissa tomatoes.

NOTE: When choosing eggplants, look for those that are shiny.

CONTINUES

MAKE THE SAFFRON YOGURT: The night before you plan to serve the dish, crumble the saffron threads into a medium heatproof bowl. Add the hot water and let it infuse like a tea for 5 minutes, until cool. Stir in the yogurt and salt. Cover with plastic wrap and refrigerate overnight. The yogurt mixture will turn a strong shade of yellow and infuse with the flavor of saffron.

MAKE THE ROASTED EGGPLANT: Preheat the oven to 450°F.

Partially peel the eggplants by removing a 1-inch strip of skin lengthwise, alternating with a 1-inch strip of skin on, creating long, zebra-like stripes. Cut the eggplants into 1-inch dice.

In a large bowl, toss the eggplant with ¼ cup of the olive oil and 1 teaspoon of the salt. Spread on a rimmed baking sheet in a single layer and roast until golden and soft, 20 to 30 minutes, flipping halfway through. Let cool.

In the same large bowl, combine the parsley, green onions, lemon juice, remaining ½ cup olive oil, and remaining ½ teaspoon salt. Scrape in the roasted eggplant and stir.

SAFFRON YOGURT

¼ teaspoon saffron threads

1 tablespoon hot water

1 cup strained (Greek-style) yogurt

Pinch kosher salt

ROASTED EGGPLANT

2 large purple eggplants

¾ cup olive oil, divided

1½ teaspoons kosher salt, divided

1 bunch flat-leaf parsley, finely chopped

1 bunch green onions, roots trimmed, white and green parts finely chopped

5 tablespoons lemon juice

HARISSA TOMATOES

2 medium Roma tomatoes

2 tablespoons harissa

2 tablespoons olive oil

¼ teaspoon kosher salt

MAKE THE HARISSA TOMATOES: Bring a small saucepan of water to a boil over high heat. Prepare an ice bath by filling a medium bowl with cold water and ice cubes. With a small paring knife, cut a shallow X just through the skin on the bottom of each tomato. Carefully lower the tomatoes into the boiling water just until the skin around the X begins to curl back, 20 to 30 seconds. Using a slotted spoon, transfer the tomatoes to the ice bath. Once cool enough to handle, peel each tomato starting with the X. The skin should come off easily.

If you like, cut the tomatoes in half crosswise and use your fingers to scoop out the seeds. (I usually leave them in, but Ron and Leetal remove them.) Dice the tomatoes into ¼-inch cubes. Combine in a small bowl with the harissa, olive oil, and salt.

ASSEMBLE: Use the back of a spoon to smooth the cold saffron yogurt across a small platter, creating slightly raised edges. Top with the roasted eggplant. Spoon the harissa tomatoes over to finish.

IRANIAN COMFORT FOOD: CHIPS AND YOGURT

MAKES 1 SERVING

This simple snack is a contrast in textures: cool creamy yogurt slathered on crunchy potato chips. It is indecently delicious. A staple of Iranian comfort foods, it's a satisfying munchie while watching TV or a cheeky appetizer to serve with cocktails at a dinner party. It is also an excellent introduction to having your yogurt in a savory way. This snack works with plain yogurt or the savory Maast-o-Moosir (page 64). Which consistency of yogurt to use is up to you, but I suggest a plain, unstrained, saucy yogurt as it will coat the chips better than a thicker Greek-style yogurt. If you're doing this right, you really are coating them liberally. (This is not a demure snack. Go to town!)

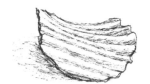

I give the recipe for one person, but it's easy to scale up for a party—or just for seconds.

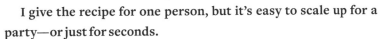

1 individual-size bag plain salted potato chips

1 cup plain yogurt or Maast-O-Moosir (page 64)

Put the chips in a bowl and douse—not drizzle, but douse, *subsume*, *smother*—them with the yogurt. Serve with a spoon for the maximum yogurt-to-chip ratio.

Soups

and Stews

For Feasts and Celebrations

For Everyday

I open this chapter with traditional Iranian soups and stews for feasts and celebrations because it takes me back in time.

I remember them being cooked in cauldrons with a dozen people all contributing. The cauldrons would be filled at dawn with herbs and meats and vegetables. The exact quantity of ingredients was always different, so these recipes have been difficult to capture in words. If there was too much parsley, someone would balance it with more beans. If there was too much rice, we would add more yogurt or broth. Somehow, these stews tasted exactly the same each time, but each time the process of getting there took a different path.

The large serving sizes and techniques for building these stews may seem intimidating, and that's understandable. But part of my goal here is to present these recipes as I experienced them. The main lesson I want to convey is that nothing ever goes to waste. You put everything in the pot—from the stalks of the herbs to any overabundance you may have of a particular ingredient, even if the "recipe" calls for less. You cook the soups for so long and become so familiar with their essence that you learn to balance out the flavors toward the end. For some Iranians, this tasting and adjusting is intuitive. For others, Iranian or not, it's a learned skill that comes from experience, some courage, and a palate that develops over time.

The second portion of this chapter is dedicated to everyday soups that are simpler to make, most of which have been inspired by the whey. They feel and taste more modern and unique, while still bringing a sense of comfort and familiarity. These soups include contributions from members of my Brooklyn community (Whey-Enhanced Summer Gazpacho, page 112, and Cauliflower Whey Soup, page 118) and one from a dear family member (Mother-in-Law's Cold Cucumber Soup, page 114).

These everyday soups have varying yields, serving two to eight people depending on the recipe. When I was a single woman living in a tiny New York City apartment, I never made soups in consistent serving sizes. On colder days, or on days I knew I had a hard week coming up, I would make soup for the whole week ahead, secure in the comfort that an easy dinner was waiting for me at home. On other days, I had time at the end of the day to simmer up a smaller pot without worrying so much about the days ahead. I've remained true to that spirit here, offering a variety of options in a variety of yields. Each one gets tastier over time as the flavors continue to mingle. As an added bonus, all these everyday soups freeze well.

A NOTE ON WHEY: You may substitute whey wherever a recipe calls for water, as in the Dizi (page 105)—or use a combination of whey and water as an economical and tasty way to use up all the whey you may have. Whey adds three things to a soup stock: subtle creaminess, body, and a hit of acid. Where normally you'd add this acid in the form of lemon juice, vinegar, or even tomatoes, whey can play that same role while also adding some creaminess, elevating even the simplest of soups. All that said, if you don't have sufficient whey when it's called for, you're always welcome to substitute water.

For Feasts and Celebrations

AASH-E-MAAST (YOGURT STEW)

SERVES 10; MAKES ABOUT 5 QUARTS

Plan ahead! Allow 4 hours for the chickpeas to soak.

Yogurt and rice are a staple pairing in Iranian comfort food. This homey stew incorporates both, plus herbs, and is an excellent way to use up leftover and/or imperfect versions of all three ingredients. Broken or dulled rice grains, tough or bruised herbs, and unevenly textured yogurt when combined here will still make a perfect pot of stew. The joy of this recipe is in its chaos, and it's very forgiving.

Yogurt is the most important element here, though it's added at the last moment. It's especially important to use unstrained yogurt in this recipe. Do not substitute Greek yogurt, as it will make the stew too thick.

The second most important factor is time. You can take a lot of liberties with the quantity of herbs or rice or whatever you are trying to use up, but the timing is crucial because that is what gives this soup its thick, porridge-like consistency. Note that you will need to plan ahead: The chickpeas need to soak for 4 hours before cooking,* and the stew simmers for 90 minutes.

In this stew, the rice isn't meant to be too discernible; it simply gives the stew a nice thickness. Use long-grain rice; while even broken grains are fine, avoid risotto-style rice and Japanese sushi rice as both will be too firm.

---

* I know you are thinking of subbing canned chickpeas and skipping the soaking step. Don't do it. You have to soak the rice anyway, so just soak the chickpeas, too. Soaking reduces the cooking time and gives the appropriate texture to the stew.

CONTINUES

In addition to the fresh leafy herbs listed below, this stew welcomes adding any combination of other tender-leafed herbs and greens, including spinach, green onions, fenugreek, tarreh, and standard leeks. When preparing your herbs, do not discard their stems, even if they're woody; the point of Persian stews is to boil otherwise tough ingredients down into tender morsels. Finely chop the stems and proceed with confidence.

This stew is fun to make and, with at least one other person in the kitchen, a bit of a dance.

Here's how we make this stew on a typical evening in the Dashtaki household. The division of roles and responsibilities rarely varies, so the scene plays out the same each time. Be aware that the number one frustration of ever eating over at my place is that we run late; even if we are on time we are late. (That's why we serve the good liquor.)

IF YOU'RE AIMING TO EAT AROUND 9:30 PM, START AT 3:00 PM

PERSON 1: Put the chickpeas in a medium bowl. Cover with several inches of cool water and leave to soak for about 4 hours.

6:00 PM

PERSON 2: When you've got 1 hour left for the chickpeas to finish soaking, put the rice in a separate medium bowl and cover with several inches of cool water. Leave in the soaking water until directed in the recipe.

7:00 PM

PERSON 1: Sound the alarms that we're starting to cook! Bring 4 quarts water to a boil in a large (ideally 8-quart capacity) pot.

Drain the chickpeas, add them to the boiling water with a pinch of salt, return the water to a boil, and simmer over medium-high heat until tender, about 1 hour.

PERSON 2: Wash the fresh herbs and set aside to dry (see page 30 for instructions). Remove the yogurt from the fridge so it has time to come up to room temperature.

1 cup dried chickpeas

2 cups long-grain white rice

1 bunch parsley (2 to 3 cups loosely packed stems and leaves)

1 bunch cilantro (about 2 cups loosely packed stems and leaves)

½ bunch dill (about 1 cup loosely packed stems and fronds)

¼ bunch mint (about ¼ cup loosely packed stems and leaves)

2 quarts plain whole milk yogurt

3 tablespoons plus ¾ cup vegetable oil

2 medium yellow onions, diced

4 garlic cloves, roughly chopped

½ teaspoon kosher salt, or more to taste

1 teaspoon freshly ground black pepper, or more to taste

1 tablespoon ground turmeric

½ cup dried mint

7:45 PM

PERSON 1: Heat the 3 tablespoons oil in a large skillet over medium heat. Add the onions and sauté, stirring frequently, until moderately browned, 15 to 20 minutes.

While you're at it, check the chickpeas. They should be almost fully cooked. (There is little risk of overcooking them, and the stock they give off makes the aash's texture silky. Keep cooking!)

Turn on some music. Hayedeh is our favorite.

PERSON 2: Reduce the heat under the skillet slightly and add the garlic, salt, pepper, and turmeric to the onions. Cook, stirring constantly, until fragrant and a bit dry, about 1 minute. Remove the skillet from the heat.

PERSON 2: Chop the herbs and any other tender-leafed greens that you washed and dried earlier. Run an extra chop over any hardy stems.

PERSON 1: When you're sure the chickpeas are tender, drain the rice and add it to the chickpeas. The rice will thicken the stew as it cooks.

Cook for 15 minutes, then add all the herbs. Continue cooking until the starches in the rice release and make the broth sticky and thick, and the bubbles on the surface become more visibly viscous, about 10 minutes longer, stirring frequently so nothing sticks to the bottom of the pot. You'll know you're ready to move on when the light, bright bursts of bubbles give way to thick, syrupy burps at the top of the water line.

9:00 PM

PERSON 1: Reduce the heat to low and add the onion mixture to the pot. Simmer gently, stirring frequently as you don't want the thickening stew to settle on the bottom of the pot and burn, about 10 minutes. Taste for seasoning, adding some salt and pepper, if you like. (You'll have another chance to correct the seasoning at the end.) Remove from the heat. Cover to keep warm.

CONTINUES

9:10 PM

PERSON 2: Heat the ¾ cup oil in a medium skillet over medium heat. When the oil is hot but not smoking, add the dried mint. Fry for only a few seconds, as dried mint burns quickly. Quickly transfer the mint oil to a heat-resistant bowl to stop the cooking. The infused dark green oil will smell deeply aromatic and earthy. You'll use it shortly. Hang tight!

By 9:20 the stew will be super thick. Keep it over low heat and keep stirring.

PERSON 1 OR 2: Wash a few dishes to get ahead of the game. Set the table.

9:30 PM

AASH IS READY! Pour the stew into a large serving bowl and stir in the yogurt. This will make it the correct—looser—consistency. Adjust the salt and pepper to taste one last time, if necessary. Drizzle about half the minty oil over the top. Put the rest of the minty oil in a small dish for folks to drizzle on top of their own bowls of stew.

Serve and enjoy! Be prepared for PERSON 1 to take all the credit.

This stew will last for 1 week in the refrigerator. To reheat, add a touch of water and warm gently in the microwave or on the stovetop over low heat, stirring occasionally.

AASH-E-RESHTEH (STEW OF MANY THREADS)

SERVES 16; MAKES ABOUT 8 QUARTS

Plan ahead! You'll need the chickpeas and kidney beans to soak overnight. The kashk sauce needs to start at least 1 day prior to serving and may be made up to 1 month ahead and stored in the fridge. Consider making See-Rogh (page 178), too. It usually accompanies aash-e-reshteh at major Zoroastrian feasts

Aash-e-reshteh is generally reserved for religious holidays, weddings and other special occasions, and the New Year. It's a stew meant to be prepared *by* a crowd and served *to* a crowd. Making it is a party where everyone plays a role: the leafy greens need cleaning and chopping, the noodle dough must be kneaded, rolled, and cut, and there is much stirring. The labor in this soup is the joy. (It's the most pleasurable work there is!)

The large quantity of herbs and spinach gives this meatless stew a lot of body, the kidney beans and chickpeas lend it a hearty warmth, and a confetti of condiments—kashk, fried garlic, onion, and hot mint oil—give it a bright and particularly Iranian flavor.

The from-scratch noodle threads (reshteh) in this recipe are the climax of the cooking festivities. In my family, men and women gather to cut the noodle threads together, making the noodles as diverse as the hands that cut them. When the noodles are ready, we take turns scattering a handful at a time into the soup to the soundtrack of our hooting and hollering and group prayer.

As you drop the noodles into the soup, it's customary to make a wish with each handful. I attribute many of my life's blessings—from my career to my babies—to this stew.

NOTE: The noodles, the stew, and the condiments are at times simultaneously prepared by your crew. Look for timing cues in the noodle preparation. Once you get a feel for this recipe, the dance can have many variations and always come out the same.

CONTINUES

STEW

1 cup dried chickpeas

1 cup dried kidney beans

2 cups all-purpose flour,
plus more for dusting

1 cup whole wheat flour

2 teaspoons kosher salt,
divided, plus more to taste

½ cup grapeseed oil
or vegetable oil

4 large yellow onions, halved
and thinly sliced lengthwise

2 teaspoons ground turmeric

1 teaspoon ground coriander

1 teaspoon ground cumin

1 teaspoon freshly ground
black pepper

2 cups dried brown lentils

3 pounds mature or savoy spinach,
stems included, washed of
all grit, finely chopped

3 bunches flat-leaf parsley,
with stems, washed (see
page 30) and finely chopped

2 bunches cilantro, with
stems, washed (see page 30)
and finely chopped

4 bunches green onions,
roots trimmed, green
parts thinly sliced, white
parts roughly chopped

CONDIMENTS

2 cups grapeseed or vegetable oil

4 large yellow onions, halved and
very thinly sliced lengthwise

3 heads garlic, individual
cloves peeled and minced

½ cup dried mint

1 quart Kashk Sauce (page 57
or store-bought)

TO PREP THE STEW: The night before you plan to cook and serve the stew, put the chickpeas and kidney beans in a large bowl. Cover with several inches of cool water, cover, and leave to soak overnight at room temperature.

MAKE THE NOODLES: In a medium bowl, whisk together the all-purpose flour, whole wheat flour, and 1 teaspoon of the salt. Pour in 1 cup water and knead by hand until you have a smooth and elastic dough, about 3 minutes. Cover the bowl with a dish towel and allow to rest for at least 1 hour at room temperature. This is a good time for someone to start making the stew.

Divide the dough into fourths. Lightly flour a work surface and, working with one piece of dough at a time, roll it into a ball and sprinkle with flour. (Keep the other 3 portions covered.) Use a rolling pin to gently roll the ball into a very thin round, as thin as you possibly can, aiming for a thickness of $\frac{1}{16}$ inch. Dust the dough heavily with flour and fold into thirds, like a letter. Dust the dough again with flour and fold in half the long way. Set aside and cover loosely with plastic wrap to prevent it from drying out. Repeat the process with the remaining 3 portions of dough. Let rest for 30 minutes.

Gather the troops! This next step benefits from as many people as want to participate. Sprinkle a baking sheet with flour and set aside. Gently lift one of the folded dough sheets onto a floured work surface. Use a sharp knife (a chef's knife works well) to cut the dough into ⅛-inch-thick slices, narrower than fettucine and a little wider than linguine. Transfer the noodles to the floured baking sheet and gently fluff and separate them, making sure they are well floured so they don't stick together. Work with the second and third dough sheets in exactly the same way, forming noodles. Once you reach the last sheet, begin cutting noodles as before, but stop before you reach the end and pinch off a 1-inch nub of dough. Add the cut noodles to the rest of the noodles on the baking sheet.

Form the nub into the shape of an oil lamp. The person who gets to drop in the oil lamp is considered an honored guest, one who gets to make a special wish to put in the magical stew. As with the small trinket in a King Cake, whoever receives the dough oil lamp in their soup is also considered lucky and their wishes deemed to be extra blessed.

Allow the noodles and the oil lamp to dry (uncovered) on the baking sheet for at least 30 minutes. This is a good time for some people to start making the condiments.

MAKE THE STEW: Drain the chickpeas and kidney beans and rinse. Transfer to a large pot (at least 12-quart capacity), cover with 8 quarts water, and bring to a boil over high heat. Reduce to a simmer and cook until the beans are tender, about 1½ hours.

Meanwhile, in a large skillet, heat the oil over medium-high heat. Add the onions and sauté, stirring as necessary, until the onions are deeply caramelized and almost crispy, about 35 minutes. Watch carefully to prevent burning. Turn the heat down to medium, add the turmeric, coriander, cumin, pepper, and the remaining 1 teaspoon salt. Cook, stirring frequently, for 3 to 5 minutes, until the spices are fragrant. Remove from the heat.

Once the chickpeas and kidney beans are tender, add the lentils, spiced onions, spinach, parsley, cilantro, and green onions to the pot. Add another 2 quarts water and bring to a quick boil. Reduce the heat to medium and continue to simmer until the lentils are tender, about 30 minutes.

CONTINUES

ADD THE NOODLES: Raise the heat ever so slightly to bring to a steady boil. Gather every-one together to start adding the noodles. Taking turns, each person sprinkles a handful of noodles into the pot, while saying prayers and/or meditating and/or making earnest silent wishes. Someone should be stirring the pot constantly and gently from the bottom. After all the noodles are added, have a beloved community member (or yourself) drop the oil lamp into the stew and make a wish. Simmer until the noodles are tender, continuing to stir from the bottom so they don't settle, 20 to 30 minutes. Check for salt. (I add about 3 tablespoons, but add it to your own taste.) Reduce the heat and gently simmer, stirring occasionally to prevent settling and burning at the bottom of the pot, as you finish off the condiments. (It doesn't matter if the noodles overcook.)

PREPARE THE CONDIMENTS: Heat 1 cup of the oil in a large skillet (mine is 14 inches in diameter) over medium-high heat. Add the onions and cook, stirring frequently, until crispy, 35 to 40 minutes. Using a slotted spoon, transfer the onions to a bowl. Add another ¼ cup oil and the garlic and cook, still over medium-high heat, until the garlic is golden and crispy. Transfer the garlic with a slotted spoon to the bowl with the onions. Add the remaining ¾ cup oil to the skillet. When the oil is hot, fry the dried mint for just a few seconds (it burns very quickly). Transfer the mint and its now-dark-green oil to another heat-resistant bowl.

SERVE: Each serving of aash-e-reshteh is topped with caramelized onions, fried garlic, kashk sauce, and fried mint oil. You as the host can do this for your guests, creating decora-tive patterns, or let guests garnish their own bowls to taste. Either way, present the remain-ing condiments at the table.

DIZI

*Plan ahead! You'll need the chickpeas and white beans to soak
overnight. The entire dish takes at least 4 hours to stew slowly.*

Ceremonial and fatty, this soup is eaten with such flair that con-
suming it is an event in itself. It is traditionally cooked over the
fire in earthenware crocks called dizi, which is how the dish got its
nickname. Lamb bones, fat, and slow-simmered meat mingle with
chickpeas, white beans, potatoes, and tomatoes. The solids are
separated from the broth, mashed and presented with an ornate
display of condiments and a good dose of pomp.

If I could guide your first bites of dizi, I would recommend you to
place a slice of onion and a pinch of herbs in your mouth and chew.
Then take a scoop of the meat with some bread and invite it to join
the onion and herbs. Chew. Close your eyes in delight. Take a sip of
the rich broth to punctuate the bite. Repeat with a different combination of herbs.

A serving of tea and honey-drenched sweets called bamieh
typically finish the meal.

NOTE: The most reliable source of lamb in my experience in America is a
Middle Eastern halal butcher. The added benefit of finding one is that they
will have lamb neck and bones and not think it's weird or bat an eyelash at
the quantities requested. Either way, choose meat that is fresh and not previ-
ously frozen. Follow the weight cues on the ingredients below; the quantity
of lambs shanks and potatoes can vary at this scale.

CONTINUES

2 cups dried chickpeas

2 cups dried white beans
(such as cannellini)

2 or 3 lamb shanks (about
4 pounds total)

2 pounds lamb necks

1 pound lamb bones

2 large yellow onions,
roughly chopped

2 teaspoons ground turmeric

3 tablespoons kosher salt,
plus more to taste

1 tablespoon freshly ground black
pepper, plus more to taste

8 whole dried (Omani)
limes (see page 29)

1 quart boiling water

6 medium tomatoes (about
2 pounds), quartered

8 Yukon Gold potatoes (about
3 pounds), halved (unpeeled)

2 tablespoons tomato paste

CONDIMENTS

3 small white onions,
quartered and sliced

2 bunches of any combination
of green onions, tareh
(Persian leeks, see page 30),
cilantro, flat-leaf parsley,
fenugreek, and/or basil

1 bunch radishes

Bread—ideally sangaak
or lavash or pita, in that
order of preference

The night before you plan to cook and serve the stew, put the chickpeas and white beans in a large bowl. Cover with several inches of cool water, cover, and leave to soak overnight at room temperature.

The next day, put the lamb shanks, necks, and bones in a large stockpot (at least 12-quart capacity). Add 8 quarts water, the onions, turmeric, salt, and pepper. Bring to a boil over high heat. Lower the heat and simmer at a slow, gentle bubble until the meat is very tender, about 2 hours, occasionally skimming off any foam that rises to the top.

While the stew simmers, carefully puncture the dried limes in several places with a paring knife and put them in a small heatproof bowl. Pour the boiling water over them and let soak for 30 minutes. Add the limes and their soaking water to the stew.

Once the meat is tender, drain the chickpeas and white beans and add them to the pot, along with the tomatoes and potatoes.

Put the tomato paste in a small bowl and stir in ½ cup of the warm broth until smooth. Scrape the mixture back into the pot and season with salt and pepper to taste. If you notice that the water has reduced to less than 6 quarts, add more water here. Simmer until the potatoes are tender and the meat has completely fallen off the bones, about 1 hour longer.

Place a colander over a large bowl or pot (Bowl #1). Set another large bowl, ideally one with a flat bottom (Bowl #2), next to you on the counter. Working in batches, ladle the stew into the colander, draining the broth into Bowl #1. Most of the meat will fall off the bones, but work into the crevices of the neck bone to salvage all of the meat. Do not discard any of the fat. Pick the cleaned bones and dried limes out of the solids in the colander and discard. Transfer the remaining solids in the colander to Bowl #2 and repeat the process until all the stew has been strained.

Now comes the fun part, where we mash together all the meat, beans, and vegetables in Bowl #2. If you don't have a traditional goosht koob, you can use a potato masher or the bottom of a sturdy cup. Keep mashing until the potatoes and beans are no longer distinct and you have a thick paste, about the consistency of raw hamburger meat.

Serve the mashed meat and the broth in separate bowls. Arrange the onions, sabzi (fresh herbs), radishes, and bread on a communal platter for people to help themselves.

Dizi may be made up to 3 days ahead, but store the soup in a single container, without separating the meat and potatoes. To serve, reheat gently on the stovetop, then separate and mash right before serving.

For Everyday

PERSIAN EGG DROP SOUP

SERVES 2; MAKES ABOUT 1½ QUARTS

This is a wonderfully simple, savory, and tart wintertime favorite featuring herbs and yogurt. I highly recommend making this when you are fighting a cold. There is very little prep work, as this recipe calls for dried herbs exclusively. The trickiest part of this soup is heating up the yogurt because you don't want it to curdle. Take your time and follow the instructions below carefully.

2 tablespoons vegetable oil

1 large yellow onion, diced

2 tablespoons all-purpose flour

1 tablespoon dried ziziphora (kakooti; see My Pantry, page 33) or dried fenugreek

1 tablespoon dried mint

1 teaspoon ground turmeric

2 cups plain whole milk yogurt

Kosher salt and freshly ground black pepper

2 large eggs, whisked

Heat the oil in a medium pot over high heat. Add the onion and sauté, stirring occasionally, until golden brown, 5 to 10 minutes. Add the flour, 1 tablespoon at a time, stirring to absorb into the oil and onions, about 5 minutes longer. Add the ziziphora or fenugreek, dried mint, and turmeric. Cook, stirring, so the herbs release their flavors, 5 minutes longer.

Add 1 quart water and bring to a gentle simmer. Reduce the heat to low. Add the yogurt very slowly in 4 additions, stirring constantly and between each addition. Move slowly and gently so the yogurt doesn't separate or curdle. (Think of adding cold water to a warm bath—you want to do it so slowly that it is almost imperceptible that the temperature of the water is changing.) Continue cooking until it has fully warmed up, about 5 minutes total. Season with salt and pepper to taste.

Ever so slowly dribble the eggs into the soup, stirring as you pour so the eggs disperse evenly and form ribbons rather than clumps. Bring back to a simmer and serve immediately.

SHOOLEY YAZDI

SERVES 6; MAKES ABOUT 3 QUARTS

*Plan ahead! You'll need 1 hour for the lentils to soak
(use this time to prep the rest of your ingredients).*

Shooley is a meatless soup with ingredients that are easy to ration during lean winter months. Across the many regions of Iran, there are many different varieties of shooley. Beets, turnips, lentils, flour, dried herbs, and tangy liquids like pomegranate molasses, sour grape water, or vinegar form the backbone of its flavor.

My dad was born during the cold month of December, in Yazd, Iran. He is the second-youngest of nine children, and of the stories we have heard, if you were born in the wintertime you were delivered in the barn with the donkeys and hay keeping you warm. If you were born in the summertime, you were delivered in the yard in the shade. From a very young age my dad and his siblings all worked on the farm and would often joke that watered-down shooley was all they got to eat and sometimes this shooley was nothing more than stone soup.

I've improvised this recipe from stories my dad and my uncles have told over the years. I have intentionally not dressed it up to be something other than it is: a very simple, nutritious, satisfying, and wildly variable soup.

1 cup brown lentils

1 pound beets or turnips, with
   stems and leaves attached

3 tablespoons vegetable oil

2 large yellow onions, chopped

1 tablespoon ground turmeric

1 tablespoon kosher salt,
   plus more to taste

1½ teaspoons freshly ground
   black pepper, plus more to taste

1 cup all-purpose flour

1 teaspoon dried oregano

1 teaspoon dried dill

1 teaspoon dried parsley

1 teaspoon dried fenugreek

⅔ cup sour grape juice (see My
   Pantry, page 32) or white vinegar

Noon-e-khosk (see My Pantry,
   page 29), for serving

Sort and rinse the lentils. Put them in a medium bowl, cover with 2 inches of cool water, and set aside to soak for 1 hour. Meanwhile, wash and quarter your beets or turnips (no need to peel) and finely chop the leaves.

In a large soup pot, heat the oil over medium heat. Add the onions, season with the turmeric, salt, and pepper, and cook until browned, about 10 minutes. Drain the soaked lentils and add to the onions. Add 2 quarts water and the beets or turnips with their greens and bring to a boil. Lower the heat to a simmer and continue cooking until the beets or turnips are tender, about 40 minutes.

Carefully remove 1 cup of the simmering liquid (which is now your broth) and transfer it to a medium bowl. Add 1 cup water, then whisk in the flour in 4 additions until smooth. Scrape the mixture back into the stew and continue to stir until fully incorporated. Add up to another 2 cups water here if you prefer a soup consistency rather than a stew consistency. Simmer for 20 minutes. Add all the dried herbs and the sour grape juice or vinegar and simmer for an additional 20 minutes. Season to taste with salt and pepper.

Serve hot with noon-e-khosk.

BORSCHT BY WHEY OF BROOKLYN

SERVES 8; MAKES ABOUT 4 QUARTS

As I looked outside my own culture for inspiration for whey-based recipes, I came across Eastern European traditions for making spring-time borscht using whey or buttermilk. Borscht includes a whole family of soupy dishes that range in color from deep reddish-pink to off-white and in texture from thin and brothy to thick and stew-like. Most red borscht recipes (those that contain beets) call for vinegar to provide a zingy contrast to the sweet beets and the addition of mild, sturdy potatoes and cabbage. The chunky, meaty version of borscht I offer here uses whey rather than vinegar to give the soup a gentle, pleasing tang.

2 pounds English-cut (bone-in, separated along the bone) beef short ribs

Kosher salt and freshly ground black pepper

3 tablespoons olive oil, divided

1 quart beef broth

8 medium beets (about 4 pounds), stems and roots trimmed, bulbs scrubbed

2 medium yellow onions, diced

4 garlic cloves, minced

1 tablespoon whole coriander seeds

4 medium waxy potatoes (about 1½ pounds total), scrubbed and cut into 1-inch dice

½ head large green cabbage, shredded

1 quart yogurt whey, or more for a brothier consistency

1 cup strained (Greek-style) whole milk yogurt, for garnish

½ cup chopped fresh dill, for garnish

Generously season the short ribs on all sides with salt and pepper. Heat a large heavy-bottomed soup pot or Dutch oven over medium-high heat, add 1 tablespoon of the olive oil, then add the short ribs one at a time with tongs, maintaining some space between them. Sear for 3 to 4 minutes on each side, until they reach a deep caramel color all over. Turn off the heat and carefully pour in the broth, scraping up the browned bits on the bottom of the pot with a wooden spoon. Bring it back to a boil over high heat, then reduce the heat to medium-low and cover the pot. Simmer for about 2 hours, until the meat turns tender and sticky and is easy to pierce with a fork.

While the meat cooks, roast the beets. Preheat the oven to 400°F. Place the beets in a glass baking dish and add water to a depth of ¼ inch. Cover tightly with aluminum foil and roast until they offer no resistance when pierced with a paring knife, 45 to 60 minutes. (When checking them, lift the foil *carefully* to avoid steam burns.). Set aside to cool, reserving the beet liquid.

Once cool enough to handle, pick up the beets one at a time and slip off their skins. (If you don't want pink hands, use latex gloves.) Cut into 1-inch pieces.

When the ribs are tender, transfer them to a plate, let cool slightly, and shred with 2 forks, or cut into ¼-inch dice. Discard the bones or save them for another use, such as making more broth. Set the Dutch oven with its liquid aside, as you'll soon cook the rest of the soup in there. Stash the meat in the fridge for now.

Heat a large skillet over medium heat and pour in the remaining 2 tablespoons oil. Add the onions and a pinch of salt and sauté, stirring frequently, until they begin to brown, about 20 minutes. Add the garlic and coriander seeds and cook, stirring, until fragrant, about 1 minute.

Scrape the onion mixture into the Dutch oven with the beef broth. Add the beets and the reserved beet liquid, potatoes, and cabbage. Pour in the whey (adding more whey for a soupier consistency) and bring to a simmer. Cover and simmer until the potatoes are soft and the cabbage is limp and tender, checking for soft resistance with a paring knife or fork, about 25 minutes. Add the shredded short ribs and simmer for a few more minutes, until the meat is warmed through. Season with salt and pepper to taste.

To serve, spoon into bowls and top each serving with a dollop of yogurt and a sprinkling of fresh dill.

If not serving immediately, this soup keeps well and the flavor will continue to improve after resting overnight in a covered container in the fridge. This soup also freezes well for up to 3 months. If freezing, do so without the yogurt or dill garnish and add them just before serving.

WHEY-ENHANCED SUMMER GAZPACHO

SERVES 2; MAKES ABOUT 1½ QUARTS

*Plan ahead! The soup needs at least 4 hours to chill
in the refrigerator to amplify the flavors.*

I met Chef Rob Newton, an Arkansas native, at the Taste of Red
Hook. This annual fundraiser benefited the Red Hook Initiative, a
neighborhood youth advocacy and education nonprofit. Rob was
serving up his southern specialties and I was offering my whey
drinks. Rob owned several restaurants in Brooklyn over the years
and has long championed local food producers, including me.

Rob was intrigued by the possibilities of cooking with whey
and experimented quite a bit. This gazpacho recipe is one of his
many inspired creations, and it's now one of my favorite versions
of this classic soup. Because the whey is never heated, the probiotics remain fully alive. On a hot summer day, this chilled soup
packed with peak-season farmers' market produce both refreshes
and hydrates.

3 pounds good, fresh, ripe
  tomatoes (any variety)

1 jalapeño, stemmed, seeded,
  and roughly chopped

1 long European cucumber,
  peeled and roughly chopped

6 to 8 fresh mint leaves,
  plus more for garnish

6 to 8 fresh basil leaves,
  plus more for garnish

1 small shallot, roughly chopped

1 small garlic clove,
  roughly chopped

1 to 2 cups yogurt whey

Juice of 1 lemon

½ teaspoon kosher salt,
  or more to taste

Good olive oil and crushed
  red pepper, for garnish

Fill a stockpot halfway with water and bring to a boil. Cut a small X just through the skin on the bottom of each tomato. Create an ice bath by placing a few handfuls of ice in a large bowl and filling it halfway with cold water.

Carefully drop the tomatoes, 5 or 6 at a time, into the boiling water and blanch until the skin is beginning to curl back at the X, about 20 seconds. Remove with a slotted spoon and transfer to the ice bath. Repeat with the remaining tomatoes.

Remove the tomatoes from the ice bath and use a paring knife to peel off the skins, starting at the X. Cut the tomatoes in half horizontally and use your thumbs to scoop out the seeds. Discard the skins and seeds (or save them for vinaigrettes or tomato sauce).

Roughly chop the tomatoes and put them in a large bowl, along with the jalapeño, cucumber, mint, basil, shallot, and garlic. Puree until smooth using an immersion blender, or in batches using a countertop blender. (If using a countertop blender, do not fill more than halfway.) If you'd like a smoother texture, strain through a fine-mesh sieve.

Whisk in 1 cup of the whey. Add up to 1 cup additional whey slowly, stopping once you achieve the texture you like. Season with the lemon juice and salt until it tastes perfectly balanced. (If it tastes underwhelming, it's probably underseasoned.) Cover and refrigerate for at least 4 hours to amplify the flavors.

When ready to serve, drizzle with olive oil, scatter with basil and mint leaves, and sprinkle with crushed red pepper.

MOTHER-IN-LAW'S COLD CUCUMBER SOUP

SERVES 4; MAKES ABOUT 2 QUARTS

Plan ahead! The soup needs to chill in the refrigerator for 12 to 24 hours.

You should know a few things about my mother-in-law. She was born and raised in Germany during World War II. She has four children, my husband being her favorite (of course). She is highly critical of everything, as a matter of sport. She likes fine chocolate and white wine and is obsessed with manners. She loves my Maast-o-Moosir (page 64), but she does not like plain whey. Not at all. Still, after I explained to her all the different uses for whey, she adapted this delicious cold summer cucumber soup to use both whey and yogurt. This soup is near and dear to me, because it finally persuaded my mother-in-law to embrace using whey in the kitchen.

The soup should ideally be chilled overnight, or you can make it in the morning for that evening's meal. The combination of the sautéed cucumbers, whey, and yogurt makes for an exceptionally refreshing soup with a creamy texture.

4 tablespoons (½ stick) unsalted butter

4 garlic cloves, chopped

1 medium shallot, diced

2 tablespoons fresh thyme leaves (or 4 to 5 sage leaves)

Kosher salt and freshly ground black pepper

4 long European cucumbers, halved lengthwise and cut into ½-inch chunks

1 cup fresh mint leaves, plus more for garnish

⅓ cup fresh dill fronds, plus more for garnish

2 cups yogurt whey, divided

2 cups plain whole milk yogurt

¼ cup Maast-o-Moosir (page 64) or additional plain whole milk yogurt, for garnish

Cooking the cucumbers will feel very, very wrong.

Melt the butter in a large sauté pan over medium heat. Add the garlic, shallot, and thyme (or sage) and sauté until the shallot is translucent, 8 to 10 minutes. Season with salt and pepper to taste. Add the cucumbers and sauté until they begin to soften and become slightly translucent, 8 to 10 minutes longer. (If you are Iranian, cooking the cucumbers will feel very, very wrong, but the soup tastes better this way and I was too scared to question my mother-in-law on this.) Add the mint and dill and stir for 2 to 3 minutes to release their flavor. Add 1 cup of the whey and bring to a simmer. Remove the pan from the heat and let cool for 30 minutes.

Stir in the remaining 1 cup whey and the yogurt. Puree until smooth using an immersion blender, or in batches using a countertop blender. (If using a countertop blender, do not fill more than halfway.) Cover and refrigerate for at least 12 hours or overnight.

Serve cold with a dollop of savory moosir yogurt or plain yogurt and sprigs of dill or mint.

TOOT! TOOT! BLACK BEAN SOUP WITH WHEY

SERVES 8; MAKES ABOUT 4 QUARTS

Plan ahead! The beans need 12 to 24 hours to soak.

Hearty spoonfuls of black beans, pork, and carrots spiced with cumin, coriander, smoky-spicy poblano peppers, and tangy whey combine in a big-batch soup to last all week. Serve with a dollop of savory yogurt, a handful of tortilla chips, or a wedge of warm Whey Cornbread (page 177) for a satisfying meal. You can omit the pork for a vegetarian option.

NOTE: To maximize efficiency, roast the poblano peppers while the beans simmer.

3 tablespoons kosher salt, plus more to taste

1 pound dried black beans, picked over

2 poblano peppers

2 tablespoons olive oil, divided

8 ounces pork belly, cubed

2 medium onions, diced

4 garlic cloves, minced

1½ teaspoons ground cumin

1 teaspoon ground coriander

4 medium carrots, diced

6 cups yogurt whey

1 cup roughly chopped fresh cilantro, leaves and tender stems

Yogurt, for garnish (strained or unstrained; your preference)

Fill a 1-gallon container or large bowl with 3 quarts lukewarm water. Add the salt and stir to dissolve. Add the beans and cover the container. Set aside at room temperature to soak overnight.

Drain the beans and rinse well. Put the beans in a large pot and cover with at least 2 inches of water. Bring to a boil over high heat, then reduce to a gentle simmer. Cover with the lid slightly askew so steam can escape. Simmer until the beans are tender, about 1 hour, adding more water if needed to keep the beans just covered. Taste the beans a few at a time for doneness. When they are fully cooked but not falling apart, drain them.

Meanwhile, roast the poblanos: If you have a gas stove, set the peppers directly on a burner over a high flame and rotate with tongs every 30 seconds, until the skin is blackened all over. This process will take 5 to 7 minutes per pepper. (If you have an electric stove, move an oven rack to the top position and turn on the broiler. Place the peppers on a foil-lined baking sheet and broil until blackened all over, turning as needed.) Transfer the blackened peppers to a glass bowl and cover with a lid to allow them to steam and soften for 15 to 20 minutes. At this point you can slip the skins off with your fingers or rub them off with a paper towel. Cut out the stems and remove the seeds. You may also remove the membranes if you like things less spicy. Dice the peppers and set aside.

Heat a large soup pot over medium heat and pour in 1 tablespoon of the olive oil. Add the pork belly and cook until the fat has rendered and the meat begins to caramelize, 5 to 7 minutes. Use a slotted spoon to transfer the pork to a plate and set aside.

Add the remaining 1 tablespoon olive oil to the rendered pork fat in the pot. Once hot, add the onions with a pinch of salt and sauté, stirring occasionally, until lightly browned, 15 to 20 minutes. Add the garlic, cumin, coriander, and diced poblanos. Sauté until fragrant, about 1 minute. Add the carrots, reserved pork belly, whey, and drained beans. Turn the heat up to high and bring the soup to a boil. Reduce the heat to low and cover the pot. Simmer until the carrots are tender but not mushy, about 45 minutes. Just before serving, stir in the cilantro.

If you prefer a thicker soup, you can add body by using an immersion blender to partially puree it. (Or blend about one-quarter of the soup in a countertop blender, making sure not to fill the blender more than halfway. Return the puréed soup to the pot.) Garnish each bowl with a dollop of yogurt.

CAULIFLOWER WHEY SOUP

SERVES 4; MAKES ABOUT 2 QUARTS

This recipe hails from Nekisia Davis, the owner of Early Bird Granola. The White Moustache shared one of our early production spaces with Early Bird, and Nekisia kindly helped me figure out new uses for our whey by taking some home and playing around with it. This recipe was the most delicious result of that partnership. This simple soup comes together quickly and uses a Parmesan rind for extra flavor.

2 medium leeks

4 to 5 tablespoons olive oil

4 garlic cloves, roughly chopped

Kosher salt and freshly ground black pepper

1 teaspoon crushed red pepper

1 medium head Romanesco cauliflower, chopped

8 cups yogurt whey or water, divided

3 or 4 thyme sprigs

Parmesan rind (optional)

Trim just the roots off the leeks. Cut the leeks in half lengthwise and rinse under cold water to remove the dirt. Slice crosswise into half-moons.

Heat the oil over medium heat in a Dutch oven or large, deep frying pan. Add the leeks and garlic, season with a generous pinch of salt and the crushed red pepper, and cook slowly until the vegetables are translucent, about 15 minutes. Do not let them brown.

Add the Romanesco and stir to coat evenly with oil. Season with salt and black pepper and add more oil if it seems necessary. Cook until the cauliflower turns soft and takes on a bit of color, 5 minutes or so. Add 6 cups of the whey, the thyme, and the Parmesan rind, if using.

Turn the heat up until the whey bubbles a bit, then turn it down to the gentlest of simmers. Cover with the lid slightly askew so steam can escape and simmer for 25 minutes.

Remove the pot from the heat and allow to cool for 10 minutes. Remove the herbs and the Parmesan rind, if you used it. Puree until smooth using an immersion blender, or in batches using a countertop blender. (If using a countertop blender, do not fill more than halfway. Remove the cap in the center of the lid and firmly hold a folded towel over the hole while pureeing.)

Add the remaining 2 cups whey slowly, stirring, until you achieve the texture you want. (You may not use it all.) Adding this whey at the end will brighten the soup and keep the probiotics alive! Store leftovers in a covered container in the refrigerator for up to 2 days.

ROASTED CARROT AND RED CURRY SOUP WITH WHEY

SERVES 8; MAKES ABOUT 4 QUARTS

This simple soup shows how whey can make a bare-bones (or no-bones, in this case) recipe sing. Roasting the carrots before adding them to soup deepens and concentrates their flavor, and Thai curry paste lends a nice heat. This soup taught me how to use whey as a base to impact both the texture and the taste of a soup in a quiet yet powerful way. Much less heavy-handed than adding cream or milk to a soup, whey provides a nice tang and complements rather than cuts the creaminess of the coconut milk, which lets all the ingredients shine brightly. It is the perfect team player.

3 pounds carrots (about
    5 large), scrubbed, trimmed,
    and cut into large dice

4 tablespoons olive oil, divided

1 teaspoon kosher salt,
    plus more to taste

½ teaspoon freshly ground
    black pepper

1 large yellow onion, diced

4 garlic cloves, minced

2 tablespoons peeled and
    grated fresh ginger

3 tablespoons Thai red curry paste

1 (14-ounce) can full-fat
    coconut milk

3 cups yogurt whey

Chopped fresh cilantro
    leaves, for garnish

Preheat the oven to 400°F. Line a rimmed baking sheet with parchment paper or aluminum foil.

Spread out the carrots on the prepared baking sheet, drizzle with 2 tablespoons of the olive oil, and sprinkle with the salt and pepper. Roast until the carrots are tender and browned in spots, 25 to 30 minutes, turning once.

Meanwhile, heat a large soup pot or Dutch oven over medium heat. Add the remaining 2 tablespoons olive oil. Add the onion and a pinch of salt and sauté, stirring frequently, until light tan and starting to soften, 6 to 8 minutes. Add the garlic, ginger, and curry paste and stir until fragrant, about 3 minutes longer.

When the carrots are ready, add them to the soup. Stir in the coconut milk and whey. Bring to boil over high heat, then reduce to a simmer. Cover and simmer, stirring occasionally, for 20 minutes.

Puree the soup until smooth using an immersion blender, or in batches using a countertop blender. (If using a countertop blender, do not fill more than halfway. Remove the cap in the center of the lid and firmly hold a folded towel over the hole while pureeing. You do not want a hot soup volcano erupting in your kitchen.) Correct the seasoning with additional salt and the texture with additional whey, if desired.

Garnish with chopped cilantro and serve. The soup will keep in the refrigerator for up to 3 days or in the freezer for up to 3 months.

Rice

We Iranians take our rice, and particularly our tah-diq, seriously.

The most coveted part of Iranian rice, the tah-diq is the crunchy, crispy layer at bottom of the pot. *Tah* means "bottom," *diq* means "pot." Recent generations have turned the unveiling of the tah-diq into a show, one with drama, suspense, and a grand, satisfying reveal. Find my technique for creating a showstopping tah-diq on page 124.

Yogurt features prominently in this chapter, as rice and yogurt are longtime partners with much in common. Both are usually present in some form during lunch and dinner, both celebrate a single ingredient where heat and time do most of the work, and both tend to provoke some anxiety because you don't know for sure if you've made them right until the very end. Making rice, like making yogurt, is a finesse-heavy technique. This is my opportunity to pass on my tips and tricks for preparing both. As with the magic of yogurt-making, once you get the technique of rice-making down, you can't ever unlearn it. It will seep into your bones.

Topped with a few cracks of black pepper, yogurt and rice is the ultimate comfort food. I remember eating this rice-yogurt combination as a child to calm a tummy ache and as a young adult to calm a broken heart. If you need further proof that they create extra-special magic together, look to Tachin (page 136) and Biryani (page 139). And even though yogurt is already incorporated into these dishes, both beg for an extra bowl of yogurt on the table as well.

I've included a few kababs and stews in this chapter as well. They make the ideal accompaniment to a perfect pot of Persian rice.

PERSIAN RICE
(Tah-Dah! Tah-Diq!)

MAKES ABOUT 8 SERVINGS

Plan ahead! The rice needs to soak for 1 hour.

As the basic building block of every Iranian meal, this staple rice dish is an art form. My parents, in their old age, now use a rice cooker that attempts to mimic this artistry. I have never forgiven them for this, especially because I know they can make a better pot of rice using this very technique below, which they taught me. I suppose what I really won't forgive them for is getting old in the first place.

This technique-heavy rice is cooked in two stages. In Stage 1, you'll boil the rice to soften it slightly; in Stage 2, you'll let the rice steam until it's tender and fluffy and develops a golden, crispy bottom layer. Tah-diq may consist of plain rice or another starch, such as potatoes or a thin white bread like lavash or pita. (See my pita and potato variations below.) For beginners I would stick to just a rice tah-diq as I offer in the main recipe, but over time, you may want to play with other starches to add new textures. Anything that will crisp up will work. There are even some serious pro moves where people make a whole fish tah-diq. I've never even attempted to do that.

My party-sized recipe here can be scaled up or down, as needed. Serve with Ghormeh Sabzi (page 132), Fesenjān (page 134), or Kabab Koobideh (page 128). Serve it all with yogurt, usually plain unstrained yogurt, or even Maast-o-Moosir (page 64).

NOTE: The pot you use is extremely important here. First, you want enough surface area so the rice can turn crispy on the bottom. I recommend a pot with a diameter of at least 12 inches. Mine holds 7 ½ quarts, in case that's helpful. Second, avoid cast-iron if you can. It conducts heat completely differently from what you need here, and it's really heavy to flip for a tah-diq reveal. Third, the pot needs a tight-fitting lid. Finally, in terms of scaling this recipe, a good rule of thumb is to allot ½ cup dry rice per person.

Put the rice in a large bowl. Fill the bowl two-thirds of the way with water and wash the rice, giving it a little massage with your hands. Tip the bowl carefully to drain out the water while leaving the rice in the bowl. Repeat this process twice more, until the water runs clear. Rinsing rids the rice of excess starch (and any dirt) and is a simple but important step.

Cover the rice with cool water by 1 inch. Stir in ¼ cup of the rock salt and let it soak for at least 1 hour.

STAGE 1: Half-cook the rice. If you're planning to use the saffron, crumble it into a small heatproof bowl and pour in the boiling water. Set aside to steep for at least 20 minutes.

Bring 10 to 12 cups fresh water to a boil over medium-high heat in a large, wide pot with a tight-fitting lid. Gently drain the water from the soaking rice and rinse with cold water to get rid of the rock salt residue; drain again. Add the rice to the pot, making sure that there is at least 1 inch of water above the rice. Add the remaining ¼ cup rock salt. Bring the water back to a simmer, stirring occasionally. About 5 minutes later, check the rice for the half-cooked stage by doing the "squish test": Pluck a grain of rice out of the pot and squish it between your thumb and forefinger. If the grain of rice simply breaks in two, it's not ready yet and you should check again in 2 or 3 more minutes. What you want when you press the grain between your fingers is to kind of flatten it, revealing a spine of multiple hard pieces along the entire grain. You do not want to let it get fully translucent and soft—that will make the rice grains stick together and be soggy. When the rice is done, drain it in a large fine-mesh strainer. If you are worried you have overcooked the rice, run some cold water over it. Rinse the pot thoroughly to remove any starchy residue.

4 cups long-grain basmati rice (do not substitute a different variety)

½ cup rock salt, divided (see My Pantry, page 32)

¼ teaspoon saffron (optional)

3 tablespoons boiling water

4 to 8 tablespoons (½ to 1 stick) unsalted butter, divided

CONTINUES ⚜

STAGE 2: Steam the rice to completion. Heat the same pot over medium-high heat until it is dry. Depending on the size of your pot, add 4 to 6 tablespoons of the butter, enough so that when it melts, it covers the entire bottom of the pot with a healthy layer of fat. The butter will help crisp the bottom layer of the rice, creating a buffer between the flames and the rice. If you like, at this point you can add potato slices or pita triangles to form your tah-diq (see the Variations below), then continue with the recipe from here.

Return the drained rice to the pot—still over medium-high heat—and use a wooden spoon to form a pyramid of rice. Keeping the rice away from the edges as much as possible will help direct the steam the rice creates through the center of the pot. Use the handle of the spoon to make six holes around the pyramid and stuff roughly one teaspoon of butter into each hole. If using, drizzle the precious steeped saffron liquid over the top of the pyramid, trying to get as much coverage as possible.

Lay a large, clean dish towel on the counter and place the pot lid facedown in the center. Gather up the edges of the towel around the lid and tie the corners together on top. Place the now-insulated lid on the pot. The towel absorbs steam and creates a tight seal. Cook the rice for 8 minutes to lock in a crispy crust on the bottom, then turn the heat down to low. Cook for an additional 20 to 25 minutes, then remove from the heat. You should start to smell it about 5 minutes before it is ready—don't panic and turn off the heat, just let it keep going for a touch longer. My experience has been that beginners tend to take the rice off the heat too early, creating an underwhelming tah-diq. Be brave!

STAGE 3: Highly Anticipated Presentation. And now, for the moment of truth—the reveal to show how well the tah-diq came out. Each and every tah-diq is different. Remove the lid carefully, watching out for steam. Invert a serving platter or large plate over the top of the pot (the platter should be larger in circumference than the pot). Using oven mitts, grab the pot handles and platter at the same time and flip the pot over so the platter is on the bottom. Use the handle of a spoon or knife to gently tap the pot to loosen any rice that may be sticking to the roof of the pot. Carefully lift the pot off the platter in the most dramatic way possible.

Variations for Potato or Pita Tah-Diq

IF USING POTATO: While your rice is soaking, peel and slice 1 small russet potato into ⅛-inch rounds. Soak them in water until you need them to prevent oxidization. Add the potatoes to the melted butter in the pot and cook over high heat until the potatoes turn translucent and the edges start to crisp. Flip them with a spatula and rearrange them in a single layer with some space between them on the bottom of the pot, then top with the rice. You want some rice to fill in the gaps so you'll get both crispy potatoes and crispy rice when the dish is done.

IF USING PITA: Split 1 pita in half and tear into small triangles. When the butter melts, lay the pita pieces in the butter and immediately top with the rice, allowing it to fill in the gaps between the pita triangles.

KABAB KOOBIDEH

SERVES 6

If heaven and hell planned a dinner party, they would serve this impossibly tender dish with rice. The proper kabab koobideh ("ground meat kabab") is cooked over an open flame that licks the skewers of meat to tantalize them into the perfect juicy texture, with the cool winds of a hand fan to save them from a fiery death.

It is thought that the gift of making this kabab is genetic. It takes patience and intuition to know how to pack the skewers with the meat, how to make the fire, when to turn the skewers, when to fan the flames, and how to avoid overcooking the meat. If someone is good at preparing this dish, the entire community—friends and enemies alike—encourages them to make it. And to have lots of kids to carry on the tradition.

To cook kabab koobideh, you'll need to lay the skewers over a manghal (shallow fire pit) filled with hot coals. Unlike a standard American charcoal grill, a manghal holds the skewers just 1 to 2 inches above the flames, close enough so the fire can kiss the meat. If do not own a manghal, it's pretty easy to craft one if you have a charcoal grill and can get your hands on a few bricks (see below). I'm also providing an alternative prep method using an oven.

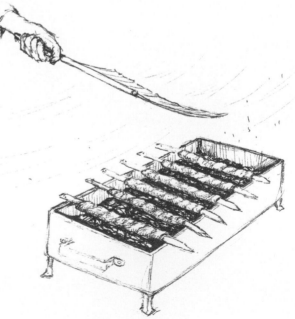

My recipe features all beef, but a combination of beef and lamb is also nice.

Serve kabob koobideh atop a pile of fluffy Persian Rice (page 124), sprinkled with ground sumac and accompanied by a refreshing glass of Doogh (page 235). Make sure there's a platter of fresh herbs (sabzi khordan, page 30) on the table, as well as a bowl of Maast-o-Moosir (page 64).

RECOMMENDED TOOLS AND EQUIPMENT

Since you'll be suspending skewers directly over the fire, with no grill grate in between, I recommend you get a hold of the following items:

Natural hardwood briquettes: "Natural" is the key word here since the flames are so close to the meat.

Extra-wide skewer (called a sikh): The proper skewer for forming this kabab is about 1 inch wide and 18 inches long. Don't choose a skinnier skewer as you'll be forming each kabab with a substantial amount of meat.

Hand fan: When prepping your fire and cooking the skewers, you'll want to fan the flames. Any hand fan or even a sturdy piece of cardboard will get the job done.

Charcoal grill or DIY manghal: To set up a makeshift grill for kababs, wrap four bricks in aluminum foil. Remove the grill grate and stack two bricks on each side of the grill, spacing them so that you can prop each end of the skewers on the bricks.

4 large white or yellow onions

3 pounds ground beef (20 percent fat is ideal)

3 tablespoons kosher salt

1 teaspoon freshly ground black pepper

6 Roma tomatoes (optional)

2 pieces lavash bread

Doogh (page 235), sabzi khordan (see My Pantry, page 30), Maast-o-Moosir (page 64), Persian Rice (page 124), and ground sumac, for serving

Peel the onions, then grate them on the small holes of a box grater. Using your hands, squeeze the juice out of the grated onion, a handful at a time, over a bowl. Alternatively, wrap the grated onions in a fine-mesh cloth or clean kitchen towel and twist it over a bowl to squeeze out the juices. Transfer the squeezed onions to a large bowl and use the reserved liquid to flavor a pot of soup (or just drink it as a shot—this is what I do). (If you don't squeeze the onions, the meat mixture will be very wet and might slide off the skewers.)

Add the ground beef, salt, and pepper to the bowl with the onions. Knead the mixture mercilessly with your hands for at least 8 minutes (or 5 minutes per pound of meat if you're scaling up), massaging the meat by scooping and rounding it with your fingers and flattening it with the heel of your hand. (Avoid squishing the meat through your fingers.) Whereas the rule when making great burgers is to handle the meat as little as possible, the rule for making kababs is to work, work, work the meat until the fat is well incorporated and the meat is nicely "knitted" together. Knead it until you feel like you're done, and then knead it twice as long. The more you knead it, the more integrated the kabab will be.

Wash your hands (which should be covered with a nice layer of fat if you've done this properly).

CONTINUES

MANGHAL/GRILL COOKING METHOD: Make a charcoal fire in a manghal or on your grill. Using a hand fan, fan the flames until the briquettes have a relentless orange glow. It can take a while to get a very hot fire, so you may want to have someone else start it while you prepare the meat (or vice versa).

Have a rimmed baking sheet or platter with raised edges handy. Fill a bowl with warm water. Dip one hand in the water to moisten it, then grab a handful of the meat mixture (about the size of a tennis ball) and form it into a rough ball in your dominant hand. Press a skewer into the middle of the ball and use a gentle massaging and squeezing motion to mold the meat around the skewer, sealing the meat on all sides of the skewer and molding it so it is 6 to 8 inches long and about ½ inch thick all around. Because the mixture is so wet, use a light touch. Create indentations along the length of the kabab by pressing the meat gently at ½-inch intervals with your index finger and thumb. Secure the ends of the meat onto the skewers by squeezing the meat about 3 inches before both of the top and bottom ends of the skewers (you want to leave the ends of the skewers free because they'll be resting directly on the sides of the fire pit or bricks). Your goal is to create an evenly weighted kabab, which will have the best chance of staying on the skewer and not fall into the flames. Lay the kabab on the baking sheet or platter and repeat with the remaining skewers. You should get 12 to 14 skewers. If using the tomatoes, skewer them lengthwise and take everything to the fire.

To begin cooking, have a platter handy to place the cooked kababs on. Line it with a layer of lavash bread. When your fire is very hot, place the skewers on the bricks, 1 to 2 inches from the fire and begin to fan the flames to keep the heat on the meat. The more vigorous the flame fanning in the beginning, the better as it will cast off a lot of the cinders so they don't end up all over the meat. Part of the kababs' smoky richness comes from the proximity to the flames.

As it cooks, the soft, wet meat will want to fall off the skewers and into the pit, so turn the skewers every 5 to 10 seconds. Once the meat begins to firm up and lock itself onto the skewer, you can turn the skewers every minute or so, and gradually less frequently. Continue cooking until the meat is cooked all the way through, 7 to 10 minutes total.

To remove the cooked meat from the skewers, grasp the meat with the other piece of lavash bread, using it like oven mitts, and pull the skewer out. Put the meat on the prepared platter. Continue until all the meat skewers are cooked. The bread will soak up the meat juices, which is a highly coveted perk of this process. (Weird colloquialism: The nickname for sister-in-law is "bread under the kabab." That's supposed to be a major compliment.)

If using, place the skewered tomatoes directly over the fire and cook for about 10 minutes, rotating them a few times and letting their skins char a bit toward the end.

OVEN METHOD: Preheat the oven to 400°F with a rack on the highest rung. Line a rimmed baking sheet with aluminum foil.

Put the meat mixture on the prepared baking sheet and form it into oblong patties, 6 to 8 inches long and ½ inch thick. Leave 1 inch space between each patty. You should have 12 to 14 patties.

Bake for 10 minutes without turning or flipping, then turn the broiler on high and broil for an additional 2 to 3 minutes, until the meat is lightly browned.

You can still have a tasty "sister-in-law" with this method, as the juices will pool up in the baking sheet, just waiting for you to sop them up with lavash.

TO SERVE: Place a pitcher of doogh, a tray of sabzi khordan, and a bowl of savory moosir yogurt on the table. Grab a plate and pile it with Persian rice. Then add a kabab and a whole tomato, and sprinkle the entire plate with sumac. Naptime will commence shortly.

A Little Something Extra

If you're walking on the wild side these days with your cholesterol intake, treat yourself and your guests to the added luxury of adding egg yolks and butter to the rice: Before plating the meat, advise guests to make a little hole in the top of their rice mound. Drop in a pat of room-temperature butter and mix up the rice until beaming, shiny, and happy. Mound the rice again and drop in an egg yolk. Mix once more to give the rice a glistening sheen and rich texture.

GHORMEH SABZI

SERVES 6

Plan ahead! The kidney beans need to soak for 4 hours. Start about 6 hours before serving, and plan on 2 to 3 hours for cooking.

Ghormeh sabzi, a two-thousand-year-old dish, refers to bunches of chopped herbs that transform into tender spoonfuls once stewed. Making it is not meant to be a solo project; you need a few people around. There's loads of chopping, plenty of washing up, and a whole lot of waiting while things simmer away. I think Iranian cuisine developed because of our need for community and entertainment. Getting a wheelbarrow full of parsley, cilantro, and other herbs from the fields, chopping them into super fine pieces, and letting it stew for hours and hours—*this* is how we love spending time with friends or family. This stew is heavy with flavorful juices from both the meat and the herbs and is ideal served over a scoop of Persian Rice (page 124) with a dollop of Maast-o-Moosir (page 64).

Pull down your largest stockpot for this recipe. And when shopping, you'll find the weight measurements in parentheses a better indicator for how much to buy, so use the store's scale if they have one.

Ghormeh sabzi can be made a day or two in advance—in fact, it tastes better that way. Just reheat and serve atop a fresh batch of rice.

NOTE: Seek out Omani limes, fenugreek, and tareh (see My Pantry, page 29) at a Persian market. There is no substitute for any of these ingredients. For the Omani limes, choose the brown Ping-Pong–size dried limes over the more bitter black racquetball-size dried limes. My trusted brand for these is Sadaf.

1½ to 2 cups dried kidney
  beans (½ to ¾ pound)

6 to 8 bunches flat-leaf parsley
  (about 1¾ pounds)

3 to 4 bunches tareh
  (⅓ to ¾ pound)

2 bunches fenugreek
  (about 10 ounces)

2 tablespoons unsalted butter

2 to 3 pounds bone-in lamb
  shanks, with marrow, cut
  into 2-inch chunks

2 tablespoons kosher salt,
  or more to taste

1 tablespoon freshly
  ground black pepper

¼ cup vegetable oil

8 whole dried (Omani) limes

1 quart boiling water

Persian Rice (page 124)
  and Maast-o-Moosir
  (page 64), for serving

Put the dried kidney beans in a medium bowl and cover with cool water. Set aside at room temperature to soak for about 4 hours.

Trim off the bottom inch from the parsley stems (and reserve for stock, page 150, or pickles, page 74). Fill the sink or a large container with cool water and dump in all the fresh herbs. Swish it around to loosen the dirt and sand. Rinse in 3 changes of water or until completely clean. Spread the herbs on clean towels to air-dry for at least 30 minutes.

Finely mince the parsley, tareh, and fenugreek, a handful at a time, transferring the minced herbs to a large bowl as you go.

In a large stockpot, melt the butter over medium-high heat and add the lamb. Season with 1 tablespoon of the salt and the pepper. Brown the lamb on all sides, stirring occasionally, about 10 minutes. Add 3 quarts water. Drain the kidney beans, add to the pot, and bring everything to a simmer.

In a second large pot or frying pan, heat the oil over medium heat and add all the herbs. Cook, stirring constantly, until the herbs turn dark green and begin to give off liquid, 10 to 12 minutes. This is the only opportunity for your ghormeh sabzi (literally "green herb stew") to turn sabz—a deep aromatic green. If you do not cook the herbs long enough, they will remain brilliant green with a raw flavor—the telltale sign of a rookie stew maker. If you don't feel your frying pan or pot is large enough for all the herbs, cook them in batches. Transfer the herbs to the lamb pot. Simmer the stew until the kidney beans and lamb are tender and the herbs are soft, about 1 hour.

While the stew simmers, carefully puncture the dried limes in several places with a paring knife and put them in a small heatproof bowl. Pour the boiling water over them and let soak for 30 minutes. Add the limes and their soaking water to the stew and continue to simmer the stew for at least 1 hour longer, so the flavors come together and the water reduces to a more substantial consistency. Season with the remaining 1 tablespoon salt, or more to taste. Serve with the Persian rice and savory moosir yogurt.

FESENJĀN

This ancient, celebratory stew is my sister Nahid's favorite dish. It's the one my parents would make for her birthday or whenever she came home from college. I'd even cook it for her to bribe her to help me with something. Nahid has never made this dish for herself, because she's never had to. And we don't mind at all because we've always loved surprising her with it.

Fesenjān celebrates the heady flavors of rich walnuts and tangy pomegranate molasses. Because it simmers a good, long while and it uses up your precious pomegranate molasses (page 31), it's usually saved for very (*very*) special occasions. The slow-cooking process yields layers of complex flavors even though the ingredients list is nice and short. Serve with Persian Rice (page 124).

Back in the olden days, this dish was made with duck, and while most modern fesenjān recipes call for chicken, I grew up making it with beef meatballs. Nahid loves it with meatballs, too, and now that this recipe is published here, maybe she can get some of her friends to make it for her!

Preheat the oven to 350°F.

Spread the walnuts in a single layer on a rimmed baking sheet and toast until browned and fragrant, about 10 minutes, turning and tossing twice. (Toasting draws out their oils.) Cool completely, then transfer to the bowl of a food processor. Pulse several times, until the nuts are finely chopped but not a paste. They will help thicken the stew.

Combine the ground beef, onion, garlic, turmeric, salt, and pepper in a medium bowl. Form the mixture into 1-inch meatballs. (You should have 25 to 28.)

Heat the oil in a large skillet over medium-high heat. Cook the meatballs in batches, turning occasionally, until browned on all sides, 8 to 10 minutes per batch. Transfer to a paper towel–lined plate and set aside.

In a large pot, combine 5 cups water and the ground walnuts. Bring to a boil, then reduce the heat to a steady simmer. Continue to simmer, stirring occasionally, until the walnuts soften into the water and are fully integrated, about 30 minutes.

Stir in ¾ cup of the pomegranate molasses and reduce the heat to maintain a gentle simmer. Simmer, stirring occasionally, until the broth is very thick and a layer of oil forms on top, 45 minutes to 1 hour longer. Taste for balance, adding up to ¼ cup more pomegranate molasses for a tarter pucker, if desired. Just before serving, add the meatballs to the stew to heat through fully, 5 to 10 minutes.

Taste for salt, adding more if needed. Serve with Persian rice, a few slices of feta, and an assortment of sabzi khordan.

1 pound chopped walnuts

1 pound ground beef

1 large yellow onion, minced

4 garlic cloves, minced

1 teaspoon ground turmeric

1 teaspoon kosher salt, or more to taste

½ teaspoon freshly ground black pepper

1 tablespoon vegetable oil

¾ to 1 cup pomegranate molasses (page 31 or store-bought)

Persian Rice (page 124), feta cheese, and fresh herbs (see sabzi khordan in My Pantry, page 30), for serving

TACHIN

SERVES 8

Plan ahead! The rice needs to soak for 1 hour.

Rice and yogurt, soulmates at the Iranian table, formalize their love affair in this gloriously decadent casserole-type dish. Lush quantities of yogurt, butter, and egg yolks—plus a regal helping of saffron—enrich a "cake" of rice. This casserole should occupy center stage, with pickles (page 74) and yogurt as supporting players. It features commonly used Iranian ingredients, including barberries (page 29), is easy to make, and delivers the highly coveted crispy golden tah-diq on the bottom. Chicken adds further texture and richness, but if you'd like to leave it out for a vegetarian version, you're welcome to do so.

4 cups long-grain white rice

2 tablespoons rock salt

4 to 5 pounds bone-in, skin-on chicken parts (any combination of white- and dark-meat pieces)

1 teaspoon ground turmeric

4½ teaspoons kosher salt, divided

½ teaspoon freshly ground black pepper

1 large onion, sliced

½ teaspoon saffron threads

¼ cup boiling water

2 cups plain whole milk yogurt (do not substitute Greek)

4 large egg yolks

4 tablespoons vegetable oil, divided, or more as needed

6 tablespoons (¾ stick) unsalted butter, divided, or more as needed

2 cups barberries (see My Pantry, page 29)

Maast-o-Moosir (page 64), for serving

CLEAN AND SOAK THE RICE: Put the rice in a large bowl and cover with cool water. Swish it with your hands, then pour off the water. Repeat this process 2 more times, until the water runs clear. Cover the rice once more with cool water by about 1 inch. Stir in the rock salt and set aside at room temperature to soak for 1 hour.

SIMMER THE CHICKEN: Combine the chicken, turmeric, 1 teaspoon of the kosher salt, pepper, and sliced onion in a medium pot. Add cool water to cover. Bring to a boil over high heat, then reduce to a simmer. Put on the lid slightly ajar to allow steam to escape and simmer until the chicken is tender, 20 to 25 minutes for white meat and 40 to 45 minutes for dark meat. Remove the chicken from the pot (remove the white meat first, as needed) and set aside on a plate to cool. Pull and shred the meat from the skin and bones and transfer to a bowl (discard the skin and bones).* Set aside a few tablespoons of the poaching liquid and refrigerate or freeze the rest as a rich base for future soups. The onion can

---

* Truth be told, I keep as much of the skin in as possible. It adds texture, flavor, moisture. I just take a bit of the skin and chop it up and add it to the rest of the shredded chicken. I'm hiding my love for boiled chicken skin here in the footnote, in hopes that it speaks to only fellow kindred spirits. The rest of you, keep it moving along now.

either be drained and kept with the chicken for added flavor and texture (my preference) or stored with the broth.

COOK THE RICE: Crumble the saffron into a small heatproof bowl and pour in the boiling water. Steep for at least 20 minutes.

Bring 4 quarts water to a boil in an 8-quart pot with a tight-fitting lid. Drain the rice and rinse with cold water to get rid of the rock salt residue. Add the rice to the boiling water and return to a boil. Cook the rice until half-done, about 8 minutes. To check for half-doneness, squeeze a grain of rice between your fingers until it breaks in a few spots along its spine but is not yet fully translucent (see page 125 for the full description of the "squish test"). Drain the rice and douse it with cold water to cool it down.

Combine the yogurt, egg yolks, remaining 3½ teaspoons salt, and saffron with its soaking liquid in a large bowl. Add the rice and turn to coat evenly. It should almost feel like the rice is getting fluffier.

Make sure your pot has no rice grains or residue, then return the pot to high heat and add 2 tablespoons each of the oil and butter. Once melted, it should coat the bottom of the pot completely; add more if necessary. When the fat is hot (throw a grain of rice in there to see if it sizzles), spoon one-third of the rice mixture into the fat and spread it evenly across the bottom all the way to the sides. Set a timer for 8 minutes. Arrange the shredded chicken on top of the rice, leaving a ½-inch border of rice around the edges. Layer on the remaining rice.

Cut another 2 tablespoons butter into 4 blobs. Dab the separate blobs on top of the rice close to the center. Drizzle the reserved few tablespoons of chicken poaching liquid over the rice. Place a large, clean towel on your counter and put the pot lid face-down in the center of the towel. Gather up the edges of the towel around the lid and tie the corners together on top. Place the now-insulated lid on the pot.

CONTINUES

When the timer beeps, reduce the heat to low and cook for 30 to 40 minutes longer, until the entire house smells like fragrant rice. (You will start to smell it as it finishes up cooking.) As you become more experienced cooking rice in this Iranian style, your sense of smell will become more reliable. In any case, do not cook the rice for longer than 40 minutes.

PREPARE THE BARBERRIES: While the rice is cooking, flash-fry the barberries. Barberries burn quickly, so have all your gear ready: a colander or strainer, a small saucepan, a wooden spoon, and a medium bowl.

Sift through the barberries to remove any stems or stones. Transfer them to the colander and rinse under cool water. Drain well.

Heat the remaining 2 tablespoons each oil and butter in the saucepan over medium-high heat until shimmering. Carefully add the barberries all at once and begin stirring. Cook, stirring with the wooden spoon, just until the barberries plump up, about 20 seconds. Turn off the heat and continue to stir for 2 minutes. Transfer the barberries to the bowl and reserve for dressing the tachin.

HIGHLY ANTICIPATED PRESENTATION: When the rice is ready, choose a serving platter large enough to fit over the top of your pot. Remove the lid and run a knife along the inside edge of the pot. Place the platter upside-down over the pot. Using oven mitts, pick up the pot and platter together and, working quickly and carefully, invert the pot onto the platter. Set the platter on the counter and bang on the bottom of the pot a few times with a spoon. If you're a true exhibitionist, do the reveal in front of your guests: Slowly lift the pot, revealing the tachin and the crispy tah-diq in one piece. Sprinkle with the barberries. Cut into wedges and serve with savory moosir yogurt alongside.

BIRYANI

SERVES 10 TO 12 (MAKE IT A FEAST!)

Plan ahead! You'll need 12 hours for the meat to marinate.

It was only when I was in my twenties that I found out that my mom was actually born and raised in India—where there are clusters of Iranian Zoroastrians among the Indian Zoroastrians (Parsis). It seems obvious now, since I was exposed to Bollywood films and chaat and biryani and gujrati growing up—but at the time, I just thought my mom was a worldly Iranian lady.

Because this traditional Indian dish is made in an Iranian style, it is the perfect representation of my mother's heritage. It features the same two-step rice cooking technique as Persian Rice (page 124) and Tachin (page 136) and eventually settles into its rich flavors by cooking in its own aromatic steam.

I have made biryani with my mom dozens of times and learned how to make this dish through osmosis by standing beside her. But in an effort to capture the precise steps for this book and to preserve this piece of our family's culture, I nearly killed the woman. Every single time we make it, she changes her mind on what should happen.

How long do I put the biryani in the oven? "It depends on how you marinate the chicken." Okay, then, how do I marinate the chicken? "It depends on the chicken!" When I couldn't get the recipe down in practice or verbally from her or her sisters, I consulted her notebook. She has a beautiful notebook filled with handwritten recipes. I've seen her consult it many times over the years, so I thought I would just lift the biryani recipe from it. How very naïve of me! There is zero helpful guidance in there; it all reads like secret code. Instead of ingredient quantities, she wrote "onions" or "meat." When I ask her how many onions, she says "enough." At the risk of sounding like a grumpy teenager: I hate her.

Somehow, despite all the arguments we have had over this dish, it always turns out spicy, tangy, colorful, and tender. It is a very Iranian-Indian dish, just like my mom. Serve with a bowl of cool Maast-o-Khiyar (Cucumber Yogurt, page 66), topped with a pinch of ground cumin if you like.

CONTINUES ⚬

NOTE: Garam masala from scratch will bring a significantly more robust flavor and aroma to this biryani. To make the exact amount of garam masala for this recipe, you will need 3 bay leaves, 1 cinnamon stick, 2 whole cloves, 4 cardamom pods, ½ teaspoon ground mace or 1 whole mace, and ½ teaspoon whole black peppercorns. Grind everything together in a spice blender, forming as fine a powder as possible. Please (please) give it a go.

CHICKEN

1 cup vegetable oil or ghee, or more as needed

8 medium yellow onions, halved and sliced into thin half-moons

2 tablespoons grated fresh ginger

5 garlic cloves, grated

1 bird's eye or Thai chile, grated

2 tablespoons kosher salt, or more to taste

1 tablespoon garam masala (see Note)

2 teaspoons ground cumin

1 teaspoon ground turmeric

1 teaspoon ground cayenne pepper

1 teaspoon ground coriander

3 cups plain whole milk yogurt

4 to 4½ pounds bone-in, skin-on chicken thighs (10 to 12 thighs)

MARINATE THE CHICKEN: Heat the oil in your largest skillet over high heat. Wait at least 3 minutes as you want it quite hot. To test readiness, add a sliver of the onion; it should sizzle immediately. When the oil is ready, add all the onions and fry, stirring frequently, until they are deep brown (verging on charred) and slightly crispy, about 45 minutes. Use a slotted spoon to transfer the onions to a bowl large enough to eventually hold the chicken, reserving the oil in the skillet. Turn the heat down to medium.

In a small bowl, combine the ginger, garlic, chile, kosher salt, garam masala, cumin, turmeric, cayenne, and coriander and stir. Add the spices to the reserved oil in the skillet. Cook, stirring constantly, just until fragrant, about 3 minutes, being careful not to let them burn. Remove the skillet from the heat and let cool.

Add the yogurt to the bowl with the cooled onions and stir thoroughly. Add the spiced oil and stir well to incorporate evenly. Add the chicken and turn to coat completely. Cover and refrigerate overnight.

SOAK THE RICE (ABOUT 3 HOURS BEFORE DINNER): Put the rice in a large bowl and cover with cool water. Swish it with your hands, then pour off the water. Repeat this process 2 more times, until the water runs clear. Cover the rice with 1 inch of cool water and sprinkle with the rock salt. Set aside at room temperature to soak for 1 hour.

ASSEMBLE AND BAKE: Fill a large pot with 4 quarts water and the 1 tablespoon kosher salt. Cover and bring to a boil over high heat. Place a colander in the sink.

Meanwhile, in a large skillet, heat the oil over high heat. Add the potatoes, season with the 1 teaspoon kosher salt, and cook, stirring often, until they are about three-quarters cooked, about 15 minutes. Turn off the heat and let potatoes cool in the skillet.

Crumble the saffron into a small heatproof bowl and pour in the boiling water. Set aside to steep and bloom for 20 minutes.

Preheat the oven to 375°F. Place a rack in the lower third of the oven.

Cut each tomato lengthwise into four pieces and toss with the cooling potatoes. Transfer the tomato-potato mixture to a very large baking dish or foil pan (about 17 x 12 inches). Add the contents of the chicken bowl, including the marinade. Stir everything together and arrange the chicken in a single layer, with the tomatoes and potatoes evenly distributed throughout. Set aside.

When the water is boiling, drain the rice by gently tipping its water into the sink and rinsing off any rock salt residue. Add the rice to the boiling water and boil for 5 minutes. Add the bay leaves, cinnamon sticks, cardamom pods, and star anise and cloves, if using. After about another 2 to 3 minutes, check the rice for half-cooked status by plucking a grain of rice from the pot and pressing it between your fingers. It should break in a few spots along its spine but not yet be fully translucent. When the rice is done, scoop out 1 cup of the rice cooking liquid and set aside. Drain the rice in a colander and run under cold water to stop the cooking process.

Spread all but 2 cups of the cooked rice over the chicken. (Reserve those 2 cups in a small bowl.) Cut the butter into tablespoon-size pats and scatter over the rice. Add the saffron water to the reserved rice in the bowl, stir, and scrape over the biryani. Drizzle the top with the reserved rice water. Cover tightly with aluminum foil and bake until the rice around the perimeter starts to look roasted, about 1½ hours.*

To serve, ease a spatula down to the bottom of the dish and scoop up a portion, much as you would serve lasagna. You're serving from the bottom up, making sure to get moist chicken and cooked rice in every serving. Serve with cucumber yogurt and cold beer.

Leftovers may be stored, covered and refrigerated, for up to 3 days. I do not recommend freezing.

---

* If this is your first time making biryani in your oven, test a piece of chicken by fishing it out and cutting to the bone to check for doneness. Add 15 minutes more if needed.

BIRYANI

6 cups long-grain basmati rice

2 tablespoons rock salt (see My Pantry, page 32)

1 tablespoon plus 1 teaspoon kosher salt

¼ cup vegetable oil

3 large waxy yellow potatoes, such as Yukon Gold, peeled and cut into 2-inch chunks

½ teaspoon saffron threads

½ cup boiling water

2 Roma tomatoes

4 bay leaves

2 cinnamon sticks, broken in half

6 green cardamom pods, cracked but left whole

2 star anise (optional)

4 whole cloves (optional)

8 tablespoons (1 stick) unsalted butter

Maast-o-Khiyar (Cucumber Yogurt, page 66) and cold beer, for serving

Meat and Fish

Dairy is a common marinade ingredient, and yogurt marinade in particular is well known as a meat tenderizer. In side-by-side comparisons, I found that whey actually delivers a more noticeable effect than yogurt. Due to its viscosity, whey infuses more deeply into meat, especially the fatty parts of the meat, and imparts a lemony flavor that lingers longer than yogurt. Yogurt marinades, on the other hand, have the benefit of providing extra body that creates a creamy sauce surrounding the meat. Both yogurt and whey marinades make for soft meat and crispy exteriors because the dairy sugars begin to caramelize during cooking. The longer the soak, the better. Most of the recipes that follow call for marinating the meat for at least 12 hours. Unlike with lemon or vinegar, there is little risk of over-marinating with yogurt and getting a rubbery texture.

Overall, my experiments led me to conclude that whey was the more versatile of the two—with pleasantly surprising hits using pork (see Whey-Brined Pork Chops with White Wine Shallot Sauce, page 153, and Slow-Cooked Pulled Pork with Whey Caramel Barbecue Sauce, page 155) and fish (see Whey Ceviche, page 162).

Brine with Whey

Brining makes meat juicier and more flavorful. The process entails dissolving salt (and sometimes sugar) in water, maybe adding spices and aromatics, and submerging raw meat in it for several hours before cooking. A traditional salt brine pulls moisture and flavor into the meat, but a problem with salt brine is that the resulting pan drippings are often too salty for gravy and pan sauces.

Another common brining method involves dairy, such as using buttermilk to make fried chicken. Many Indian and Middle Eastern recipes for grilled meats begin with a yogurt marinade to tenderize the meat. Whereas marinades made with vinegar or citrus juice are so acidic that they begin to break down the surface of the meat after a short amount of time and ultimately render it mushy, buttermilk and yogurt are more mildly acidic, and the presence of calcium activates enzymes in the meat that begin to break down tough muscle fibers.

Because whey has a similar tenderizing effect on meat as buttermilk or yogurt, but is also much higher in water content, it has a similar juicifying effect as a brine, without added salt or sugar. As a bonus, whey gives meat an alluring, slightly lemony tang, and makes the skin brown faster and crisper. And oh, those pan drippings make the best gravy ever!

JUICIEST-EVER WHEY-BRINED ROAST TURKEY WITH LIFE-CHANGING GRAVY

MAKES 1 (14- TO 18-POUND) TURKEY; SERVES 9 TO 12

Plan ahead! You'll need to let the turkey brine for 18 to 24 hours.

This recipe was a revelation. For months my team and I had been playing around with the different flavors of whey drinks we could make, but this turkey was our first attempt at cooking with whey. We were dually inspired by the trend of salt-brining a Thanksgiving turkey, as well as the familiar use of a buttermilk brine to make southern fried chicken. We set out to discover what would happen if we brined a turkey in whey.

When that first whey-brined turkey came out of the oven, dark bronze and sizzling, we picked at the skin first, and found it savory, crispy, and flavorful. The meat was aggressively juicy. The pan drippings were the best we'd ever had. Behind the flavor of turkey and butter was a distinct and deeply savory twang, which was so pleasantly surprising.

Serve turkey alongside Whey-Creamy Mashed Cauliflower (page 88) and Whey Cornbread (page 177). Any leftover meat and the reserved solids from the gravy can go into the Leftover Turkey and Dumplings (page 151), and the remaining turkey carcass and leftover brining whey makes for a tart turkey stock (page 150).

NOTE: If you are sourcing whey like an environmental advocate (see page 21), get a 5-gallon bucket of whey. You'll use 3 gallons of whey for the turkey (don't throw it away after you soak your turkey—it will be repurposed to make gravy and stock) and the remaining 2 gallons to make mashed cauliflower, cornbread, lemon meringue pie for dessert, and/or bloody Marys for the leftover brunch gathering. If you have any leftover turkey meat, Turkey and Dumplings (page 151) will keep this party going.

CONTINUES ⟩

NOTE: This recipe calls for a 5-gallon bucket (or a lobster pot) for brining. You can also use a brining bag and store it in the refrigerator or in a cooler with ice packs. Keep in mind that the bird must be fully submerged in the whey liquid and remain at or below 40°F during the brining process.

EQUIPMENT

5-gallon food-safe bucket with lid

Roasting pan and rack

Meat thermometer

TURKEY

3 gallons yogurt whey

4 garlic cloves, peeled and smashed

2 tablespoons whole black peppercorns

Handful thyme sprigs

4 bay leaves, crumbled

1 (14- to 18-pound) whole turkey, thawed if frozen, neck and giblets reserved for gravy

8 tablespoons (1 stick) unsalted butter, softened

Kosher salt and freshly ground black pepper

GRAVY

1 yellow onion, cut into eighths

1 carrot, cut into 4 pieces

1 celery stalk, cut into 4 pieces

5 tablespoons cornstarch

BRINE THE TURKEY: Combine the whey, smashed garlic, peppercorns, thyme, and bay leaves in a 5-gallon bucket. Slowly lower in the turkey, neck cavity first, holding on to its legs and jostling it a bit as you lower it in (this allows air to escape from the cavity). Make sure the bird is completely submerged. Put the lid on the bucket and store in a cool place for 18 to 24 hours. (If you are lucky enough to have that much refrigerator space, put the bucket there. If the temperature stays below 40°F where you live, stash it outside on your fire escape, balcony, or porch away from sunlight. If not, pack the bucket into a cooler or a large garbage can filled with ice.)

Carefully remove the turkey from the bucket (save the whey for the gravy) and place it on a rimmed baking sheet. Let the turkey sit out at room temperature for about 1 hour to lose its chill.

START THE STOCK FOR THE GRAVY: While the turkey is coming to room temperature, get a head start on the gravy. Put the reserved neck and giblets, onion, carrot, and celery in a large saucepan and cover with 2 quarts of the reserved whey used for brining. (Refrigerate the rest of the whey to make stock, page 150.) Bring to a near boil over high heat, then reduce the heat to low. Remember: whey is still milk and will behave as such when boiling, so be careful that it doesn't froth over. Simmer until reduced to 4 to 5 cups total stock, about 1 hour. Allow to cool a little, then strain into another pot or container. Snack on the solids, especially if you are a giblets lover like me. Once the stock is completely cool, cover and refrigerate until the turkey comes out of the oven.

ROAST THE TURKEY: Position a rack in the second-lowest position in the oven and remove the other racks. Preheat the oven to 400°F.

Pat the turkey completely dry with paper towels. Tuck the wing tips under the turkey, securing the skin flap at the neck, and truss the legs together with kitchen twine. Rub the entire bird evenly with the softened butter and season generously with salt and pepper.

Place the turkey, breast side up, on a rack in a sturdy roasting pan and roast for 35 to 40 minutes, until it begins to turn a deep brown. Because whey contains natural sugars, some spots will be browner than others—this is perfectly normal, but check the turkey periodically to monitor the browning.

Lower the oven temperature to 375°F. Take the bird out briefly to baste it with the pan drippings, tent any spots that are deep brown with aluminum foil, and return the turkey to the oven. Roast, basting every 30 minutes and re-covering any dark spots with foil each time, until a meat thermometer inserted in the thickest part of the thigh reads 165°F, another 2 to 2 ½ hours.

Remove the pan from the oven and lift the rack and turkey onto a cutting board (preferably one with a moat to catch the juices). Tent loosely with foil and allow to rest for 30 minutes before carving.

CONTINUE MAKING THE GRAVY: While the turkey rests, continue with the gravy. In a small bowl, slowly whisk 1 cup of the chilled gravy stock into the cornstarch and set aside. Place the roasting pan with the turkey drippings across two burners. Turn the burners up to high, bring the drippings to a boil, and slowly whisk in the remaining gravy stock, scraping the bottom of the pan to loosen up the browned bits. Gradually whisk in the cornstarch mixture and simmer over medium heat, whisking often, until it is thickened to the desired consistency. Strain through a fine-mesh strainer and adjust the seasoning with salt and pepper if necessary.

Carve the turkey, sneaking the crispiest parts of the skin for yourself. Serve the gravy alongside.

LEFTOVER WHEY
TURKEY STOCK

MAKES 5 TO 6 QUARTS

Thanksgiving leftovers have always led, for better or worse, to some really inventive meals come Saturday and Sunday of the holiday weekend. Here we're going to make a bright and tangy stock from the reserved whey brine used when making the Thanksgiving turkey (page 147). Think of it as a flexible base for any soups you'll make in the coming months. Any leftover vegetables lingering in your refrigerator are welcome here.

When your stock has fully cooled, freeze in separate one-quart containers and pull them out one at a time whenever you need chicken or turkey stock. If you strain away all the solids, you can even reserve the cooked vegetables for the turkey and dumplings recipe that follows (page 151).

NOTE: This stock is a companion recipe to the Juiciest-Ever Whey-Brined Roast Turkey with Life-Changing Gravy on page 147. It requires the leftover turkey carcass from that meal, and the "reserved whey brine" refers to the whey (along with any aromatics) you soaked your Thanksgiving turkey in and were smart enough to save.

1 leftover turkey carcass (hacked into pieces with a cleaver to release more gelatin and flavor into the stock)

8 to 10 quarts reserved whey brine (see Note)

1 or 2 celery stalks, cut in half

1 or 2 carrots, chopped

1 large yellow onion, cut in half

2 teaspoons kosher salt

Combine all the ingredients in a large stockpot and bring to a boil over high heat. Turn the heat down to medium-low and simmer until the remaining meat falls off the bones, about 4 hours. Let cool slightly. Strain out all the solids, first through a colander and then a second time through a fine-mesh strainer. Snack on the soft vegetables and any meat that has fallen off the bones, if desired, or combine both with a little of the stock for a quick soup!

Cool completely, then transfer to quart-size containers. Cover and refrigerate for up to 4 days or freeze for up to 6 months.

LEFTOVER TURKEY AND DUMPLINGS

SERVES 6 TO 8

We Iranians drag out our holidays for days if not weeks on end—in the best way possible. Meals are made for feasting on for days as people continue to visit one another even after a holiday "officially" ends. As with our poetry and storytelling, Iranians like to make sure the lovely things in life last as long as possible. Thanksgiving is the one nonreligious American holiday that lends itself quite well to my love of languishing in the holiday spirit.

For Thanksgiving, I always buy a larger bird than I need for that night's meal so I have plenty of leftover turkey to make this easy, cozy meal.

You'll need about 3 cups of mixed veggies for this dish. I've given my suggestion below, but you can use any vegetables left over from your feast so long as you've got about 3 cups total. Frozen vegetables also work in a pinch.

NOTE: I recommend making the turkey filling right away and freezing it to make this dish within 3 months. Then make the dumplings fresh when you are ready to assemble the whole dish. Thaw the filling and cook as usual according to the instructions.

DUMPLINGS

1¾ cups all-purpose flour

½ teaspoon baking powder

¼ teaspoon baking soda

½ teaspoon kosher salt

1 stick (8 tablespoon) unsalted butter, cold and cubed

¾ cup chopped fresh herbs, such as chives and/or flat-leaf parsley, divided

¾ cup yogurt whey

1 large egg

TURKEY FILLING

1 stick (8 tablespoon) unsalted butter, divided

1 large yellow onion, diced

2 medium carrots, peeled or scrubbed and thinly sliced

2 medium celery stalks, thinly sliced

1 teaspoon kosher salt, divided, plus more to taste

4 large garlic cloves, minced

¼ cup all-purpose flour

3 cups Leftover Whey Turkey Stock (page 150) or chicken stock

1 cup fresh or frozen corn kernels *or* 1 large potato, scrubbed and cut into ½-inch pieces

1 tablespoon chopped fresh thyme leaves

2 bay leaves

Freshly ground black pepper

4 cups shredded cooked turkey

CONTINUES

MAKE THE DUMPLINGS: Sift the flour, baking powder, baking soda, and salt into a large bowl. Add the butter and, using a fork, integrate it fully into the flour until you have little butter-flour granules. Stir in ¼ cup of the herbs. Cover and refrigerate while you make the filling. (You'll add the whey and egg to the dumplings just before the dish hits the oven. Don't add them yet.)

Preheat the oven to 375°F with a rack in the top third.

MAKE THE FILLING: Melt 4 tablespoons of the butter in a 4-quart saucepan over medium-high heat. Add the onion, carrots, celery, and ½ teaspoon of the salt and sauté, stirring occasionally, until softened and beginning to turn golden, about 7 minutes. Stir in the garlic and cook for 3 to 4 minutes, stirring so the garlic doesn't burn. Transfer the vegetables to a plate.

In the same saucepan, melt the remaining 4 tablespoons butter over medium heat. Slowly whisk in the flour until smooth, about 1 minute. Add the stock, ½ cup at a time, whisking vigorously to even out the texture and prevent lumps. Add the corn or potatoes, thyme, bay leaves, reserved sautéed carrot mixture, remaining ½ teaspoon salt, and a few grinds of pepper and simmer over medium heat for 15 to 20 minutes, until all the vegetables are fork-tender.

Stir in the turkey and the remaining ½ cup chopped herbs. Taste and adjust seasonings, if necessary.

ASSEMBLE THE DISH: Transfer the filling to a 9 x 13-inch casserole dish. Whisk the whey and egg together in a medium bowl and stir into the dumpling mixture until fully incorporated. Plop 12 spoonfuls of the dumpling batter over the filling, spacing evenly and leaving a bit of room between each plop since the dough will expand as it cooks.

Bake the dish until the dumplings are baked through and golden, about 30 minutes. Serve immediately.

WHEY-BRINED PORK CHOPS WITH WHITE WINE SHALLOT SAUCE

SERVES 6

Plan ahead! You'll need 6 to 12 hours for brining.

Once you try whey-brined pork chops, you're not going to be able to shut up about how delicious they are. Pork chops are too often bland and dry, easy to overcook because they're so lean. Whey cures what ails your chops, giving them a juicy boost. While you can add your favorite spices and aromatics to the whey brine, plain whey makes a brilliant brine all on its own.

6 cups yogurt whey

4 garlic cloves, peeled and smashed

1 tablespoon ground (powdered) mustard

1 teaspoon whole celery seed

6 (8-ounce) bone-in pork chops (loin or rib chops)

2 tablespoons kosher salt

2 tablespoons freshly ground black pepper, or to taste

2 tablespoons olive oil, divided

2 medium shallots, minced (about ½ cup)

½ cup leftover* dry white wine

1 tablespoon Dijon mustard

2 tablespoons unsalted butter, sliced

---

* "Leftover" because of the impressive amount of willpower not to drink all the wine the night before because you really want to make these pork chops.

CONTINUES

In a large, flat-bottomed plastic or glass container, combine the whey, garlic, mustard, and celery seed. Add the pork chops, cover the container with a lid, plastic wrap, or aluminum foil, and refrigerate for a minimum of 6 hours up to a maximum of 12 hours.

Remove the chops from brine, set on a rimmed baking sheet in a single layer, and allow to come to room temperature, about 30 minutes. Discard the brine. Pat the chops dry with paper towels. Combine the salt and pepper and rub liberally on both sides of each chop to season.

Heat a 12-inch cast-iron skillet over medium-high heat until very hot, about 5 minutes. Swirl in 1 tablespoon of the olive oil and add 3 of the pork chops. Sear until golden-brown, about 4 minutes, then turn the chops over with tongs. Continue to cook until just slightly pink in center, about 4 minutes more, lowering the heat if the exterior of the meat gets too brown before it's cooked through.* Transfer the chops to a clean plate and repeat with the remaining 1 tablespoon oil and 3 chops.

When all 6 chops are cooked and have been removed from the skillet, reduce the heat to medium and add the shallots. Sauté, stirring frequently, until the shallots are soft and caramelized, about 10 minutes. Deglaze the skillet with the wine, using a spatula to scrape up all the browned bits from the bottom of the pan. Once the wine is reduced by half, 2 to 3 minutes, turn off the heat and stir in the Dijon mustard and butter. Pour the sauce over the pork chops and serve.

---

* If your chops have luxuriated in the whey for closer to 12 hours, they will have absorbed more of the natural sugars found in the whey and will caramelize faster; turn the heat down here if necessary.

SLOW-COOKED PULLED PORK WITH WHEY CARAMEL BARBECUE SAUCE

SERVES 10

Plan ahead! The barbecue sauce (page 156) needs 8 hours to chill before serving. (The sauce may be made up to 1 month in advance.)

This one-pot dish makes an easy, sumptuous meal. Pork butt (also known as pork shoulder) is fatty and has abundant collagen, which breaks down and becomes tender and sticky during long, slow, moist-heat cooking. Though this is a trendy cut now, the butt used to be a cheap, "second choice" piece of the pig, as opposed to the more desirable lean and quick-cooking tenderloin and chops. Using yogurt whey as the cooking liquid gives the pork a hint of zest, and the whey's acid helps tenderize the meat. Liquid smoke evokes a satisfying barbecue flavor, and I don't recommend leaving it out.[*]

The accompanying barbecue sauce also uses whey; cooked with sugar, it makes a tangy caramel.

NOTE: If you don't have a Dutch oven or prefer to use a slow cooker, place the meat in the slow cooker and cook on the low setting for 8 to 10 hours, until the meat is tender and falling off the bone.

---

[*] Yes, barbecue snobs, I see you. I am with you. I still stand by this recommendation.

1 (4½-pound) bone-in pork butt, cut in half

2 teaspoons kosher salt

1½ teaspoons freshly ground black pepper

1 large onion, cut into large dice

1½ cups yogurt whey

2 tablespoons liquid smoke

10 potato buns, for serving

Whey Caramel Barbecue Sauce (recipe follows), warmed, for serving

Whey-Fermented Sauerkraut (page 78), for serving (optional)

Preheat the oven to 300°F.

Season the pork on all sides with the salt and pepper. Evenly distribute the onion in the bottom of an 8-quart (or larger) Dutch oven. Place the pork on top of the onion, then pour in the whey and liquid smoke. Cover and bake until the pork is tender and falling apart, about 4 hours. Transfer the pork to a shallow dish or rimmed baking sheet and shred with two forks. If you like, reserve some of the onions to mix with the shredded pork, or save the onions and the drippings and use it as the flavorful oil to roast or fry vegetables with in the weeks to come. Discard the bones.

Pile the shredded pork onto potato buns and dollop with barbecue sauce. I like to add a spoonful of sauerkraut, too.

WHEY CARAMEL BARBECUE SAUCE

MAKES ABOUT 1½ CUPS

Plan ahead! The sauce needs to chill for 8 hours.

The sauce tastes best after the flavors have mingled for several hours. You can make it up to 1 month in advance. Keep refrigerated.

1½ cups yogurt whey

¾ cup sugar

1 cup ketchup

2 tablespoons molasses

1 tablespoon Dijon mustard

1 individual canned chipotle chile in adobo, finely minced

½ teaspoon sweet paprika

1 teaspoon kosher salt

Combine the whey and sugar in a small saucepan and bring to a boil over high heat, watching carefully to make sure the liquid doesn't foam up above the rim of the saucepan. Reduce the heat to medium, maintaining a gentle boil. Do not stir. Check the pan at least every 5 minutes to make sure it's not boiling over or burning. If the mixture begins to foam up, pull the pan off the heat until it settles down, reduce the heat a little, and return the pan to the burner. Over the course of 40 to 50 minutes, the liquid will cook off, the sugar will caramelize, and the mixture will gradually turn from pale yellow to light gold to amber and become viscous. As soon as the caramel turns a deep honey color, turn off the heat and remove the pan from the burner.

Stir in the ketchup, molasses, mustard, chipotle, paprika, and salt. Taste and add more salt if you like. Allow the sauce to cool to room temperature, then transfer to a storage container, cover, and refrigerate for at least 8 hours before serving. Warm the sauce over gentle heat before serving.

FRIED TONGUE SANDWICH WITH LABNEH

SERVES 4

In the 1960s, when my teenage dad worked summers at Parsian, a sandwich shop in Tehran, the place was a popular watering hole. Though Iran's population was already predominantly Shi'ite Muslim, alcohol was legal at that time. The store was owned and operated by young Zoroastrians, a religious group that didn't prohibit alcohol, so the alcohol flowed freely and drew in customers.

My dad's own experience with alcohol had been limited to a few sips of homemade wine (page 250), and getting accidentally drunk one time after quenching his thirst with the "liquid fire" from a satchel strapped to his donkey. (He thought it was water.) So he was ill prepared to learn that the most important menu item at Parsian was beer: Shamsh beer, Majidiyeh beer, Argo beer.

Parsian decided to serve some snacks with the beer. Tongue sandwich was easy, pragmatic, and effortlessly delicious. The tongue wasn't even in a sandwich to begin with. It was just boiled tongue sliced up in its own broth, with a side of baguette. The tongue had a delicate texture and a pleasing salty flavor, complementing the beer perfectly. It was an easy, no-fuss option to sling at the drunken clientele.

CONTINUES

Eventually, that clientele became too much to handle, so my dad, now co-owner of the shop, stopped serving alcohol in 1978.

Without the easy revenue from booze, Parsian had to focus on its food. They began by making a more refined version of its tongue dish, turning it into a proper sandwich. While always delicious, the tongue was no longer slopped on a plate but now thoughtfully sliced and fried up in butter and tucked *inside* the baguette, with onion, tomato, lettuce, and a lemony homemade mayonnaise. It was their bestselling sandwich for decades.

Once we moved to the States, when my dad would make this sandwich at home, I would pretend to be too American to eat it. But now, as an adult, I'm embracing it once again. It's not just nostalgic but delicious—and always a hit at adult gatherings. I offer it here as a way to honor my dad and his own journey running a food business.

The tongue takes several hours to simmer and a gamey smell fills the entire house as you cook it. There is a sense of ceremony in watching a whole tongue boil, then anxiously peeling off the skin so as not to lose any of the meat (or the shape), and finally slicing it up and frying it in butter. We smear the tender meat with tangy labneh in lieu of mayonnaise and wash it down with an ice-cold beer.

NOTE: The cooking liquid becomes a thick, creamy stock; it's delicious in soups or sipped in mugs alongside your sandwich.

Rinse the tongue very well under cold running water until no longer slippery. Put it in a soup pot and cover with cool water. Squeeze the juice of 1 lemon into the pot. Bring to a boil over high heat, then reduce the heat to a gentle simmer. Cover and continue cooking over low heat for 3 to 4 hours, until you can easily sink a fork into the tongue and the skin peels off easily. To test, look closely at the skin in the back part of the tongue. Once cooked through, the leathery skin will turn white and opaque as it naturally separates from the meat. If the skin is sticking or pulling on the meat, it is not ready and you will need to continue simmering. While it is not necessary for the tongue to remain submerged, there does need to be liquid in the pot at all times; if necessary, add ½ cup water at a time.

Remove the tongue from the broth and transfer to a plate (serve the broth in a mug with your sandwich, or save it for your next pot of soup). Let rest just until cool enough to handle. It's important to peel the tongue while still warm; a cold tongue is very hard to peel.

Peel all the skin from the tongue, starting at the back. You can use a sharp paring knife or your hands; the skin should easily come off. Once the tongue is peeled, you can fry it right away or wrap it tightly in plastic wrap or seal in a lidded container and refrigerate it for up to 1 day.

Slice the tongue crosswise into ¼-inch-thick slabs. Melt 2 tablespoons of the butter in a large skillet over medium heat. When the butter is sizzling, lay half the tongue slices in the skillet, leaving some space between each slice. Fry for about 1 minute, until the meat is nicely browned and a little crispy, then flip and brown the other side. Transfer to a plate. I prefer not to line the plate with a paper towel as the residual butter adds wonderful flavor to the sandwich.

Wipe out the skillet with a paper towel to mop up any burnt butter. Melt the remaining 2 tablespoons butter and fry the remaining tongue slices as before. Sprinkle the crispy tongue medallions with salt and the juice of the remaining lemon.

Cut the baguette lengthwise, taking care not to cut all the way through, so there's still a little bread hinge on one side. Spread both halves with labneh, then layer on the fried tongue, tomato, onion, and lettuce. Cut into 4 pieces and eat immediately or wrap up to take on a picnic. Sandwiches should be eaten the same day they are made.

1 fresh (not frozen) beef tongue (they range in size, but aim for an average 2-pounder)

2 lemons

4 tablespoons (½ stick) unsalted butter

Kosher salt

1 very good baguette

½ cup plain Labneh (page 53)

Ripe tomato, thinly sliced

Red onion, thinly sliced

Romaine lettuce leaves

YOGURT-MARINATED FRIED CHICKEN WITH SAFFRON HONEY

SERVES 4

Plan ahead! The saffron honey needs 8 to 12 hours to infuse, and can be made months in advance. Chicken requires at least a 4-hour marinade.

One of the products we make at The White Moustache is a labneh flavored with Aleppo pepper. The pepper is well rounded, spicy, oily, and distinctly Middle Eastern. Aleppo peppers hail from Aleppo, Syria, and their origins can be traced to a time when the city was the center of the Silk Road spice trade. This pepper is grown in the arid mountains and dried in the hot sun using salt and oils to bring out its earthy flavor. Its heat level is relatively mild, but its flavor is pungent and its history meaningful to many.

Distinct cultural influences converge in this recipe: Middle Eastern flavors of honey, precious saffron, complex Aleppo pepper, and a tenderizing yogurt marinade meet all-American fried chicken.

NOTE: The saffron honey will keep for at least 6 months and can be used anywhere you use honey. My favorite use of it is drizzled on buttered toast.

MAKE THE SAFFRON-INFUSED HONEY: Measure the honey into a heatproof glass measuring cup and heat in the microwave for about 45 seconds (or heat in a small saucepan over low heat for 2 to 3 minutes), until runny but not boiling. Crush the saffron threads between your fingertips as you add them to the honey, then stir well. Cover and leave at room temperature for at least 8 hours or overnight. The saffron will color the honey a rich amber, with pops of red that announce its presence.

MAKE THE MARINADE: Stir the yogurt, garlic, and 1 teaspoon of the salt together in a wide, shallow dish (such as a 9 x 13-inch baking pan). Add the chicken and turn to coat thoroughly. Cover and refrigerate for at least 4 hours or up to overnight.

MAKE THE FRIED CHICKEN: Remove the chicken from the refrigerator 1 hour before you're ready to start cooking so it can come to room temperature. This is important so it cooks evenly. Set up 2 cooling racks with baking sheets under them.

Pour the oil into a 12-inch cast-iron skillet and heat over medium until it reaches 375°F on a candy thermometer.

While the oil is heating, combine the flour, remaining 2 teaspoons salt, Aleppo pepper, and black pepper in a pie pan or wide, shallow bowl and mix thoroughly. Use tongs to lift one chicken piece from the marinade, allowing the excess to drip back into the dish, and transfer to the flour mixture. Coat thoroughly on all sides, then lift again and very gently tap to allow the excess flour to fall off (you don't want to knock all of it off—this is what forms the crispy crust!—just let the loose bits come off so they don't float away in the oil and burn). Transfer to one of the prepared racks. Repeat with the remaining chicken pieces.

Working in batches so as not to crowd the pan, lower the chicken pieces skin-side down into the hot oil. Once you add the chicken, the oil's temperature will drop, so adjust the heat if necessary to maintain a steady temperature of at least 325°F. Flip the chicken pieces every few minutes to allow for even cooking without burning. Cook until the chicken is golden brown all over and a meat thermometer inserted into the thickest part of each piece registers 165°F. This will take anywhere from 8 to 15 minutes, depending on the size of the piece. Transfer the cooked chicken to the clean rack and allow to cool for at least 10 minutes before serving.

To serve, drizzle each piece of chicken with saffron honey.

SAFFRON HONEY

⅔ cup mild-flavored honey
(such as clover)

1/8 teaspoon saffron threads

FRIED CHICKEN

2 cups plain whole milk yogurt

3 tablespoons minced
garlic (about 8 cloves)

3 teaspoons kosher salt, divided

1 (3-pound) chicken, cut into
8 pieces, or any 8 bone-in,
skin-on chicken parts

3 cups peanut or canola oil
(or enough to fill a 12-inch
skillet one-third of the way)

2½ cups all-purpose flour

1 tablespoon Aleppo pepper,
more or less, depending
on desired intensity

½ teaspoon freshly ground
black pepper

WHEY CEVICHE

SERVES 4 TO 6 AS AN APPETIZER

Plan ahead! The fish needs to soak in the whey for 24 hours.

This recipe was a complete surprise and one I struggled with for many years. In experiment after experiment, while the yogurt whey did not cook the fish the same way that lime juice does in traditional Latin American ceviche, the brightness of the whey made for a very refreshing version worth sharing.

The acidity of yogurt whey is usually between 4 and 4.6 pH. The acidity of lime juice is 2.8 pH—much more acidic than whey. Whey is still acidic enough to begin "cooking" the fish while also adding a light, bright creaminess—plus all those probiotics. Just make sure you slice your fish thinly and cut it into small dice. I do use limes for a final citrusy kick.

Use sushi-grade fish as it will not be fully "cooked."

NOTE: Leche de tigre is the name given to the liquid the fish "cooks" in. It is rumored to be an aphrodisiac and a hangover cure, and here can be reserved for taking shots, inventing cocktails (I like mine with beer and hot sauce), or adding to fish stock. Make sure to use an immersion blender or the lowest speed of a traditional blender to avoid making your leche de tigre too foamy.

LECHE DE TIGRE

½ small red onion, chopped (reserve the other half for the ceviche)

2 garlic cloves, peeled

1-inch piece ginger (no need to peel)

1 or 2 serrano chiles, chopped (remove the seeds and ribs before chopping, if desired, to tame the heat)

1½ teaspoons kosher salt

1 cup yogurt whey

CEVICHE

1 pound semi-firm, white-fleshed fish (such as sea bass or snapper, sushi grade if possible), thinly sliced and cut into ¼-inch dice

⅔ cup lime juice (from 5 or 6 limes)

½ small red onion, thinly sliced

2 garlic cloves, grated

1 pint grape or cherry tomatoes, quartered

1 cup finely chopped cilantro leaves (save the stems for pickling, see page 72), from 1 small bunch

1 serrano, thinly sliced (optional)

2 avocados, peeled, pitted, and diced

Kosher salt

Plantain chips or plain corn tortilla chips, for serving

Whey Down South of the Border Pineapple Margaritas (page 257), for serving

MAKE THE LECHE DE TIGRE: In a large bowl, combine the onion, garlic, ginger, chiles, and salt. Use an immersion blender to break down the solids while slowly adding the whey, pureeing but not over-agitating. (You want to avoid creating foam.)

MAKE THE CEVICHE: Add the fish to the bowl with the leche de tigre. Stir well. Cover and refrigerate until the fish is almost opaque, about 24 hours, stirring once or twice.

Drain the fish and transfer to a serving bowl, reserving the leche de tigre if desired (see Note). Add the lime juice, onion, and garlic and stir to coat. Cover and refrigerate for another 15 minutes so the flavors can mingle.

Add the tomatoes, cilantro, and serrano (if using). Gently mix in the avocado. Season with salt to taste. To serve, use a slotted spoon to divide among four bowls, making sure each serving includes a balance of fish, tomatoes, and avocado.

Serve with plantain chips and tequila cocktails.

BREAK
FAST
___

BREADS
BUTTERS

Breakfast is the most lawless meal of the day. It can be hot or cold. It can be sweet or savory. It is appropriate at 6 AM or 10 PM. Anything goes.* This chapter celebrates the spirit of breakfast and breads by boosting familiar recipes with whey. When you have a little bit of whey on hand, I hope it is with these recipes that you see the magic at work.

Do not miss the Whey Pancakes (page 174) that are so easy and delicious to make from scratch, the whey sugars leaving a light texture and crispy edges. The Fluffy Whey Biscuits (page 176) are phenomenally good and will make you consider opening up your own shop. The Quick Breads (page 171–173) will give you an idea of how to easily boost other recipes in your home kitchen with whey. The Butters (page 185 and 188) aim to reclaim time as the most vital ingredient and make every drop of the final result magnificently decadent and uniquely your own.

This ethos, to worship every single ingredient—including your own vibe that infuses into the food you make—is one of our driving principles, and I hope to inspire you in these pages that follow.

---

* Well, almost anything. The one food I never ate, and never eat, for breakfast is yogurt. We Iranians eat yogurt to help digest our food and, when I first wake up, well there is no other food in my stomach to digest yet. That is why I'm more likely to eat other forms of dairy in the morning (such as butter and cheese), but save the yogurt for later in the day. This is the greatest irony for me as an artisanal yogurt maker in Brooklyn, where I know most of my product is enjoyed for breakfast.

SEV

SERVES 4

In India, Zoroastrians enjoy these sweet noodles tossed with butter and sugar for breakfast on auspicious occasions. This dish is one my mother particularly loved to prepare on birthdays, where we woke to the smells of butter, cardamom, and toasted noodles, telltale signs that sev was underway.

The trick with cooking sev is to stir diligently (and to use a lot of butter!) to prevent the noodles from clumping together. My family serves it with cool yogurt on the side and tops it with fried slivered almonds and raisins.

NOTE: Parsis seem to exclusively use and have luck with the Elephant brand of roasted vermicelli. It is available in most Indian grocery stores. I've had good results with Shan brand roasted vermicelli from online outlets. You want to make sure the vermicelli is brittle and very thin. If you cannot find Elephant or Shan brands, look for vermicelli that is "roasted." If it says it's for desserts, even better. Break down the noodles if they are too large for your skillet.

TOPPING

½ cup unsalted butter

¼ cup slivered almonds

¼ cup raisins

SEV

10 to 11 ounces roasted
vermicelli noodles (see Note)

1 cup sugar

2 teaspoons ground cardamom

1½ to 2 cups lukewarm
water, divided

1 tablespoon rose water
(see My Pantry, page 32)

Plain whole milk yogurt,
for serving

Line a plate with a paper towel and set aside. Melt the butter in an extra-large skillet over medium heat. When the butter has melted, add the almonds and cook, stirring constantly, until the nuts are golden brown, about 3 minutes. Add the raisins and stir until they have ballooned, 30 seconds to 1 minute. (The raisins will burn and get very tough if overcooked.)

Using a slotted spoon, remove the raisins and nuts, leaving as much butter in the skillet as possible, and transfer them to the lined plate.

Add the vermicelli, sugar, and cardamom to the skillet. Cook over low heat until all the fat is absorbed and the sugar has melted, about 5 minutes. Continue cooking for 5 minutes longer, stirring constantly, to dry-roast the noodles, turning them a rich, deep brown. Take your time.

Add 1 cup of the lukewarm water and the rose water. Cook, still over low heat and stirring often, until the noodles absorb all the water. This is the step where your attention is key, as forgetting to stir will make the noodles clump together.

When the water has been fully absorbed, add another ½ cup lukewarm water and stir. Continue to cook for another 10 minutes, stirring frequently, until the noodles are fully cooked. They should be soft rather than crunchy. If they are still feeling too firm, add up to ½ cup additional lukewarm water and cook for another 5 minutes, stirring as before, until fully cooked.

Transfer to a plate and sprinkle with the fried nuts and raisins. Serve warm with a side of cool yogurt.

BREAKFAST-ON-THE-WHEY WHOLE WHEAT BLUEBERRY MUFFINS

MAKES 12 MUFFINS

Simple, moist, reliable, always good. Despite the fact that these muffins are made with 100 percent whole wheat flour, they're not at all dry thanks to the whey. The acid in whey delivers moisture to these muffins without the added fat that yogurt or sour cream would. I love blueberries in these muffins, but you can substitute just about any kind of fruit you like, including raspberries, blackberries, diced peaches, plums, or apples—whatever strikes your fancy.

Nonstick spray or soft butter, for greasing the muffin tin

2¼ cups whole wheat flour

1 cup packed light brown sugar

1 teaspoon baking powder

½ teaspoon baking soda

¾ teaspoon kosher salt

½ teaspoon ground cinnamon

1 cup blueberries, fresh or frozen (if using frozen, do not thaw)

Grated zest of 1 orange

1 large egg, at room temperature

1 teaspoon vanilla extract

⅓ cup olive oil

1¼ cups yogurt whey

Preheat the oven to 400°F. Spray a 12-cup muffin tin with nonstick cooking spray or grease with softened butter.

In a large bowl, whisk together the flour, brown sugar, baking powder, baking soda, salt, and cinnamon. Gently stir in the blueberries and orange zest until evenly distributed.

In a medium bowl, whisk the egg, vanilla, oil, and whey until pale and smooth. Pour the whey mixture into the flour mixture and stir just until combined.

Use an ice cream scoop to portion the batter into the prepared muffin tin. Fill almost to the top as these muffins don't rise very high.

Bake until the tops of the muffins no longer look wet and a toothpick inserted into the center comes out clean, about 25 minutes. Transfer to a rack to cool completely, then pop out each muffin and serve.

The muffins will keep in an airtight container at room temperature for up to 3 days. They also freeze beautifully in a zip-top freezer bag.

WHEY QUICK BREADS

If you have only a small amount of whey on hand, these are the recipes I would insist you make. Requiring only ¼ to ⅓ cup of whey, these everyday loaves show how effectively whey lends moisture and a hint of tanginess to baked goods. Plus, if I've done my job up to this point, you'll always keep a little jar of whey on hand.

Each of the following recipes yields a single 9 x 5-inch loaf, but all of them double nicely. If doubling, divide the batter between two loaf pans and keep an eye on baking times. A fuller oven often means your baked goods will need a few extra minutes.

Leftovers can be stored at room temperature, tightly covered, for up to 2 days.

BANANA BREAD

MAKES 1 (9 X 5-INCH) LOAF

Softened butter, for
  greasing the pan

1 cup all-purpose flour,
  plus more for dusting

3/4 teaspoon baking soda

11/4 teaspoons kosher salt

2 large eggs, at room temperature

1/2 cup packed light brown sugar

2 teaspoons vanilla extract

1/2 cup neutral oil (such as
  sunflower, canola, or grapeseed)

⅓ cup yogurt whey

3 very ripe medium
  bananas, mashed

1 cup pecans or walnuts, toasted
  and coarsely chopped (optional
  but highly recommended)

Preheat the oven to 350°F with a rack in the top third. Coat a 9 x 5-inch loaf pan with softened butter, then dust with flour.

Sift the flour, baking soda, and salt into a medium bowl.

In a large bowl, whisk the eggs, brown sugar, and vanilla until smooth. Slowly whisk in the oil until fully emulsified. Whisk in the whey. Once it is fully incorporated, add the mashed banana. Add the wet ingredients to the flour mixture and stir with a silicone spatula just until combined. Gently fold in the nuts, if using.

Pour the batter into the prepared loaf pan and bake until a toothpick inserted in the center comes out with moist crumbs, 50 to 55 minutes. Cool on a rack for 15 minutes. Run a knife around the edges of the pan to loosen the bread, then remove from the pan to finish cooling. Let cool for at least 1 hour before slicing.

ZUCCHINI BREAD

MAKES 1 (9 X 5-INCH) LOAF

Softened butter, for
  greasing the pan

1¾ cups all-purpose flour,
  plus more for dusting

1 teaspoon baking powder

¼ teaspoon baking soda

1 teaspoon kosher salt

2 teaspoons ground cinnamon

¼ teaspoon ground nutmeg

2 large eggs, at room temperature

¼ cup yogurt whey

⅓ cup neutral oil (such as
  sunflower, canola, or grapeseed)

2 teaspoons vanilla extract

⅔ cup packed light brown sugar

1½ cups shredded zucchini
  (about 2 small zucchini)

⅔ cup add-ins of your choice, such
  as coarsely toasted chopped
  nuts (walnuts, pecans, and/or
  pine nuts) or dried fruit (cherries,
  raisins, cranberries, and/or
  chopped apricots) (optional,
  but highly recommended)

Preheat the oven to 350°F with a rack in the top third. Coat a 9 x 5-inch loaf pan with softened butter, then dust with flour.

In a large bowl, whisk together the flour, baking powder, baking soda, salt, cinnamon, and nutmeg.

In a medium bowl, whisk the eggs, whey, oil, vanilla, and brown sugar until smooth and well combined. Pour the wet ingredients into the dry and whisk just until incorporated. Gently fold in the zucchini, as well as the nuts and raisins, if using.

Pour the batter into the prepared pan and bake until a toothpick inserted in the center comes out clean, 50 to 60 minutes. Cool on a rack for 15 minutes. Run a knife around the edges of the pan to loosen the bread, then remove from the pan to finish cooling. Let cool for at least 1 hour before slicing.

PUMPKIN BREAD

MAKES 1 (9 X 5-INCH) LOAF

Softened butter, for greasing
 the pan, plus 6 tablespoons
 (¾ stick) unsalted butter, melted

1⅔ cups all-purpose flour,
 plus more for dusting

1½ teaspoons baking powder

¼ teaspoon baking soda

2 teaspoons ground cinnamon

½ teaspoon ground nutmeg

¼ teaspoon ground cloves

½ teaspoon kosher salt

1¼ cups plus 2 tablespoons
 pumpkin puree (about half of
 a 15-ounce can, see Note)

1 cup packed dark brown sugar

2 large eggs, at room temperature

¼ cup yogurt whey

¾ cup chopped, pitted
 dates (optional)

1 cup walnuts or pecans, toasted
 and chopped (optional)

Preheat the oven to 350°F with a rack in the top third. Coat a 9 x 5-inch loaf pan with softened butter, then dust with flour.

In a large bowl, whisk together the flour, baking powder, baking soda, cinnamon, nutmeg, cloves, and salt.

In a medium bowl, whisk the pumpkin puree, brown sugar, eggs, melted butter, and whey until smooth. Pour the pumpkin mixture into the flour mixture and whisk gently just to combine. Fold in the dates and nuts, if using, until evenly distributed.

Pour the batter into prepared pan and smooth the top. Bake until a toothpick inserted in the center comes out clean, 55 to 60 minutes. Cool on a rack for 15 minutes. Run a knife around the edges of the pan to loosen the bread, then remove from the pan to finish cooling on a rack. Let cool for at least 1 hour before slicing.

NOTE: The leftover pumpkin puree makes a great quick snack. Spoon it over thick yogurt, sprinkle with a little brown sugar and cinnamon, and top with toasted nuts. This combo also makes a satisfying dipping sauce for the pumpkin bread.

WHEY-TO-START-THE-WEEKEND PANCAKES

MAKES ABOUT 8 (4-INCH) PANCAKES

The first time I had pancakes in America, it felt gloriously naughty. Cake! For breakfast! These impossibly light, tender pancakes produce that same feeling. Using two eggs gives them a rich, custardy taste akin to French toast.

Don't skip the important step of letting the batter rest, as it gives the leaveners time to activate to make your pancakes taller and fluffier.

These are at their best when they're fresh out of the pan, while the edges are still crispy. If you must be polite and serve everyone at once, don't stack the pancakes or they'll steam and go limp. Instead, warm a baking sheet in a 250°F oven. Add the pancakes in a single layer as they come off the skillet and hold until ready to serve.

The same batter makes terrific waffles. It also doubles well.

1⅓ cups all-purpose flour

2 tablespoons sugar

1 teaspoon baking powder

1 teaspoon baking soda

1 teaspoon kosher salt

2 large eggs

1 cup yogurt whey

4 tablespoons (½ stick)
unsalted butter, melted,
plus more for the skillet

Neutral oil (such as sunflower,
canola, or grapeseed) or
coconut oil for the skillet

In a large bowl, whisk together the flour, sugar, baking powder, baking soda, and salt.

In a medium bowl, whisk the eggs, whey, and melted butter until thoroughly combined. Pour the wet ingredients into the dry and gently whisk just until incorporated. (A few lumps are okay and preferable to an overmixed batter, which will lead to denser pancakes.) Set the batter aside for 15 minutes at room temperature, until the surface is dotted with bubbles.

Heat a large nonstick skillet or griddle over medium heat. Plop in approximately 1 teaspoon butter and 1 teaspoon oil (you get the flavor and browning properties of butter, while the oil tempers burning), and swirl the pan to coat well.

Pour about ⅓ cup batter per pancake into the hot pan. Bubbles will form on the tops of the pancakes; wait to flip them until most of the bubbles have popped and the surface begins to lose its wet, shiny look, 2 to 3 minutes. If you like, use a spatula to peek underneath when you think the pancakes are getting close—the bottom should be golden brown. Flip and cook for another 1 to 2 minutes, just until golden. Transfer to a plate and repeat to cook the remaining pancakes, adding more butter and oil as needed.

Serve with maple syrup, jam, yogurt, fresh fruit, or lemon juice and sugar . . . or all of the above. Or just stand at the stove and eat them with your hands. Hey, it's the weekend.

FLUFFY WHEY BISCUITS

MAKES 10 BISCUITS

Martha Stewart and I made these biscuits on television and her whole team loved them. I am shamelessly bragging here in hopes that this recipe will become your go-to biscuit recipe—and, if you are like me, you will start to make these biscuits on the regular.

This recipe was inspired by the brilliant and charming Shirley Corriher, author of *CookWise* and *BakeWise*. A scientist and baker, Corriher approaches biscuits by making an exceptionally wet dough so the liquid steams up and the biscuits become fluffy and tender. In my twist, whey serves as the liquid and creates unbelievably tender results. Rather than adding more flour to make the dough easier to handle, embrace the sloppiness: wet dough, handled minimally, will reward you with biscuits that are light and moist, cakey rather than flaky.

3 tablespoons unsalted butter, melted, plus 6 tablespoons unsalted butter, chilled and cut into ½-inch cubes

2¼ cups all-purpose flour, plus more for dusting

1 tablespoon baking powder

½ teaspoon baking soda

1 tablespoon sugar

1 teaspoon kosher salt

1 cup yogurt whey

Preheat the oven to 450°F. Brush the bottom and sides of a 9-inch round cake pan or pie plate with just enough of the melted butter to coat. Reserve the remaining melted butter.

In a medium bowl, whisk together the flour, baking powder, baking soda, sugar, and salt in a medium bowl. Add the cold cubed butter and work it into the flour mixture with a pastry cutter or by rubbing lightly between your fingers, until the mixture resembles coarse meal. Pour in the whey and, using a silicone spatula, mix quickly and gently just until combined. The dough will be very wet.

Put about a cup of flour in a wide, shallow dish. Using a greased ¼ cup measuring cup, portion out biscuits a few at a time, dropping the dough gently into the flour-filled dish. Sprinkle more flour on top of the dough. Pick up scoops of dough one at a time, gently shaking off the excess flour. Place the biscuits in the prepared baking pan, evenly spaced, first around the perimeter, then in the middle; the biscuits will be touching. When the pan is filled with biscuits, brush the tops with the reserved melted butter (rewarmed if necessary).

Bake until the tops of the biscuits are golden brown, 15 to 20 minutes. Allow to cool for 10 minutes. Serve warm.

WHEY CORNBREAD

MAKES 1 (9-INCH) PAN

Adding whey to a simple staple like cornbread is an example of how whey can turn up the volume on both texture and taste. Like a good DJ playing on both the treble and the bass on a favorite classic. Whey-boosted cornbread strikes a happy medium between the crumbly, savory, southern-style cornbread and the cake-in-disguise variety. It is soft and slightly sweet, with a satisfying cornmeal crunch. Whey makes this super-quick-to-whip-up cornbread moist and tangy. It's just the right accompaniment to any of the everyday soups on pages 107 to 119.

8 tablespoons (1 stick) unsalted butter, melted

1½ cups medium-grind cornmeal (such as Bob's Red Mill)

1 cup all-purpose flour

2 teaspoons baking powder

½ teaspoon baking soda

3 tablespoons sugar

1 teaspoon kosher salt

1½ cups yogurt whey

2 large eggs, at room temperature

Preheat the oven to 450°F. Generously brush the bottom and sides of a 9-inch round or square baking pan with some of the melted butter, reserving the remaining butter for the batter.

In a large bowl, whisk together the cornmeal, flour, baking powder, baking soda, sugar, and salt.

In a medium bowl, whisk together the whey, eggs, and reserved melted butter. Pour the wet mixture into the dry and whisk just until incorporated.

Scrape the batter into the prepared pan and bake until golden brown and a toothpick inserted in the center comes out clean, about 25 minutes. Allow to cool for 15 minutes before cutting. Leftovers can be stored at room temperature, tightly covered, for up to 2 days.

SEE-ROGH

MAKES 9 (6- TO 8-INCH) DISKS

Plan ahead! The dough needs to rise for 1 hour.

See-rogh is a Zoroastrian fry-bread, shaped in disks of variable sizes and usually served on celebratory occasions, including funerals.* Each time I make these, I make a variety of sizes, but in this recipe, you can expect to make about nine individual breads. Of course, your yield will depend not only on the size of your frying pan but on the experience of the hands that help you.

My favorite memories of making this bread are at the San Jose Zoroastrian Youth camps in northern California. The adults would wake up early and start heating oil for frying. The aash-e-reshteh would be slowly cooking nearby. Despite being almost biologically allergic to the early morning, I was always the first one up, eagerly pacing the cooking area so I could get my hands in the dough, flatten out the breads, and drop them in the hot oil myself. The dozens and dozens of hot, golden disks of impossibly chewy, warm, crispy bread, sprinkled with sugar, delighted me.

I loved how making see-rogh was a three- or four-person activity. The hustle and bustle of it all was so comforting and familiar.

This recipe easily doubles, or quadruples. And if you are making this as a celebration with many people, consider making some Aash-e-Reshteh (page 101) as a group as well. The combination of the hearty soup and a piece of the crispy sweet bread is a particularly auspicious one for Zoroastrians.

---

* If making for a funeral, omit the sugar.

Add the yeast to ½ cup of the warm water and stir well. The yeast will start frothing. Add the sugar and stir. Set aside for 15 minutes.

Whisk the flour and salt together in a large bowl. Add the dissolved yeast and the remaining 1½ cups warm water and knead with your hands until the dough is elastic, about 5 minutes. Cover and leave in a warm, dry place until the dough doubles in size, about 1 hour.

Pour the oil to a depth of at least 2 inches in a large, deep frying pan. Pour a little oil in a plate for your hands and coat a rimmed baking sheet with more oil. Line another baking sheet with paper towels and set aside.

Place the frying pan over high heat. When it's ready for frying, a small ball of dough (just pinch a bit off) will immediately sizzle when it hits the oil.

Dip your hands in the plate of oil. (This essentially makes your hands "nonstick.") Grab a handful of dough. Spread out the dough on the oiled baking sheet. Continue stretching the dough, lifting it with your hands to expand the disk wider. Stop when the disk is ¼ inch thick and about the diameter of your frying pan.

Now here's where other hands in the kitchen will be necessary. Ask a friend to help you guide the see-rogh into the frying pan. Let your friend oversee the frying process while you focus on stretching out the next disk of dough.

Fry each disk until browned, 2 to 3 minutes per side, turning once. Transfer to the paper towel–lined baking sheet and, if desired, sprinkle with sugar while the dough is still hot.

1 tablespoon active dry yeast

2 cups warm water (use the pinkie test, page 48), divided

1 tablespoon sugar, plus more for optional sprinkling

4 cups all-purpose flour, plus more for dusting

1 teaspoon kosher salt

Vegetable oil, for frying

Sugar, for sprinkling (optional)

"SOURDOUGH" SICILIAN PIZZA DOUGH

MAKES 1 (10 X 15-INCH) PIZZA
SERVES ABOUT 4

Plan ahead! The dough requires 2 ½ hours to complete its two-phase rise.

No Brooklyn-based cookbook would be complete without a pizza recipe. Pizza is a big point of pride around here—we puff our chests at the fact that our per-capita pizzeria count is the envy of the world. In addition to the array of New York's iconic thin-crust Neapolitan pies, every pizza joint worth its mutz has a Sicilian pie on offer—a rectangular, thick-crusted pizza that stands out as an island of chewy loveliness for us bread fiends. (This style of pizza is often just called a "square pie," and nobody makes a better one than Dom De Marco, owner and sole pizza maker at the legendary Di Fara Pizza in Midwood, Brooklyn. He parbakes the crusts for his square pies and leaves them in the baking pans, stacked up next to the oven, waiting for an order to come in before he tops and bakes each one to order. Get one if you ever have the chance.)

Many great Brooklyn pizzerias ferment their dough, and I tried a few variations during my experiments in the kitchen. The final, best version I offer here substitutes whey for water. It gives the crust a sourdough-like tang, without all the trouble of feeding and maintaining a starter.

Sprinkle the yeast over the warm whey in a small bowl. Let stand for about 1 minute, until the yeast is creamy, then stir to dissolve.

In the bowl of a stand mixer, combine 3 ½ cups of the flour, the salt, and the olive oil. Add the yeast mixture and mix on medium speed with the dough hook attachment until smooth and elastic, adding up to ½ cup more flour if necessary, about 5 minutes. (If you don't have an electric mixer with a dough hook, stir with a wooden spoon until smooth, then turn out onto a generously floured surface and knead by hand, adding more flour as needed, until you have a smooth, satiny dough.)

Lightly coat a large bowl with olive oil. Put the dough in the bowl and turn to coat. Cover with plastic wrap and let rise in a warm place until doubled in volume, about 1 ½ hours.

Lightly oil a baking sheet. Gently flatten the dough with your fist and transfer to the baking sheet, continuing to press and flatten it out to reach the edges of the baking sheet. Cover again with plastic wrap and let rise for another hour, until nearly doubled in bulk.

Preheat the oven to 450°F with a rack in the lower third.

Press the dough with your fingertips to make dimples at 1-inch intervals. Top the pizza to your liking and bake until the crust is golden brown on the edges and bottom, about 20 minutes for a pizza with minimal toppings or about 30 minutes for a fully loaded pizza. Allow the pizza to rest for a few minutes before slicing.

1 envelope (2 ¼ teaspoons) active dry yeast

1 ⅓ cups yogurt whey, warmed to 110°F (or use the pinkie test, page 48)

3 ½ to 4 cups all-purpose flour

2 teaspoons kosher salt

2 tablespoons olive oil, plus more for greasing the bowl and pan

Pizza toppings of your choice

SOUR-FAUX
NO-KNEAD BREAD

MAKES 1 LOAF

Plan ahead! You'll need to allow for 18 to 24 hours for the initial rise, an additional 2 hours for the second rise, and another 2 hours for the bread to cool before serving.

The main difference between a homemade no-knead loaf and a traditional loaf you'd get from a proper bakery is complexity of flavor. Many traditional bakery loaves are made from a long-fermented starter, or levain. A longer, slower fermentation causes the bread to rise, sans commercial yeast, and the levain adds a distinctive and lively tang. Using whey in place of water allowed me to mimic the tang of a levain-based sourdough bread with far less time and effort.

The dough's high moisture content and long rise give the bread its structure—a network of irregular air pockets and crannies—and its chewy-but-light texture. A blazing-hot Dutch oven creates a spectacularly crispy crust.

The basic recipe I offer below uses all bread flour, but you may swap in up to one-third of the bread flour for any whole-grain flour you like, such as whole wheat or rye flour.

This recipe owes everything to Jim Lahey, the owner of Sullivan Street Bakery, a New York institution. Lahey's widely publicized technique for making artisan-quality bread with nearly zero effort resonates strongly with me. After all, his "set it and forget it" ethos parallels the walk-away-and-let-the-magic-happen hallmark of my yogurt-making.

In a large bowl, whisk together the flour, yeast, and salt. Pour in the whey and mix with a wooden spoon until the dough comes together and there are no visible streaks of dry flour. It will be sticky. Cover the bowl with plastic wrap and let it rest in a warmish place for 18 to 24 hours. (The most important thing is to avoid leaving the dough in a cold, drafty spot.)

Remove the plastic wrap and set aside. Lightly flour a clean work surface and scrape the dough onto it. It will be stickier and gooier and stretchier than it was when you set it to rise. Don't punch it down and try not to handle it more than necessary. Use a bench scraper to fold it over on itself a few times, turning it as you go. Sprinkle the dough lightly with flour, cover it loosely with the plastic wrap, and let it rest on the countertop undisturbed for 20 minutes.

Spread out a clean, non-nubby (*not* terrycloth) cotton towel next to the dough. Heavily coat half the towel with wheat bran or corn-meal. Sprinkle some more flour onto your work surface and move the dough onto it. Gently tuck the dough's edges underneath it to form a ball (or something vaguely resembling a child's attempt at a dome—perfection doesn't matter here, as craggy bread has its own rustic appeal). Quickly and gently move the ball of dough onto the wheat bran/cornmeal side of the towel. Sprinkle the top of the dome with a thorough coating of additional wheat bran or cornmeal, then fold the other half of the towel on top of it. Let rest for 2 hours.

3 cups bread flour (or 2 cups bread flour plus 1 cup whole wheat or rye flour), plus more for dusting

¼ teaspoon instant yeast

1½ teaspoons kosher salt

1½ cups yogurt whey, at room temperature

Wheat bran or cornmeal, for sprinkling

CONTINUES

After the dough has been resting for 1½ hours, position an oven rack in the lowest position and remove the other racks. Cover an empty Dutch oven with its lid and transfer to the cold oven. Preheat the oven to 450°F.

At the end of the dough's resting time, put on your most robust oven mitts (this isn't one of those "oh, I can use a kitchen towel" moments—you want thick, protective mitts for handling hot, heavy cast iron) and make *absolutely sure* that they are completely dry (if they're even a bit damp, you'll burn your hands). Remove the hot Dutch oven and set it on top of the stove. Remove the lid, take off your oven mitts, and peel back the towel from the top of the dough. Working quickly, scoop your hand between the towel and the counter to pick up the dough. Turn your hand over and plop the dough from the towel so it falls gently into the Dutch oven. Put your oven mitts back on and shake the Dutch oven a little if the dough landed lopsided. Cover the Dutch oven and put it back in the oven.

Bake the bread for 30 minutes, then remove the lid and continue baking until the crust is deep brown, about 15 minutes longer. Put your oven mitts back on, pull out the Dutch oven, and use the oven mitts to transfer the bread to a cooling rack. At this point, the crust will be menacingly hard, and it may have tiny cracks in it. Stand by as the loaf cools and the cracks widen. The crust will soften a little as it cools, transforming from an impenetrable shell to a crisp and friendly crust. The bread will smell amazing and look amazing and you're going to be tempted to cut into it right away, but stay strong because the texture and flavor will improve dramatically after the bread cools.

After 2 hours, reward your patience and self-restraint by slicing off a slab of bread and slathering it with butter.

WHEY SPROUTED
ALMOND BUTTER

Plan ahead! You'll need to wait 2 days for the almonds to sprout, then an additional 2 to 3 days to dehydrate the almonds before churning them into almond butter.

This recipe was inspired by a visit I had with Johnathan Adler, the chef at Franny's, the beloved pizzeria in Brooklyn. Johnathan had heard that we were offering up whey for experimenting and he wanted some. During our meeting, Johnathan casually mentioned using whey to make almond butter.

Inspired and intrigued, I experimented with different techniques. I hearkened back to longstanding family tradition, especially Persian New Year (spring equinox) and Yalda (winter solstice), for which we always soak nuts before eating them. I also consulted the Internet. Scientifically speaking, once nuts are soaked and allowed to sprout, they are easier to digest and their nutrients are easier to absorb because they lose their enzyme inhibitors. I loved this idea of sprouted almonds with probiotic whey, as everything was alive. Even though I go on to dehydrate the almonds, the sprouting process changes their chemistry.

In this recipe, it's important to use unpasteurized raw almonds, as pasteurized almonds will not sprout. However, US growers are required by law to pasteurize their almonds, using either steam or chemicals. The only exception is if you buy your almonds directly from the farmer. So, your best bet for getting a hold of unpasteurized almonds is to buy them at a farmers' market or to buy imported raw almonds. If you're looking for them online, search for "unpasteurized almonds" rather than "raw almonds" as almonds are usually called "raw" if they haven't been roasted even though they *have* been pasteurized.

In practice, soaking your nuts is much easier than sprouting your nuts.* But even if your almonds do not sprout, do not despair as there will still be notes of tangy whey in your almond butter, making the minimal added effort worth it.

This recipe scales easily, so make as much as you'd like.

---

* Oh, grow up.

CONTINUES ♪

SPROUT THE ALMONDS: Put the almonds in a bowl or jar big enough to accommodate them with at least 1 inch of headspace. Cover the almonds completely with whey. Keep at room temperature, lightly covered with a tea towel or other clean cloth, for 48 hours. As the almonds soak up the whey, add more whey so they remain completely submerged until they sprout. To confirm that they have sprouted, crack one open down the middle as you would a sunflower seed. At the tip of the almond you should be able to see a very tiny, pale nubbin of a sprout forming. That's about as much as they will bloom. Whether or not your almonds have sprouted at this point, go ahead and drain out the whey. (Reserve it for use in cooked preparations such as the quick breads on pages 171 to 173 or any of the hot soups starting on page 92.) While successful sprouting is ideal, you can make almond butter regardless.

DEHYDRATE THE ALMONDS: It is important to the shelf-life of your almond butter for the almonds to be completely dry, as eliminating moisture helps prevent spoilage. While dehydrating almonds in a dehydrator or on a baking sheet in a 125°F oven for 24 to 36 hours is ideal, many ovens don't dip that low (and many people—like me—don't own

Almonds, unpasteurized and raw

Yogurt whey, enough to cover the almonds entirely, plus more to top off the jar as they sit

a dehydrator). Here's what I do instead: I dehydrate my almonds when I know I'll be using the oven a lot over the course of a few days—to roast chicken or bake potatoes or make pie. I set my almonds on a rimmed baking sheet and leave it nearby. Then every time I'm finished using the oven and turn it off, I slide the baking sheet inside so the almonds can dry in the residual heat. I'll do this a few times, taking care not to let the almonds get dark, as the goal is to just dry them rather than roast or toast them. To confirm they are fully dry, bite into an almond. There should be no chewy give, and the nut should be almost brittle, with crunch.

MAKE THE BUTTER: Put all the almonds in the bowl of a food processor fitted with the steel blade. Run the processor until the almonds turn into a creamy butter, scraping down the sides with a spatula once or twice as you go. For the first couple of minutes the almonds will look like coarse sand and you'll wonder if they're ever going to turn into butter. Keep going! (I like my nut butter smooth, so I keep the processor going for at least 8 minutes; if you prefer yours chunky, check earlier in the process and stop when you've reached the desired texture.)

Store the almond butter in a tightly covered container for up to 1 month at room temperature or for several months in the refrigerator.

MARBLE BUTTER

FLEXIBLE YIELD

In the spirit of making amazing dairy with very little to no machinery, I love this simple butter recipe. It was introduced to me by Sabah Ashraf, a dear family friend who dreamed about opening up her own butter shop. Sabah is, at the time of this writing, the CEO of an international branding company and the type of New York City jet-setter you might only meet in movies. Her success, I am convinced, lies in her ability to truly listen to people. She picks up every nuance of a person's communication.

Sabah told me she learned to listen to people while making butter. Here's her method: Put a marble in a jar with some heavy cream. Roll it across the floor between you and someone you enjoy listening to. By the time you finish the conversation, you'll have butter and a little residual buttermilk.

NOTE: Choose a jar about twice the capacity of the amount of cream you will use. So, if you're using 8 ounces of cream, use a 16-ounce jar. Also: You will need a marble!

Put the cream in the jar so it fills it only halfway. Add 1 marble. Sit on the floor across from your friend and roll the jar with gusto back and forth. Have a lengthy conversation about something totally random and delightful. When you can't hear the marble anymore and can feel solid chunks and liquid in the jar, you are finished.

Alternatively, if you want to make this butter without a partner, you will have to exert a lot of elbow grease but you'll get results in about 15 minutes. Once the cream and marble are in the jar, shake the jar vigorously for about 2 minutes, at which point the cream will thicken to a yogurt-like consistency. You'll still be able to hear the marble, so keep shaking. Shake vigorously until you can no longer hear the marble, about 8 minutes with an extra hard dose of shaking for 1 minute longer.

At this point, you'll have butter and liquid buttermilk. Strain off the buttermilk and drink it or use it in place of the whey in the quick breads on pages 171 to 173.

If desired, mash the salt into the butter. Shape the butter into a roll using parchment paper, roll up the ends like a taffy, and store in the refrigerator.

Heavy cream

¼ teaspoon kosher salt per every 1 cup cream (optional)

Preserves

با من ترش است روی یار فدری
شیرینتر از این ترش ندیم شکری
بیزار شود شکر ز شیرینی خویش
گر زان شکر ترش بیاید نمبری

The face she shows me is a little sour,
Though sugar has never tasted sweeter.
Sugar would be bored by its own sweetness
If it ever came to know that sour flavor.

—RUMI

In Yazd, when it was time for us or our neighbors to harvest our fruits, the whole town would get together to help, counting on the future reciprocity. Sometimes family members from the cities even came back to the villages to lend a hand. While the nicest fruits were prepared for market, the "ugly" or "blemished" ones were rescued and prized for preserves.

In Iran, we would make preserves in huge quantities in copper pots. Fruit is picked, peeled, and pitted (and eaten along the way), and then a huge wood fire is lit and a cauldron that could bathe four toddlers is filled with fruit, sugar, spices, and water. The fruits are cooked down over the gentle fire well into the evening. Everyone's labor is rewarded with jams that last through the winter months until the next harvest.

Today, we make our preserves as we did in Iran—in huge pots, all in one go when produce is at its peak. We use blemished fruits that would otherwise be composted by the farms as these make the best preserves. I encourage you to source your fruit from the farmers' market rather than the grocery store. In fact, you'll get the best deal if you head to the market toward the end of its operating hours, or even call up your local farm and secure any unsold fruits at the end of the season. When cooking these produce items, I keep the fruit as intact as possible, as the soft chunks provide an appealing contrast to the silky smoothness of the yogurt.

These preserves form the basis for The White Moustache yogurt line. Adding preserves to our yogurt lets us acknowledge the American preference for sweet yogurt while remaining true to the Iranian flavors I grew up with: date, quince, sweet beet, and more.

The recipes that follow might seem simple, even boring—after all, they consist of little more than fruit and sugar. I don't like to overwhelm or complicate the preserves with spices or other add-ins. They're as simple as the yogurt I pair them with. In some ways, the complexity lies in the fruit itself—at what stage of ripeness it is plucked, at how much inherent sweetness it has, in its texture.

The process is tedious but also meditative. And the reward is great. Making preserves lets me capture a season in time for yearlong enjoyment. Each time I scoop preserves onto a bowl of yogurt, or scrape them over an indulgent slice of buttered toast, I taste the harvest once again.

QUINCE PRESERVES

FLEXIBLE YIELD

*Plan ahead! This preserve will take about 1 ½ hours
of cooking time and several hours to cool.*

Beh is the Iranian word for quince. *Beh-hesht* is the word for
heaven. So heaven must be a quince orchard. This positively
intoxicating fruit is from the pome (apple) family of fruits. Those
unfamiliar with it may mistake it for a stubby pear or a mis-
shapen Golden Delicious apple, but give it a sniff and the smell
will transport you. A sack of quince will perfume your entire
kitchen. Honey? Pineapple? Bananas? Gardenias? Strawberries?
Gummy bears? The quince's scent is so alluring, you'll want to
take a big bite, but as with any siren's song, immediate surrender is not recommended. The white flesh is chalky and astringent
when raw, but when cooked it transforms, turning a deep, dark
red and taking on a floral flavor that is, well, just as heavenly as
it smells.

This recipe is for the preserve that we make for The White Moustache. My family gathers in the early fall to harvest the quince and
make the jam. The weather is just starting to cool, and the air is
perfect for grilling kababs or heating up a cauldron of stew and
chopping and chatting through bushels and bushels of quince.

Perfectly ripe quince is firm (but not rock-hard) and banana-
yellow and will practically knock you over with its fragrance.
I once drove from a farm in upstate New York to the factory in
Brooklyn with quince and nearly passed out from the delicious
aroma that filled the car. If quince is picked green (or half-green),
it will continue to soften a little, though it will not fully ripen. You
can still make jam with it, though. You'll just need to coax it along
with some additional sugar.

I like to leave the skin on for added flavor and nutrients. If you
get your quince from a neighbor's backyard tree (lucky neighbors! lucky you!), or from the farmers' market, it will most likely
be covered in fuzz. Remove the fuzz by rubbing the fruit with a
towel before you proceed with the recipe. If the quince is from the

CONTINUES

grocery store, it'll probably be smooth and shiny already, so you'll just have to remove the sticker.

Spoon the preserves over yogurt or enjoy on buttered bread with a cup of tea. Use the leftover syrup to sweeten teas, cakes, and drinks or to make Quince Soda (page 241).

A general note on measuring ingredients: Any bowl or vessel can serve as an accurate measuring cup for this recipe. For example, let's assume you bought 16 quince and chopped them up and they   your favorite ceramic bowl (the oddly shaped one your niece made in pottery class) 4 times. You would then transfer the quince to a large pot and use that same bowl to measure 2 bowls of sugar and 1 bowl of water. In other words, the ratio among the ingredients is key. Go hunt for as many quince as you can find during harvest time and scale the quantities up or down accordingly.

The cardamom is to taste, but my general guideline is 1 cardamom pod for every quart of cut fruit. Make sure the cardamom is fresh, as stale cardamom will be too subtle for this preserve.

2 parts cored and chopped quince (see directions)

1 cardamom pod per every 4 cups chopped raw quince

1 part sugar

½ part water

Cut each quince in half and scoop out the core with a melon baller or a knife, making sure to get all the tough membrane-y bits in addition to the seeds. To ensure you got it all, you can let your halved quince sit for a few minutes, and the surface will oxidize a little, but the tough membrane will remain a stark white and alert you to its presence. Cut each quince half lengthwise into 4 slices, then cut each slice crosswise into ¼-inch cubes.

Crush each cardamom pod so it's open but still intact. Tie them up in a little sachet of cheesecloth for easy retrieval or drop in directly (in which case you'll have to later retrieve the pods).

Put the quince, sugar, water, and cardamom sachet in a pot; choose one that is large enough to allow at least 5 inches headspace as quince tends to float when it cooks. Cover the pot and bring to a boil over high heat, then lower the heat to medium and uncover so steam can escape. Your

task now is to maintain a constant simmer throughout cooking, even if you have to toggle the heat. Keep cooking, stirring occasionally and pressing the fruit down with a spatula when it floats to the top, for 1 ½ to 2 hours.

Watch as the quince turns from white to gold to blush and eventually to a brilliant coral-maroon. The fruit will volunteer some of its own juices to the syrup, creating a delicious abundance of liquid for it to cook in. The quince is done when it's tender but not falling apart (similar in texture to a poached pear) and tastes like strawberries and pineapple and honey all at once.

Allow the preserves to cool at room temperature, which will take several hours. Remove the cardamom sachet (or pods). Transfer the preserves to glass jars or plastic containers, cover, and store in the refrigerator for several months.

CARROT PRESERVES

MAKES ABOUT 1½ QUARTS

My family will make jam out of anything. Carrots are naturally sweet and take well to the heady, floral additions of rose water and cardamom. This sweet jam, with some added texture from toasted pistachios, hits the spot on a spring morning when slathered on fresh bread with a clump of clotted cream. Don't have clotted cream? Ah, but you do. The next time you make yogurt, skim the cream off the top of the milk as it's cooling and set it aside in the fridge. Voilà.

Carrot Preserves also works well in a layered cake, such as A Simple Cake Either Whey (page 218).

2 to 3 cups sugar, depending on how sweet your carrots are and how sweet you like your jam

6 cups grated carrots (from about 6 large, peeled carrots)

5 cardamom pods, cracked

2 tablespoons rose water (see My Pantry, page 32)

½ cup shelled pistachios, toasted and chopped

In a large saucepan (3 quarts or larger), combine 1 quart water and the sugar over high heat, stirring constantly until the sugar melts. Reduce the heat slightly, add the carrots, and maintain a steady simmer until the carrots are tender but not mushy, about 1 hour.

Secure the cardamom in a cheesecloth sachet or tea ball and add to the carrot pot. (You can also drop them in directly and then fish them out at the end—just be prepared for a little surprise when eating the jam in case you miss one.) Continue to simmer until most of the liquid has cooked off and the jam is thick, fragrant, and deep orange, about 1 hour longer. Begin stirring constantly toward the final 20 minutes or so of cooking, when the liquid starts becoming as thick as corn syrup and gentle bubbles emerge throughout. Otherwise the carrots will stick to the bottom of the pot.

Stir in the rose water and cook for 5 minutes longer. Remove from the heat and allow to cool to room temperature. Remove the cardamom. Stir in the pistachios.

Transfer to airtight glass jars or plastic containers and store in the refrigerator for several months. The jam makes a great gift.

SWEET BEET PRESERVES AND BEET SYRUP

MAKES ABOUT 1 QUARTS

In 2014 I was invited by Whole Foods Market to come up with an exclusive new yogurt flavor for their Brooklyn opening. They suggested several options, including blueberries, passionfruit, and mango—but these are not fruits or preserves that I was familiar with. So I told them I needed to stay true to my strengths and my Iranian flavors. I chose beets.

I knew choosing beets was going to be risky. But yogurt and beets are a staple combination in Middle Eastern and Iranian fare. I took inspiration from my own people.

These sweet beet preserves are so earthy, in the best possible way. Brown sugar amplifies beets' natural sweetness, making them an especially good partner for creamy, tangy yogurt. The color combination of bright purple against stark white yogurt is an added bonus.

NOTE: There will be ½ to 1 cup of syrup leftover, which I recommend straining off and reserving so you can make the Sweet Beet Probiotic Whey Tonic (page 246). It's a great example of using two byproducts (beet syrup and whey) to make something completely new and totally refreshing.

CONTINUES

If your beets still have their greens attached, trim off and wash for use in salads. Trim off the stems and root tails. Put the beets in a large pot, cover with water by about 1 inch, and cover the pot. Bring to a boil over high heat, then reduce the heat to a heavy simmer. Simmer until the beets are tender and can be easily pierced with a paring knife. This will take at least 30 minutes but may take much longer depending on the size and age of the beets.

Turn off the heat. Use a slotted spoon to transfer the beets to a 9 x 13-inch baking dish. Reserve 1 cup of the cooking water from the pot. Let the beets sit for at least 15 minutes, until they're cool enough to handle, then slip off the skins with your hands or a paring knife.

Preheat the oven to 325°F.

Shred the beets on the large holes of a box grater or using a food processor's shredding attachment. This is a messy job, and beets stain, so keep away from any fabric or wooden cutting boards you want to keep pristine! Return the shredded beets and the reserved cooking water* to the baking dish and stir in the brown sugar. Cover the dish with aluminum foil, poke a few holes on top, and bake until the sugar and beet juice have formed a thick syrup, about 30 minutes. Remove the foil and let cool to room temperature.

Transfer the beet preserves to airtight glass jars or plastic containers and store in the refrigerator for up to 3 weeks. Make sure to have a fresh batch of yogurt on hand. There is no better destiny for these preserves.

---

* If you would like a preserve to pair with your yogurt, add only ¼ cup of the cooking water. If you plan on needing syrup to make pitchers of Sweet Beet Probiotic Whey Tonic (page 246), add the full cup.

2 pounds red beets, scrubbed

¾ cup packed light brown sugar

RHUBARB PRESERVES

FLEXIBLE YIELD

With only three ingredients (one of them being water), these preserves are not complex. The short—even boring—ingredients list is misleading, as when combined, rhubarb, sugar, and water produce something unexpectedly magical.

The technique of cooking rhubarb down slowly and having it retain some of its shape is an important one, as most rhubarb recipes call for this tart vegetable to almost dissolve under heat so it becomes a loose mush. My method, which leaves the rhubarb in slightly larger pieces and calls for as little stirring as possible, is one I want to pass down to my children, and so here I pass it down to you as well.

I prefer to give ratios rather than specific amounts here, so you can decide how much to make.

1 part sugar

1 part water

2 parts rhubarb, washed and coarsely chopped into rough 1-inch pieces

Depending on how much you're making, choose a saucepan large enough so all the ingredients won't occupy more than two-thirds its capacity. Combine the sugar and water and set the saucepan over medium-high heat. Stir just until the sugar is dissolved.

Add the rhubarb. As soon as the mixture comes to a boil, lower the heat so just a few bubbles break on the surface. (You may have to wait and watch for a few minutes to get the heat right, as sugar syrups hold heat well and take time to cool down.) Cook until the liquid becomes a thick syrup, stirring very gently every 15 minutes or so. Be patient. It will take about 1 ½ hours to get it to where you want it—that is, with the liquid cooked down to a thick, hot-pink syrup. Don't try to speed things up by turning up the heat or the rhubarb will taste candied, which will get in the way of its bright, tart flavor.

Remove the saucepan from the heat. Allow the preserves to cool at room temperature. Transfer the preserves to airtight glass jars or plastic containers and store in the refrigerator for several months.

NABAAT
(CURE-ALL ROCK SUGAR)

FLEXIBLE YIELD

Plan ahead: It takes 2 weeks for the crystals to form.

Think of quartz and the precious gems you see in museums, the ones with thick blades of minerals that fused together into rock hard spikes.

Now imagine you could eat them.

This is nabaat: large, fat crystals of pure rock sugar. While Iranians consider raw sugar a cold food, nabaat is a hot food (see page 35). The theory is that when sugar is cooked, your body can digest it more easily. Tradition holds that nabaat can soothe nausea, boost energy, and even lift your mood.

I follow Iranian custom and take nabaat in my tea (page 236). I drop a few nuggets in a small teacup, pour the tea over it, and stir so it starts to melt. At the end of the journey that is my third cup of tea, the nabaat will be fully dissolved, or at least soft enough that I can suck on it comfortably.

Nabaat is a miracle to have around and takes something of a miracle to make. I have made countless batches that have gone wrong. I have destroyed pans and burned my fingertips on batch after batch of puny crystals. I finally clawed the technique out of the clenches of the oldest Zoroastrian lady I could find. (I was hard-pressed to find anyone who still made nabaat outside of Yazd.) I finally mastered it. And I've mastered failing at it, too.

Making nabaat is an art. It takes practice and patience and finesse and even a lot of luck that the wind is literally blowing in the right direction. Take comfort, though: even if you botch a batch, you can still use it to sweeten your tea.

First, prepare your work area as you would for making yogurt. Place a blanket in the center of a table, then place a towel in the center of the blanket. Lightly coat a thick, heatproof glass or ceramic square or rectangular dish with oil. Have a tray nearby. It should be large enough to cover your pan. Finally, place a spoon and small plate near your stove.

Next, make the syrup. Combine the sugar and water in a pot with high sides. (The sugar will eventually bubble up to twice its original volume, so choose your pot wisely.) Bring to a boil over medium-high heat, stirring to dissolve the sugar. Reduce the heat to medium and continue to cook for 15 to 20 minutes, stirring occasionally. The sugar-water will change dramatically as it cooks, beginning first as an opaque, white paste, turning next into a clear liquid, and eventually transforming into a soft, thick, yellow syrup with a good bit of froth. It should coat the back of a spoon.

To test if it's ready, reduce the heat to low. Using your spoon, drip a few syrupy droplets onto the nearby plate. It will be very hot, so let it cool to where you can tolerate it—masochists rejoice!—and pinch a bit between your thumb and index finger while it is still soft. As you pull your fingers apart, there should be 1 or 2 threads of stringy sugar. The string should continue to stretch as you pull your fingers farther apart. If it is not stretchy, boil the syrup a little longer and keeping testing until you've reached this consistency.

Remove the pot from the heat. Wait a few moments for the gurgling to subside and the syrup to still. Very carefully, pour the hot syrup into the oiled dish. Cover with the tray. Wrap it in the blanket, and set the bundle aside in a warm, dry place. (We put ours in a cupboard). Wait 2 weeks before even peeking at it.

When it's ready, the top of the pan will form thick, beautiful quartz-like crystals of sugar; the bottom will form a solid brick of sugar. Between the two layers will be residual syrup. (Nabaat refers to this entire mass.) To remove the nabaat, prop the vessel so that a corner of it is over a bowl or pan. You will want to capture all of the syrup that leaks out. When it is drained of this syrup, turn the vessel upside down—the crystals and block should all slide out. Crack the block into smaller pieces using an ice pick or a makeshift chisel with a sturdy knife.

Store indefinitely in an airtight container or zip-lock bag at room temperature. The reserved syrup can also be used as a sugar syrup concentrate to sweeten tea and coffee.

Vegetable or coconut oil for coating your glass or ceramic vessel

3 parts sugar

1 part water

DESSERTS

DESSERTS

While many other chapters in this book
are heavily steeped in Iranian tradition, this chapter
has just one: the Cake Yazdi (page 220).

This is the most innovative chapter in the book, as creating these recipes has allowed me to experiment and push boundaries.

Most of these dessert recipes feature whey. Whey adds a hint of dairy and natural sweetness to desserts without making them overly creamy or overly sweet. Even when frozen, its acidity shines through and makes other flavors pop. Whey-based sorbets like the Blueberry (page 210), Raspberry-Lime (page 211), and Roasted Pear (page 212) flavors are light and refreshing while still luxurious and smooth.

In cakes, like the All the Whey Upside Down Cake (page 222), whey isn't just a substitute, whether for buttermilk, yogurt, or even lemon juice. It goes well beyond that and enhances the cakes, making them lighter, brighter, and moister. Adding whey even allows you to reduce the amount of butter or oil in a recipe without making the cakes feel any less indulgent.

The Lemon-Whey Meringue Pie (page 226) is the chapter's climax recipe. I use whey in all three components: the light and tangy crust, the cheerful, citrusy filling, and even the whey-stabilized meringue. Shamelessly showing off, I know, but I couldn't help myself. Whey is truly a revelation in desserts: tangy, moist, creamy, and lemony. It just makes them better.

SALTY WHEY CARAMEL
FROZEN YOGURT

MAKES ABOUT 1 QUART

Plan ahead! This recipe takes 3 hours for the base to chill before churning, plus at least 2 more hours to freeze after churning. Do yourself a favor and start it one day ahead.

This recipe is inspired by author and food scientist Harold McGee, whose recipe for homemade yogurt with whey caramel appeared in the *New York Times*. Adding some flaky salt and freezing the yogurt made an already good recipe even better, as salt accents the yogurt and whey without overshadowing them. It's the punctuation mark at the end of a beautiful sentence.

NOTE: The whey caramel keeps well in the fridge; just warm it up in either a hot water bath or a quick microwave jolt before you drizzle on cake, pancakes, ice cream, or apples.

2 cups yogurt whey

1¼ cups sugar

Pinch kosher salt

3 cups strained (Greek-style) yogurt, divided

½ teaspoon flaky sea salt (such as Maldon)

MAKE THE WHEY CARAMEL: In a medium saucepan, combine the whey, sugar, and kosher salt and bring to a boil over high heat. Reduce the heat to medium and continue to boil, stirring occasionally. (It will foam up furiously every time you put a spoon in it, so be careful.) Boil until most of the liquid has cooked off and it turns a deep amber color, 25 to 30 minutes. Remove from the heat and allow to cool for 5 minutes.

MAKE THE FROZEN YOGURT: Put 2 cups of the yogurt in a medium stainless steel or glass bowl. Add the remaining 1 cup yogurt to the saucepan with the caramel, stirring to combine thoroughly. Scrape the caramel-yogurt mixture into the bowl with the yogurt. Stir well and refrigerate for at least 3 hours, or overnight.

Transfer to an ice cream maker and stir in the flaky salt. Churn according to the manufacturer's instructions. Transfer to a lidded freezer-safe container and freezer for at least 2 hours, or overnight, to firm up to a scoopable consistency.

WHEY SIMPLE SYRUP

MAKES 1 QUART

Like many frozen dessert recipes, my sorbets (pages 210 to 212) and pops (pages 214 to 215) call for simple syrup. My version of simple syrup incorporates whey, which adds its own natural sweetness and tang.

Whey simple syrup will keep for up to 6 months in the refrigerator, so prepare a large batch. When you have it on hand, you'll soon discover new possibilities for using it—for stirring into your iced coffee or tea, sweetening cocktails, drizzling over cakes, and more.

4 cups sugar

2 cups yogurt whey, water, or any combination of the two

Combine the sugar and whey and/or water in a medium saucepan. Bring to a simmer over medium heat, stirring just until the sugar is dissolved. Remove from the heat and let cool completely.

Transfer the cooled syrup to a jar or bottle with a lid. Store in the refrigerator for up to 6 months.

BLUEBERRY WHEY SORBET

MAKES ABOUT 4½ CUPS

Plan ahead! This recipe takes 4 hours for the base to chill before churning, plus at least 4 hours to freeze after churning. I suggest you start it one day ahead.

In Iran, you always knew when a fruit was in season and when it tasted off and what regions each fruit grew in. It's all people talked about as they rifled through the fruits at the market.

But blueberries? We didn't have blueberries in Iran, so my family had no point of reference for them when we got to America. This made them a low-stress fruit as no one complained that "they tasted better back home." We just bought the Driscoll's kind or whatever they had at Costco and ate them. Ignorance was bliss and that was pretty much that.

Today I know more: that blueberries are high in pectin, that lemon juice brightens their flavor, that whey is an especially compatible friend. It lingers in the background of this velvety sorbet, lending just a hint of extra creaminess.

3 cups fresh or frozen blueberries

1 cup yogurt whey

1 cup Whey Simple Syrup (page 209)

3 tablespoons fresh lemon juice

Combine the blueberries, whey, syrup, and lemon juice in a blender and puree until smooth. Transfer to a glass or metal bowl, cover, and refrigerate for at least 4 hours, up to overnight.

Churn in an ice cream maker according to the manufacturer's instructions, using the "sorbet" setting if available. When the sorbet has reached the consistency of a thick milkshake, scrape it into a clean glass or metal container (a loaf pan is a good choice), then press plastic wrap directly onto the surface to prevent ice crystals from forming. Freeze for at least 4 hours before scooping.

RASPBERRY-LIME WHEY SORBET

MAKES ABOUT 4½ CUPS

Plan ahead! This recipe takes 4 hours for the base to chill before churning, plus at least 4 hours to freeze after churning. Do yourself a favor and start it one day ahead.

Like the Blueberry Whey Sorbet (page 210), this recipe doesn't call for anything fancy. Its ease is part of its charm. And before you worry that tart raspberries plus sour lime plus tangy whey is too much pucker, I promise it all just works (thanks, sugar!).

NOTE: I enjoy the crunch of the raspberry seeds, but if you like your sorbet a little more refined, pass the puree through a fine-mesh strainer before chilling it.

3 cups fresh or frozen raspberries

1 cup yogurt whey

1 cup Whey Simple Syrup (page 209)

6 tablespoons fresh lime juice

Combine the raspberries, whey, syrup, and lime juice in a blender and puree until smooth. Strain out the raspberry seeds if desired. Transfer to a glass or metal bowl and refrigerate for at least 4 hours, up to overnight.

Churn in an ice cream maker according to the manufacturer's instructions, using the "sorbet" setting if available. When the sorbet has reached the consistency of a thick milkshake, scrape it into a clean glass or metal container (a loaf pan is a good choice), then press plastic wrap directly on the surface to prevent ice crystals from forming. Freeze for at least 4 hours before scooping.

ROASTED PEAR WHEY SORBET

MAKES 1 QUART

Plan ahead! This recipe takes 6 hours for the base to chill before churning, plus at least 4 hours to freeze after churning. Do yourself a favor and start it one day ahead.

This sorbet cries out for seasonal, perfectly ripe pears. Any variety will do, so long as they're at their peak. Roasting the pears with honey and vanilla bean gives them a warm, rich flavor, and the brandy adds a sophisticated edge. The texture of the final sorbet is heavenly.

NOTE: While you can omit the pear brandy, make the splurge if you can. Outside of this recipe, it is soothing to sip on its own and a warm welcome when slipped into an autumn cocktail.

4 large just-ripe (soft, but not mushy) pears

3 tablespoons mild honey, such as wildflower

½ vanilla bean, split lengthwise

¼ cup Whey Simple Syrup (page 209)

2 cups yogurt whey

2 tablespoons pear brandy (optional but highly recommended)

Preheat the oven to 400°F. Peel the pears, cut them in half lengthwise, and remove the cores. Arrange the pear halves cut sides up in a medium baking dish. Drizzle with the honey. Add the vanilla bean to the dish, along with 2 tablespoons water.

Roast the pears for 25 minutes, until lightly browned, basting the fruit with its own juices a few times to keep them from drying out. Remove from the oven and let cool to room temperature. Using the edge of a sharp knife, scrape the seeds from the vanilla bean onto the pears. Discard the pod.

In a blender, combine the pears and all their juices with the simple syrup, whey, and brandy. Blend until completely smooth. Pour into a covered container and refrigerate for at least 6 hours or overnight.

Churn in an ice cream maker according to the manufacturer's instructions. When the sorbet has reached the consistency of a thick milkshake, scrape it into a clean glass or metal container (a loaf pan is a good choice), then press plastic wrap directly onto the surface to prevent ice crystals from forming. Freeze for at least 4 hours to allow the sorbet to firm up a little. If serving sorbet that has been frozen for more than one day, leave it out at room temperature for 5 to 10 minutes for easier scooping.

WHEY POPS

There is no graceful way to tell you how these glorious pops came about so I'll just say it: My factory had a yeast infection.

In 2014, The White Moustache was smug as we had achieved the impossible: we were profitable and we were at capacity. We had proudly made a commitment to cap production of our yogurt until we could find a market for the whey (see page 21). We'd already introduced our tonics and were optimistic that sales would increase and we could start opening our wait-list up to new accounts.

So in the summer of 2016, we moved out of our shared working space and into an old but extremely sturdy Con Edison building in Brooklyn that would allow us to build a dairy room. We could build this room to our very particular specifications and keep control over our products from start to finish. Doing so would let us expand on our own terms.

Every penny I had saved up went to this expansion. I could avoid copackers who prioritized efficiency over art and truly put my personal mission of selling the whey we were producing through our yogurt-making at the center of my attention. I was so excited to start production with brand-new equipment.

Within two weeks of operating in our new space during the hottest summer on record, we got reports from customers that our yogurt jars were exploding on the shelves. Apparently, yeast was somehow getting into my yogurt, and its gases created immense pressure in the jars. So pop! pop! pop! The bulging lids just popped off. We immediately shut down the factory to investigate the source of the problem and temporarily stopped selling our products to customers.

It took us three months to figure out and resolve the source of the contamination. During that time, I had depleted all of our savings on the construction and was operating on borrowed time. One happy surprise: During this time, the only thing that was consistently testing negative for yeast was the whey—and we didn't yet have enough interest in our tonic line to make a dent in our supply. So here I am: It's summer, I'm hot, I'm broke, I'm stressed, and I'm swimming in whey. So I froze some in Popsicle molds, and they were delicious. And I put a slice of cucumber in the next one, and that was even more refreshing.

One thing led to another and that's how The White Moustache pops got started. In the middle of a crisis, we started brainstorming joyful, happy flavors for these new frozen treats. Coming up with these flavors was, in many ways, a natural evolution

CONTINUES

of what we'd already gone through with the tonics. But we had even more flexibility. Because freezing purees extends their shelf-life, we could use more perishable produce—like cucumber, watermelon, cantaloupe, and mango, for example—and not have to worry about them spoiling. I also knew that freezing whey maintained its probiotic activity, so these pops would be far more healthful than your average frozen treat. The moral of this story is: If you happen to hire a bad contractor, you may get a raging yeast infection, but you may also invent a brand-new ice pop line.

At The White Moustache, we use stainless steel pop molds that come ten to a unit. Each mold holds 3.3 ounces of puree and creates 4-inch-high pops. After blending the ingredients and filling the molds, if you have a small amount left over, you can freeze it in an ice cube tray or use it as an excuse to make a cocktail.

Finally, I encourage you to follow my proportions as a guide and to adjust the sweetness to taste—but do so within limits. The whey simple syrup affects not only flavor but texture, so don't reduce it too much. And keep in mind that the mix becomes *less* sweet once it's frozen, so when you taste the blended ingredients, you do want them on the sweeter side. In addition, if you want to make these pops next-level adult, add a splash of gin to the cucumber pops, tequila to the pineapple pops, and vodka to the watermelon pops. Just don't use too much, as alcohol in larger quantities can inhibit freezing.

PERSIAN CUCUMBER ICE POPS

MAKES ABOUT 8 ICE POPS

1 cup cucumber puree (from 3 Persian cucumbers; see directions)

1 cup yogurt whey

½ cup Sekanjabin (page 239)

3 or 4 mint leaves

To make the cucumber puree, wash the cucumbers and roughly chop before adding them to the blender. Include the peel, seeds, and even the bitter blossom ends as part of your puree—it's all fine. The skin will add nutrients and gorgeous emerald color. Then proceed as directed under "For all pops" on page 215.

WATERMELON ICE POPS

MAKES ABOUT 10 ICE POPS

2 cups watermelon puree

1 cup yogurt whey

½ cup Whey Simple
  Syrup (page 209)

MANGO ICE POPS

MAKES ABOUT 10 ICE POPS

1 cup mango puree (from 2 ripe
  mangoes, preferably Alphonso)

1½ cups yogurt whey

¼ cup Whey Simple
  Syrup (page 209)

PINEAPPLE-GINGER POPS

MAKES ABOUT 9 ICE POPS

1 cup pineapple puree

1¼ cup yogurt whey

⅓ cup Whey Simple
  Syrup (page 209)

1 teaspoon grated fresh ginger

FOR ALL POPS: Combine all the ingredients in a blender and blitz until mostly smooth with some bits of fruit still apparent. Fill the ice pop molds three-quarters of the way to the top and insert sticks. Freeze overnight. To unmold, dip the molds into hot water briefly to loosen the pops. Remove gently by the stick. Enjoy as is, or plop into a glass of Prosecco for an impromptu cocktail.

LA NEWYORKINA YOGURT-BERRY PALETAS

MAKES 8 TO 10 PALETAS

Fany Gerson is a unicorn of a human being. She owns two wildly popular New York City establishments: Fan-Fan Doughnuts and La Newyorkina. Fany was our neighbor at the famed Smorgasburg weekend food market in Williamsburg. We bartered doughnuts for yogurt. When we moved to Red Hook in 2014, La Newyorkina was across the street. My team and I took refuge from the brutal New York summers with her Mexican-inspired paleta treats. It took me a minute to put together the impossible fact that the woman responsible for the greatest doughnuts in New York City was also responsible for the most refreshing Mexican sweets and paletas. When I finally met her, I asked, "When do you ever sleep?!" and she shot back a mischievously sarcastic look: "I don't!"

Fany, born in Mexico City, started La Newyorkina in 2010 after she went on a year-long trip back home to write her first cookbook, *My Sweet Mexico*. Those memories of her childhood in Mexico and the research for her book are infused into every joyful bite of her frozen treats. This ice pop recipe is a combination of our yogurt and Fany's Mexican paleta technique. This collaboration put a knot deep down in my cynical throat that swells up with the realization that indeed the world is a big and bright place, and it can taste sweet when we realize we are in it together.

2 cups blueberries or
  blackberries or a mix

3 tablespoons confectioners' sugar

2 strips lemon or lime peel

½ cup granulated sugar

1½ cups plain whole milk yogurt

2 tablespoons honey

¼ teaspoon kosher salt

Combine the berries, confectioners' sugar, and citrus peel in a medium saucepan over medium heat. Cook, stirring, until the mixture comes to a boil and all the sugar has been dissolved. Remove from the heat and cool. Discard the peel.

While the berry mixture cools, combine ½ cup water and the granulated sugar in a small saucepan. Cook over medium-high heat, stirring, just until the sugar has dissolved. Allow to cool for 10 minutes, then whisk in the yogurt, honey, and salt.

You can use a Popsicle mold or small freezer-safe cups. You'll be making four layers in each mold or cup: yogurt, berry, yogurt, berry, from the bottom up. To make the bottom layer, divide half the sweetened yogurt mixture among the molds, pouring to a height of about ¾ inch. Freeze until it begins to set, about 40 minutes.

To make the second layer, divide half the berry mixture among the molds, adding it on top of the chilled yogurt layer. Then repeat with one more layer each of yogurt and berry puree. Leave the top quarter of the mold empty to allow room to expand. Use a toothpick or skewer to move the berries around to create a marbled effect.

If using conventional molds, snap on the lid and freeze until solid, 3 to 4 hours. If using cups or unconventional molds, freeze until the pops are beginning to set (45 minutes to 1 hour), then insert sticks and freeze until solid, 3 to 4 hours.

Dip the molds in warm water for 5 to 10 seconds to loosen the paletas, then pull up to unmold.

A SIMPLE CAKE EITHER WHEY

MAKES ONE 8-INCH CAKE

Over the years, I've had plenty of chances to bake with both yogurt and whey. Eventually I started comparing the results so I could see what kind of impact each had on flavor, texture, and crumb. Both elevate a good, even plain cake by imparting dense moisture and lemony tang. Both are even (arguably) healthier than baking with cream or buttermilk, or by adding extra eggs. The more I baked with whey, the more curious I became about what made it truly stand apart.

I made the exact same plain cake with the same quantity of yogurt and whey. While the yogurt cake was denser and slightly moister—with a sharper, tangier bite—the whey cake was lighter and fluffier, with a melt-in-your-mouth texture.

Both cakes were tangy and both took beautifully to an icing glaze and a drizzle of quince syrup from Quince Preserves (page 195). And both are equally adaptable, open to the fragrant addition of citrus zest or even rosemary. At the end of the day, whether to use yogurt or whey is really up to you—and what you happen to have more of in the fridge.

½ cup vegetable oil, plus more for greasing the pan

1¼ cups all-purpose flour

1 teaspoon baking powder

½ teaspoon baking soda

1 teaspoon kosher salt

3 large eggs, at room temperature

1 cup granulated sugar

1 cup plain whole milk yogurt or yogurt whey

ICING (optional)

1 cup confectioners' sugar

1 tablespoon yogurt whey or water

Preheat the oven to 350°F with a rack in the middle position. Cut a circle of parchment paper to fit the bottom of an 8-inch springform pan (or any 8-inch cake pan). Lightly oil the bottom of the pan, then fit it with the parchment round. Make sure it's smooth. Oil the parchment and the sides of the pan.

Sift the flour, baking powder, baking soda, and salt into a medium bowl.

In a large bowl whisk together the eggs and granulated sugar until smooth. Add the oil in a slow, steady stream, whisking until fully emulsified. Gradually whisk in the yogurt or whey. Whisk the dry ingredients into the wet until fully incorporated.

Scrape the batter into the prepared pan and smooth the top. Bake until golden and a toothpick inserted in the center comes out clean,

45 to 50 minutes.* (Do not judge doneness by color alone as the yogurt and especially the whey create some early browning before the cake is fully set.)

Set the cake pan on a cooling rack for 10 minutes, then transfer the cake directly to the rack. Gently peel off the parchment and cool completely. Because there is a lot of moisture in this cake, cooling upside-down on a rack allows the steam to escape properly and prevents the bottom from turning gummy. Do not ice until the cake is completely cooled.

If using the optional icing, whisk the confectioners' sugar and whey until smooth. Drizzle over the cake and allow to set for 30 minutes before serving.

---

* The whey version of this cake has consistently needed 50 minutes, pretty much on the dot, in my oven. The yogurt cake I would check at around 45 minutes.

CAKE YAZDI

MAKES 12 INDIVIDUAL CAKES

Yazd, Iran, where my family is from, has a desert climate. The city looks and smells sandy, its air hot and dry. This cake, which originates in Yazd, is textured with rice flour and moistened with yogurt, and carries subtle fragrances of rose water and cardamom. It is just the right texture that thirsts for a complementary cup of tea.

This cake is so sentimental to me that I had never dared to make it at home. It felt too sacred for anyone other than the bakers who have been making it for a hundred years—in their signature cake molds—to make it. Even so, when I first got the courage to make it, the results tasted nothing like the cake I recalled from Iran.

It has been years of trial and error, landing on a recipe only to come back to it knowing it wasn't right. I have even fought with my elders to give me their version of this recipe, and then I have fought with them further because those recipes were just not quite right.

Out of the wisdom of those trials and fights has come this recipe, which is the closest to home for me. And I have since patched over any hard feelings with my elders over tea and, what even they must begrudgingly admit, perfect cake Yazdi.

NOTE: These cakes are traditionally baked in fanned muffin tins, making individual tea cakes. You may use standard muffin tins.

8 tablespoons (1 stick) unsalted butter, melted, plus more for greasing the pan

1 cup all-purpose flour

2 tablespoons rice flour

1 teaspoon baking powder

½ teaspoon baking soda

¼ teaspoon kosher salt

2 teaspoons ground cardamom

2 large eggs, at room temperature, separated

½ cup sugar

½ cup plain whole milk yogurt

1 tablespoon rose water

1 tablespoon chopped pistachios

Preheat the oven to 350°F with a rack in the middle position. Grease a 12-cup muffin tin with butter.

Sift the all-purpose flour, rice flour, baking powder, baking soda, salt, and cardamom into a small bowl. Whisk thoroughly till fully combined. Set aside.

In a separate small bowl, whisk the egg whites until stiff peaks form; set aside. In a large bowl,* whisk the egg yolks and sugar until creamy, 2 to 3 minutes. Mix in the melted butter, yogurt, and rose water and gently whisk until smooth, another 2 minutes.

Slowly add the dry ingredients to the wet and mix until fully integrated. Add the egg whites until you have a uniform mixture, gently folding to not deflate the eggs. Fold in the pistachios.

Divide the batter among the muffin cups, filling three-quarters full. Bake until the tops are browned and a toothpick inserted in the center comes out clean, about 25 minutes.

Let the cakes cool completely before unmolding them. Serve with tea (this is a must). Store any leftovers in an airtight container at room temperature for up to 3 days.

---

* I know. Three bowls. I'm so sorry. You can curse me for this while you are washing the dishes, but you will forgive me once you try the cake.

ALL THE WHEY
UPSIDE-DOWN CAKE

MAKES 1 (9-INCH) CAKE

When I originally made the cake, I used pineapple, but it's great with just about any kind of fruit, any time of year. Use what's in season, or source from your freezer. Blueberries, raspberries, blackberries, halved strawberries, or sliced peaches or plums—even mixed and matched—will all be perfect.

Since this cake will be inverted, the bottom layer of fruit (which will become the top) needs careful attention. I like to meticulously prepare the fruits: slice the peaches into little wedges; halve, slice, and fan out the strawberries; and so forth. After all, I do come from a culture that obsesses over tah-diq (page 124), so the act of inverting something to oohs and aahs runs deep.

¾ cup plus 2 tablespoons (1¾ sticks) unsalted butter, softened, plus more for greasing the pan

2½ cups sliced fresh or frozen fruit

¼ cup packed light brown sugar (or more to taste if your fruit is tart)

2¼ cups all-purpose flour

1½ teaspoons baking powder

½ teaspoon baking soda

¾ teaspoon kosher salt

1¼ cups granulated sugar

3 large eggs, at room temperature

2 teaspoons vanilla extract

½ teaspoon almond extract

1 cup yogurt whey

Confectioners' sugar, for serving

Preheat the oven to 350°F. Cut a circle of parchment paper to fit the bottom of a 9-inch springform pan (or any 9-inch cake pan). Lightly butter the bottom of the pan, then fit it with the parchment round. Make sure it's smooth. Butter the parchment and the sides of the pan.

Spread the fruit in a single layer evenly across the bottom. If you are in the mood, lay it out like elaborate geometric Islamic tile art. Sprinkle it with the brown sugar.

In a medium bowl, whisk together the flour, baking powder, baking soda, and salt.

In a separate large bowl, whisk together the butter and granulated sugar until fluffy and pale, about 3 minutes. Whisk in the eggs one at a time, followed by the vanilla and almond extracts.

Gently mix in the flour mixture and whey in 3 additions, alternating between the two. Mix until just combined. Scrape the batter over the fruit and smooth it out with a small spatula or the back of a spoon dipped in warm water.

Bake until the cake is pale gold and a toothpick inserted in the center comes out clean, about 1 hour. Set the pan on a cooling rack for 20 minutes. Run a thin knife around the perimeter of the pan to loosen the cake. If using a springform pan, open the clamp and lift off the rim. Place a serving platter or large, flat plate over the cake, grasp both the sides of the platter and the bottom of the pan and flip the whole setup with confidence so the pan is now on top. Carefully lift the pan from the cake and gently peel off the parchment. Allow the cake to cool for at least 1 hour before serving.

Just before serving, put the confectioners' sugar in a small strainer or tea ball and generously dust the top of the cake. (Don't do this in advance or the juice from the fruit will absorb the sugar and you won't be able to see it.)

Store any leftover cake, covered, in the refrigerator for up to 4 days.

CARROT CAKE WITH YOGURT FROSTING

MAKES 1 (9-INCH) CAKE

My introduction to carrot cake was traumatic. It happened at the very first birthday party my parents allowed me to plan. I was in sixth grade, and I had invited all the cool girls (even the ones who had already French-kissed boys). I showed off my New Kids on the Block gear, and we proceeded to have a very on-trend pizza party with games and soda. Then my mom came in with the cake. It was supposed to be the chocolate fudge cake from Costco we had agreed on, but she went rogue and splurged on a "very special" spiced gourmet carrot cake instead. None of the girls touched it, which put a swift end to my very first American birthday party.

The sixth grader in me was mortified. I could not easily forgive my mom's deviation from our plan, and for years afterward, carrot cake would stir up the trauma of that weird day between us. Looking back, I'd been convinced that she and my dad were out to sabotage my attempts to fit in.

One secret, though, I've never really told anyone: that carrot cake was the most delicious thing I had ever tasted. By sharing the recipe here, I not only honor my mother's well-intentioned kindness on that ill-fated day, but I use our family's yogurt in this re-creation.

Fragrant spices make the carrots sing in this extremely moist cake. It will fit in on (almost) any occasion.

NOTE: While unstrained yogurt works best in the cake, strained Greek-style yogurt or labneh is more suitable for the frosting. See page 50 for tips on straining.

CAKE

⅓ cup vegetable oil, plus
  more for greasing the pan

1¼ cups all-purpose flour

1 teaspoon baking powder

½ teaspoon baking soda

½ teaspoon kosher salt

2 teaspoons ground cinnamon

1 teaspoon ground ginger

½ teaspoon ground nutmeg

¼ teaspoon ground allspice

1/8 teaspoon ground cloves

2 cups grated carrots (from
  about 4 medium carrots,
  peeled and trimmed)

½ cup plain whole milk yogurt
  (do not use Greek here),
  at room temperature

2 large eggs, at room temperature

½ cup granulated sugar

¼ cup firmly packed
  dark brown sugar

1 teaspoon vanilla extract

YOGURT FROSTING

1 cup strained (Greek-style)
  yogurt or Labneh (page 53)

1 teaspoon vanilla extract

3 tablespoons maple syrup
  or confectioners' sugar

Preheat the oven to 350°F. Cut a circle of parchment paper to fit the bottom of a 9-inch springform pan (or any 9-inch cake pan). Grease the bottom of the cake pan with oil, then fit it with the parchment round. Make sure it's smooth. Grease the parchment and the sides of the pan.

Sift together the flour, baking powder, baking soda, salt, and all the spices into a large bowl. Mix thoroughly. Add the carrots and stir to coat fully with the dry ingredients.

In a separate bowl, whisk together the yogurt, oil, eggs, both sugars, and vanilla. Mix the dry ingredients into the wet ingredients in two stages, stirring gently to incorporate fully.

Pour the batter into the prepared cake pan and smooth the top. Bake until a knife or toothpick inserted in the center comes out clean, about 35 minutes. Set the pan to cool on a wire rack for 10 minutes. Transfer out of the pan, gently peel off the parchment, and let cool completely on the wire rack. The cake must be completely cool before frosting.

To make the frosting, in a small bowl, whisk the Greek yogurt, vanilla, and maple syrup until smooth. Frost the cake generously and serve. Store any leftovers, covered, in the refrigerator and enjoy within 3 days.

LEMON-WHEY MERINGUE PIE

MAKES 1 (10-INCH) PIE

Plan ahead! Because the pie dough needs to chill for at least 1 hour and the lemon filling needs to chill for at least 7 hours, I recommend making the crust and filling a day ahead and assembling the pie just before serving.

In the first few years of The White Moustache, I was the only employee. Saturdays were the only day I didn't have to make yogurt in the factory, so I would treat myself to a diner breakfast in Brooklyn's Fort Greene neighborhood. I always ordered the same thing: cup of coffee, two eggs over easy, sausage, whole wheat toast, no home fries, and a side of lemon meringue pie. I'd eat that pie last, like a prize for getting through the heavy breakfast, and the heavy week.

My version of this lemon meringue pie uses whey in all three components: the crust, the filling, and the meringue. Whey makes the crust tender and light while adding some telltale tang. And because the whey also adds brightness to the filling, you only need two lemons.

Making meringue, a real science, involves just two ingredients: egg whites and sugar. Adding a few drops of whey lowers the pH of the meringue (functioning similarly to cream of tartar or lemon juice), strengthening the proteins and creating a more stable result. Make sure your utensils are clean and that there is not a drop of egg yolk in the egg whites, as any presence of fat on your spatula or other equipment will jeopardize the stability of the meringue. Similarly, make sure the whey you are adding doesn't have a drop of solids (milk fats) in it and is perfectly neon and translucent.

NOTE: Since you'll be using lemon zest here, try to buy unwaxed lemons if you can.

NOTE: To avoid a soupy filling, pay close attention to the cook times on the filling. Egg yolks have an enzyme that thins out the cornstarch, so the trick to a firm, set filling is to heat the egg yolks long enough to deactivate the enzyme.

CRUST

1¼ cups all-purpose flour

1 teaspoon sugar

½ teaspoon kosher salt

8 tablespoons (1 stick) unsalted butter, cut into ½-inch cubes and placed in the freezer until very cold and firm (about 30 minutes)

3 to 5 tablespoons cold yogurt whey

LEMON WHEY FILLING

1 cup sugar

5 tablespoons cornstarch

1 teaspoon kosher salt

1½ cups cold yogurt whey

4 large egg yolks

Grated zest and juice of 2 large unwaxed lemons (2 scant tablespoons zest and about ½ cup juice)

4 tablespoons (½ stick) unsalted butter, chilled and cut into small dice

MERINGUE

4 large egg whites

¾ cup sugar

¼ teaspoon yogurt whey

Large pinch kosher salt

MAKE THE CRUST: In a food processor fitted with the steel blade, combine the flour, sugar, and salt. Add the cold butter and pulse about 8 times, until the butter is the size of peas. (If you don't have a food processor, use a bowl and a pastry blender.) Drizzle in 3 tablespoons of the cold whey and pulse briefly, just to moisten. If it looks dry, add more whey 1 tablespoon at a time, pulsing briefly each time. Stop while the dough is still a bit crumbly but holds together when pinched. There will be small visible butter chunks. Turn out the dough onto a large sheet of plastic wrap and, with minimal handling, form into a disk about ½ inch thick and 7 inches in diameter. Wrap tightly and refrigerate for at least 1 hour, or up to 1 day. (The crust may also be frozen for up to 1 month. Thaw at room temperature for 20 to 30 minutes before rolling.)

When ready to bake, preheat the oven to 400°F with a rack in the lower third.

Let the dough soften slightly at room temperature before proceeding. On a lightly floured surface, roll the dough into a 12-inch circle. Gently fold the dough in half and then in half again, forming a wedge. Transfer to a 10-inch pie pan, placing the point of the wedge in the center and gently unfolding. Tuck the edges under and crimp or shape as you like. Place in the freezer for 20 minutes.

Using a fork, prick the dough in several places across the bottom. Crumple up a piece of parchment, large enough to cover the dough with some overhang, then line the dough with the parchment paper, pressing it into the corners as much as possible. Fill with pie weights or dried beans.

CONTINUES ⚭

Bake for 25 minutes, then remove the pan from the oven. Lower the oven temperature to 375°F. Remove the pie weights by grasping the corners of the parchment and lifting the whole setup out of the crust. Tent the edges of the crust with aluminum foil. Return the pan to the oven and continue to bake until the crust is golden brown all over, 15 to 20 minutes longer. Remove from the oven and allow to cool.

MAKE THE LEMON-WHEY FILLING: In a medium saucepan, whisk together the sugar, cornstarch, and salt. Gradually whisk in the whey until the cornstarch is dissolved. Turn the heat to high and bring to a boil, whisking often. Reduce the heat to medium-low and simmer, whisking constantly as it thickens to a gel-like consistency, 3 to 4 minutes. Remove from the heat.

In a medium bowl, whisk the egg yolks. Gradually temper the yolks by slowly whisking in some of the hot whey mixture. Pour the yolk-whey mixture back into the saucepan and return to medium heat. Continue cooking and whisking constantly, bringing it to a boil, at least 4 minutes. (Because the consistency is so thick, and you are constantly stirring it, "boiling" will look like big bubbles occasionally bursting on the surface. The filling will also become brighter and more opaque with each passing minute. Don't worry, the starch will prevent the eggs from curdling. Keep cooking!) Remove from the heat and whisk in the lemon zest and juice. Whisk in the butter cubes, a few at a time, until emulsified. Transfer to the cooled crust and shake gently to level out the filling. Press plastic wrap directly on the surface of the filling to prevent a skin from forming. Chill the pie for at least 7 hours, ideally overnight.

MAKE THE MERINGUE: Pour 3 inches of water into a medium saucepan and bring to a boil. Turn the heat to medium-low to keep the water at a simmer. In a medium heatproof bowl, whisk together the egg whites, sugar, whey, and salt. Set the bowl over the saucepan with the simmering water—make sure the bottom of the bowl is not touching the water. Using a spatula, constantly stir the mixture until the sugar is dissolved and the egg mixture is hot to the touch, 5 to 7 minutes. Test to make sure the sugar has dissolved by rubbing the mixture between your fingers—you should not be able to feel any granules.

Remove the bowl from the heat. Using an electric beater (preferably with the whisk attachment), whisk on medium-high until stiff peaks form, 5 to 7 minutes.

Place a rack in the middle of the oven. Turn the broiler on high.

Remove the pie from the refrigerator and gently peel off the plastic wrap. Spoon the meringue on top of the filling in several large plops. Push and swirl as you like—I find the back of a spoon to be helpful here. The goal is to cover the top entirely and to make sure the meringue meets the pie crust. There's no need to be too precious about how you do this. (I'm a big ugly plopper myself.)

Place the pie on a baking sheet and slip it under the broiler. Turn on the oven light so you can keep an eye on it (or just leave the oven door open while it's going)—it will take anywhere from 30 seconds to 2 minutes for the meringue to get brown and toasty without getting scorched, depending on how temperamental your broiler is.

Remove the pie from the oven. Serve immediately. This pie is best served the day it is made and best made on a day that is not humid.

DRINKS

DRINKS DRINKS DRINKS
DRINKS DRINKS DRINKS
DRINKS DRINKS DRINKS
DRINKS DRINKS DRINKS

I remember strolling through the streets of Tehran with my family in the summers. My dad would suddenly stop and announce that so-and-so lived just down the street. "Let's go visit," he'd say.

In Iran, we never called ahead and we never showed up empty-handed. We might bring flowers, we might bring pastries, but when dropping by to visit anyone—friend, relative, new acquaintance—we always came with some kind of gift.

Most of the time this gift determined what our hosts would pour. Bring flowers, they'll likely pour a sharbat, flavorful syrups thinned with cold water and ice. Bring pastries to share, they'll pour cups of tea, diluted with hot water to the preferred strength. Drinks are all based on ratios rather than set measurements. They're easy, relaxed, and accessible. Where food is the centerpiece of an Iranian party, drinks facilitate small talk and set the tone for what's to come.

Today, if you pop by to see me during the summer, I'll grab us a bottle of Cucumber Sekanjabin Sharbat (page 240) from the fridge. On other days, especially during NoRooz, I'll pour tea. I'm al ways prepared, always ready and happy to fill your cup.

Iranians drink before and after meals, but rarely during the meal itself. One exception is Doogh (page 235), a yogurt drink with mint. During a heavy meal with kababs or rice, it's typical to sip doogh to aid with digestion.

The recipes that follow in this section include both classic Iranian drinks—tea, sharbats, doogh—and the naturally fermented sodas and probiotic tonics I've created using whey. The process for developing these original whey drinks, which are not traditional in Iran, is pretty simple: I listen to the whey. It's always telling me, "I'm a little tangy, a little spicy," and over time, and a few flops (hello, whey-coffee tonic—bad idea!), I've learned to follow its lead. Ingredients with a tangy, acidic, or lemony profile make the best partners.

I'm so proud to know them. As soon as I introduced them to whey, they embraced it as a provocative new ingredient. An American Moustache (page 253), Weathered Wheyfarer (page 254), and the Symbolic Gesture (page 261) are just a few of their genius creations. Yes, some of their inventions may require investing in some less familiar bottles. Don't be intimidated! Expand your liquor cabinet slowly—it will be well worth it.

Tea and Tonics

DOOGH

**MAKES 3 CUPS (DOOGH IS RATIO-BASED.
SIMPLY SCALE UP THE QUANTITIES FOR A LARGER BATCH.)**

Doogh—a yogurt drink diluted with either whey or water and spiked with mint and salt to taste—is an example of Iranians' preference for savory yogurt.

Tangy, salty, and minty, doogh is best enjoyed with heavy dishes, especially a plate of Kabab Koobideh (page 128). Not only does it aid with digestion, doogh also refreshes your palate during a rich meal. Between bites of food, imagine a cool rush of tangy yogurt cleansing and soothing your entire digestive tract; your next morsel of food will taste as good as the first.

Doogh celebrates yogurt's sourness. If you are making yogurt specifically for doogh, try to make an extra tangy batch by leaving your yogurt under the blankets to incubate for an extra day.

NOTE: The dried herb ziziphora is often used in doogh either in combination with, or in place of, dried mint (see My Pantry, page 29). If you can't find it, just leave it out.

1 cup plain whole milk yogurt

2 cups yogurt whey or water

Kosher salt, dried mint, and
    dried ziziphora, to taste

Combine all the ingredients in a pitcher. Whisk thoroughly. Serve immediately, either at room temperature or (my preference) over ice. I stir between each sip to evenly distribute the yogurt, whey, and herbs, but that's just me.

Store in a covered container in the refrigerator for up to 2 weeks. Stir again before each pour.

TEA

For as far back as I can remember, the samovar was always on the stove, ready for breakfast. It was there in the afternoon, ready to make an unexpected guest feel welcome. Today, my samovar is the one thing that makes my house feel like a home.

A typical day at our house starts like this: I fill the large samovar with water and bring it to a boil. I then fill a small teapot with black tea and hot water. They simmer together, the teapot resting on top of the samovar, lapping up the hot steam that brews the tea leaves as we prepare breakfast, wake up the night owls of the house, and decide whether to eat inside or out in the yard. One of us pours the tea matter-of-factly as we plan our day: a splash of tea from the teapot and hot water from the samovar. Yardwork, visiting nearby aunts and uncles, shopping, studying, writing, reading, watching TV, nothing is too mundane to discuss over a cup of tea.

And when everyone goes off to have their day, that samovar stays on a low, steady simmer. Whoever needs a break uses it as an excuse to pause and have a small cup of tea. Best of all is when an aunt or friend stops by unexpectedly. They will most often say that they were just passing by, that they are in a hurry, that they don't want to stay. But then you pour them a cup a tea, and this interruption becomes the most welcome part of everyone's day.

Finally, a sage piece of advice: If you ever find yourself in the awkward position of needing to end a party, just stop serving tea. If there's one thing Iranian hospitality has taught me, it's that while a hot cup of tea is a lovely way to greet a guest, a _**final**_ cup of tea is a gracious, classy, and very clear message that the party is over. Not offering to refill an empty tea cup signals that it's time to wrap things up, sober up, and head on home. It is the polite equivalent of putting on your pajamas and turning out the lights.

EQUIPMENT

Teapot: A porcelain or ceramic teapot

Strainer: A small strainer to put over the cup to catch any errant tea leaves

Samovar/large kettle: A traditional samovar was heated with hot stones or wood. Today's samovars are either stovetop versions that sit directly on the burner or electric versions that plug in. I recommend everyone get a samovar, as it will quickly become the warm, beating heart of the kitchen. If you don't have one, you might be able to make one with everyday items at home: Remove the lid from your kettle and sit a teapot securely on top of the opening. You've essentially made a makeshift samovar.

Small glass teacups without handles: Okay, this isn't necessary, but it's a good idea. Diminutive cups encourage small, frequent sips, about four per cup. Your guest will finish a small cup faster than a big cup, giving you more opportunities to be generous by constantly offering to refill their cup. You can fill any awkward silences or change the subject with a simple, "Would you like more tea?" Social anxieties are real, and we must combat them with grace.

Loose leaf tea: The blacker, stronger, and more aromatic the leaf, the better. Any Middle Eastern store will have loose black tea.

ADDITIONAL FLAVORINGS: Tea receives spices and aromas so well that you should experiment with what you like. Some of my favorites:

Cardamom: Crack 2 or 3 pods of cardamom and brew in the teapot for at least 20 minutes.

Lemongrass: 1 or 2 green stalks of lemongrass brewed in the tea pot for the full 20 minutes will give a pleasant lightness to the tea. Crush the lemongrass stalks to extract maximum flavor from them. Find it in Asian and Middle Eastern grocers.

Fresh mint: Throw a few sprigs of mint into the teapot a few minutes before serving.

Dried rosebuds: A few buds will perfume your home and lend a subtle floral note to the tea. Find them in any Middle Eastern grocery.

MAKE THE TEA: Fill the samovar with water and bring to a boil over high heat. Put 4 tablespoons loose tea in the teapot. When the water boils, pour hot water from the samovar over the loose tea. You may hear those shriveled tea leaves, that were picked and dried, screaming back to life under the scalding water. Put the lid on the teapot. Place the teapot over the samovar. Reduce the heat to low.

Maintain a gentle flame throughout the day, so the water remains hot. The steam will bathe the base of the teapot, blooming the tea leaves into a potent brew. Let steep for at least 20 minutes before serving.

CONTINUES

SERVE: When it's time to pour, prepare your tray: Place your teacups on the tray. Place your preferred form of sugar—sugar cubes, fresh dates, or Nabaat (page 202)—on the tray. If you are feeling particularly grand and the occasion calls for it, cookies or cakes or sweets are a nice accompaniment. If I am coming over, I will want those cakey French pastries—different-flavored cakes layered thickly with cream, or éclairs—as they were fashionable and ubiquitous during my childhood in Tehran. We call them "wet cakes" (shirini-taar).

Fill a teacup one-third full with the concentrated tea from the teapot. Top it off with hot water from the samovar. You don't want it too strong, as you will likely pour many cups. (Ideally, your concentrate will be very potent, so each cup holds just a splash of tea and plenty of hot water to dilute. If you've gone too far and find it's too light in color or weak in strength, add a bit more concentrated tea.)

Be prepared for what will happen next. Teatime will bleed into snacktime, snacktime will bleed into dinner. Even if you started at 11:00 am. Even if you didn't plan on it. Even if you didn't really have anything in the fridge. These things have a way of evolving when we are together, just passing the time. Hot water and tea leaves and company make magic.

SEKANJABIN

**MAKES ABOUT 3 CUPS (LIKE DOOGH, THIS DRINK
IS RATIO-BASED AND EASILY SCALABLE.)**

Sekanjabin is a simple combination of sugar, water, vinegar, and
mint, simmered into a sweet, tangy syrup. Keep a jar or bottle of it
on hand, ready to be diluted with water for impromptu drinks or
to flavor desserts. I have a bottle in my fridge at all times. It tastes
intense, vinegary, and sweet, but balanced.

Sekanjabin is used in the summertime as a cooling food. The
Cucumber Sekanjabin Sharbat (page 240) might be my favorite
variation. For a perfect snack on a sweltering day, sekanjabin is
served in an ice-filled bowl with crisp romaine leaves for dipping.

For nontraditional uses, I love it as the base for an easy cocktail,
splashing in rum, bourbon, or vodka and serving it over crushed
ice; as a sophisticated soda with seltzer and pulpy fruit; and frozen
into ice pops (page 214).

3 cups sugar or 2½ cups honey

2 cups water or yogurt whey

½ cup apple cider vinegar

½ bunch mint, rinsed and
   tied with butcher's twine

Combine the sugar and water in a large saucepan over high heat and
bring to a boil. Reduce the heat to a rapid simmer and cook, uncovered, until the syrup has thickened but not yet begun to turn yellow,
about 25 minutes. Turn off the heat, stir in the vinegar, and add the
mint. Steep for at least 2 hours. Discard the mint. Transfer to a jar or
bottle, cover, and store in the refrigerator for several months.

CUCUMBER SEKANJABIN SHARBAT

MAKES 1 QUART

This is the sharbat I serve to guests in hot weather. Since cucumber and whey are both "cold foods" (see page 35) that chill the metabolism and soothe the spirit, it's doubly refreshing. The cucumber should be very finely shredded but still discernible. I love spooning up the bits up and sinking my teeth into them while "drinking."

6 Persian cucumbers

½ bunch mint, chopped

2 cups yogurt whey or water, plus more to taste

½ cup Sekanjabin (page 239), plus more to taste

Shred the cucumbers on the smallest holes of a box grater. Combine the cucumber, mint, whey, and sekanjabin in a pitcher. Add ice. Taste, adding more whey, water, or sekanjabin if desired. Pour into glasses and serve with spoons for scooping up the cucumber bits that fall to the bottom of the glass.

QUINCE SODA

Plan ahead! This recipe needs 3 to 10 days for fermentation.

This lightly fermented drink came about when I started innovating with whey and the syrup from Quince Preserves (page 195). It's a great example of sensitivities ingrained early in my life for minimizing waste by transforming two byproducts into something brand new.

In addition to adding flavor and brilliant color, the quince syrup serves as "food" for the whey, jump-starting the fermentation process. The fizzy, probiotic soda that results is highly aromatic and super hydrating.

In place of the quince syrup, you may substitute the syrup from any homemade jam, or even maple syrup or simple syrup.

NOTE: Because tap water may have certain chemicals that inhibit fermentation, I call for filtered water here.

¾ cup quince syrup (from
   Quince Preserves, page 195)

2 cups filtered water

1 tablespoon fresh lemon juice

3 tablespoons yogurt whey

Pour the syrup, water, lemon juice, and whey into a 1-quart flip-top bottle or canning jar and seal tightly. Don't fill the container more than three-quarters full, as the contents will expand as they ferment.

Let stand at room temperature for 3 days. Open the bottle carefully over the sink, pointing it away from your body. Give it a taste and see if you like the level of sweetness and fizz. Because the "good" bacteria in the whey consume the sugars and produce carbon dioxide, the longer it sits, the fizzier and less sweet it becomes. If you'd like it drier (less sweet) and fizzier, just keep it at room temperature for up to 1 week longer, tasting daily.

Once you're happy with it, refrigerate the bottle to slow fermentation. Enjoy within 2 weeks. (Don't be alarmed by the sediment at the bottom of the bottle. It's perfectly normal.)

BEET KVASS

Plan ahead! This recipe requires 2 weeks for fermentation.

This drink takes inspiration from Eastern European kvass, which uses rye bread as a fermentation starter and is believed to cleanse the blood and flush out the digestive system. Replacing the bread with whey also fuels fermentation and creates a fizzy, scarlet-hued drink with a deep, earthy flavor. I down a shot of it in the morning to kick-start the day with a probiotic boost. I also use it as the base for a cold soup and mix it with vodka and a squeeze of lemon for a lively brunch cocktail.

You'll need a wide-mouth, quart-size canning jar. Boil the jar and its lid to sanitize them.

NOTE: Because tap water may have certain chemicals that inhibit fermentation, I call for filtered water here.

3 medium red beets
  (about 1 pound)

¼ cup yogurt whey

2 teaspoons fine sea salt

Filtered water

Trim the greens, stems, and any root tails from the beets. (Reserve the greens for eating. They make an excellent alternative to spinach or chard.) Scrub the beets well (don't bother peeling them) and cut into 1-inch cubes. Put them in the jar. Add the whey, salt, and enough filtered water to cover the beets completely. Secure the lid tightly. Place the jar on a plate (in case it leaks). Set aside at room temperature.

Start checking the jar after 3 days. Open the lid so the gases can escape. Taste the liquid to discern the level of fizz. Continue to ferment for up to 2 weeks, opening the lid every few days to let the gases out. When the kvass has reached a lively level of fizz, pour off just the liquid into a clean jar, leaving the beets behind. (Refrigerate the beets separately and enjoy in soups or salads.)

Secure the kvass jar with a tight-fitting lid. Refrigerate and enjoy within 1 month.

TONICS

When The White Moustache first bottled up our yogurt whey as tonics, I started with the plain, unflavored version. I knew how hydrating and healthful it could be on its own and thought it was so obvious and delicious a drink. I was sure it was going to be a hit with customers as well. How could it not be? It was so clear, so pure.

It totally bombed. No one knew what to do with it! It was too weird, too foreign.

This was an uncomfortable feeling. And it felt like a very personal rejection. As an immigrant who worked really hard to figure out how to make myself palatable to a new/foreign/skeptical audience, I was now in a position to make my precious whey accessible to the American consumer. And it felt messy and clumsy and awkward at first.

"Infused beverages" had started to become quite trendy, so I threw a cinnamon stick in a bottle of whey. I infused red currants. I infused mint. But they were just too subtle, and the whey overpowered them all. As with my own assimilation efforts, I was trying too hard and nothing was working.

So, just as I embraced side ponytails and New Kids on the Block T-shirts in school, I looked to see what other trendy flavors might make my whey work in the American market. Of course, numerous disasters resulted, as they often do when people step too far outside of what feels right. My biggest disaster came when I tried a coffee flavor. This was during the summer, so I thought a yogurt-whey coffee could be a sure thing.

No! It was disgusting. Truly unsalvageable. Like, not even the biggest dose of simple syrup could rescue this combination. I was still trying too hard.

I stopped resisting so much and started embracing what the whey was telling me. I prioritized the whey—not trying to sell it, not trying to bring it to market, not trying to solve the climate crisis or food waste. I took all the pressure off and put the whey first.

Experimenting then became fun. I learned that acidic flavors work really well with the acidic yogurt whey, so I turned to familiar and simple fruit juices. Our first flavored tonic was honey-lime. It was a riff on just regular ol' lemonade. We wanted to go sugar-free, so we used honey. Our second flavor was pineapple. Again, pineapple has a very tangy-sweet flavor, which pairs perfectly with the lemony and creamy backnotes in the whey. Like, PERFECTLY.

We were on a roll! Expanding the identity of the yogurt, through its whey, felt like taking it on a parallel path to the one I myself had taken: My yogurt, which had strict Iranian flavors—date, sour cherry, quince, orange blossom honey—had a very clear and familiar identity, one that was easy for me to present to the world. But the whey, the glorious whey, allowed me to step outside my tradition and experiment with other flavors. I could add any juice that paired well flavor-wise. These were not necessarily Iranian flavors, but no matter, they all worked well with the whey.

And just like that, an entire line of White Moustache drinks was born.

The four tonic recipes that follow are our top-selling whey drinks.

HONEY-LIME PROBIOTIC WHEY TONIC

MAKES 1 QUART

While my true goal is to get everyone to love the taste of plain whey, this super thirst-quenching twist on lemonade is exactly how we like to first introduce whey-based drinks to customers at The White Moustache. It contains no sugar and is best served ice-cold. It also serves as a lovely base for a cocktail—just add tequila!

½ cup mild-flavored honey, such as wildflower

½ cup boiling water

¼ cup fresh lime juice (from about 2 limes)

3 cups yogurt whey

Put the honey in a heatproof measuring cup. Add the boiling water and stir until the honey is completely dissolved. Let cool. Transfer to a lidded jar. The honey syrup will keep in refrigerator for up to 2 months.

In a 2-quart pitcher, combine the lime juice, whey, and ¼ cup of the honey syrup. Chill for at least 1 hour. Stir, adding more honey syrup to taste. Store in the refrigerator for up to 2 weeks.

GINGER PROBIOTIC WHEY TONIC

MAKES 1 QUART

Plan ahead! This tonic needs to steep for 24 hours before serving.

This tonic has been our most successful savory flavor to date. Infuse spicy ginger into fresh whey to produce this refreshing and soothing digestive aid. Sip it on its own or add it to a smoothie for an energizing kick.

Break the ginger apart and rinse well, getting into the nooks and crannies. (This makes peeling unnecessary.) Line a small bowl with a large square of cheesecloth, at least 12 inches square.

Grate the ginger on the large holes of a box grater or in a food processor fitted with the shredding attachment. Transfer to the lined bowl. Tie the cheesecloth securely with a twist-tie or piece of kitchen twine.

Pour the whey into a large pitcher. Add the ginger bundle (and any residual juices) to the pitcher. Cover with a lid or a piece of plastic wrap.

Refrigerate for at least 24 hours. This allows the ginger to steep and maximizes its flavor. Thoroughly wring the ginger bundle over the infusion before discarding, so you capture every bit of its spicy, gingery essence. Stir well before serving. (Sediment settles to the bottom very quickly).

Store leftovers in an airtight container in the refrigerator for up to 1 month; it may take on a slightly pink tinge—a natural reaction between the ginger and acidic whey.

2 ounces fresh ginger

1 quart yogurt whey

SWEET BEET PROBIOTIC WHEY TONIC

MAKES 1 GENEROUS CUP

If you have 1 cup of whey on hand, you have endless options of concocting your own kitchen experiments. This beet tonic is the perfect example of salvaging two byproducts into a delightful drink. At The White Moustache, we make sweet beet preserves to flavor our sweet beet yogurt and combine the residual syrup from the preserves with whey for this happy result.

2 tablespoons reserved syrup from Sweet Beet Preserves (page 199)

1 cup chilled yogurt whey

Stir the beet syrup into the whey. Enjoy immediately, over ice if you like.

PINEAPPLE PROBIOTIC WHEY TONIC

MAKES 1 QUART

Pineapple and whey make fantastic partners. In fact, if you were to ask me which White Moustache whey tonic flavor is my favorite, the answer is easy: pineapple, pineapple, pineapple.

When I first started making this tonic in 2017, I used equal parts pineapple juice and whey. Over the years, I've tipped those proportions more in whey's favor, now using about 35 percent juice to 65 percent whey. Even the smaller proportion of pineapple juice gives this tonic plenty of sweetness and tropical essence. Nothing at all is lost—with more whey, it's just more hydrating and more refreshing.

Combine 2 cups whey and 1½ cups pineapple juice in a pitcher. Taste. You now have 3½ cups total, so you can customize that last ½ cup to your liking. Want it sweeter? Add the remaining ½ cup pineapple juice. Want it less sweet and more refreshing? Add that last ½ cup whey. Or use a bit of each, tasting and adjusting until it reaches your ideal level of flavor and sweetness.

Stir before serving. You can certainly serve it over ice, but I prefer it chilled. Store leftovers in an airtight container in the refrigerator for up to 3 weeks.

2 to 2½ cups yogurt whey

1½ to 2 cups 100 percent pure, no-sugar-added pineapple juice

Wine and Cocktails

This final section of my book, Wines and Cocktails, is appropriately where I find my whey to be the most at home: in a cocktail and made in community. All of the cocktails found here were made in collaboration with bartenders in New York City who were genuinely excited about whey and their creations are inspired! I'm so proud to know them. As soon as I introduced them to whey, they embraced it as a provocative new ingredient. An American Moustache (page 253), Weathered Wheyfarer (page 254), and the Symbolic Gesture (page 261) are just a few of their genius creations. Yes, some of their inventions may require investing in some less familiar bottles. Don't be intimidated! Expand your liquor cabinet slowly—it will be well worth it.

I also include my family's recipe for homemade wine, as it is one that carries many memories for me and I'd like to preserve it. It is very similar to yogurt: a single ingredient transformed over time. May we all be given the time to reach such full potential.

MOONSHINE WINE

"Drink wi he season for wine, roses, and drunken friends.
Be happy for this moment. This moment is your life."
  Omar Khayyam

If you could drink time, this is what it would taste like. The time the grapes grew in the soil, the time it took to press each one between your toes. Your feet, which have been around for so long, a part of your wretched history, now become part of this glorious wine, to be imbibed by your loved ones and become part of their bodies as well.

When red grapes are in season in late summer or early fall, the process begins. This wine does not result in a fine vintage but one that's fun to get drunk on, fun to make by squishing grapes with your feet.

This special recipe follows the thirty-day cycle of the moon, and making it is as lyrical as drinking it. As any lover knows, wanting and waiting make for longing. Every time I make it, I think about the wine every day for a whole month, wondering how it will taste, what it will make me say. It is never the "best" wine I have ever had, but it is always perfect because it is **my** wine, and I love it all the more for that.

Get a whole lot of grapes. Bushels and bushels. You can use any kind of red or black grapes here, but not green ones. And steer clear of seedless varieties as you want as much pulp as possible. This recipe's yield really depends on your patience, the size of your buckets, your feet, and your own endurance. The smallest batch I've ever made used approximately 32 pounds of black grapes. I do not recommend making less than this amount.

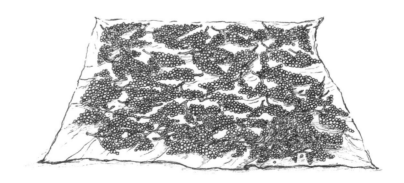

WHAT YOU'LL NEED:

A sheet or large, clean piece of fabric for spreading out your grapes.

A tarp, old plastic tablecloth, or oilcloth to spread on the floor of your work area.

A flat-bottomed plastic or steel tub big enough for you to stand in.
(We have used everything from a 10-gallon Rubbermaid plastic storage bin to a hard plastic kiddie pool.) This is your stomping tub.

A cask in which to ferment your wine. You'll need about 5 gallons of capacity for each bushel (44 to 50 pounds) of grapes. I recommend a
5-gallon plastic bucket with a lid for a small batch.
If you are doing two bushels, you'll need a 10-gallon container, and so on. You want to ferment your batch of wine all in one container.

A fermenting cloth to cover the bucket. An old dish towel or piece of cotton cloth will do.

A straining cloth. Get another old towel, piece of cotton cloth, superfine mesh fabric, or multiple layers of cheesecloth. Straining helps purify your wine when it is ready to drink.

And, of course, grapes. Source your grapes with intention. Know where they come from and trust your purveyor. (In order to preserve the yeasts that naturally collect on their surfaces, you will not wash the grapes, so make sure they've been grown without pesticides.)

Empty glass or plastic bottles with tight-fitting covers to pour your finished wine into.

In a cool, dry place (like a shaded porch or a garage), cover the floor or a large table with the sheet. Spread the grapes on top in a single layer and let stand, uncovered, overnight.

The next morning, spread the tarp on the floor where your stomping grounds will be. Set the stomping tub and your fermenting cask or bucket on the tarp. Dump some of the grapes into the stomping tub. Don't fill the tub more than one-third full. Work in batches and secure a second set of hands (well, feet really) to help. You may feel overambitious and try to stomp on all the grapes at once, but this will create more work in the long run. Pick out any large twigs and discard.

Now, the part you've been waiting for: Kick off your shoes and socks, wash your feet, hop into that tub, and start stomping. Initially it will be fun and unfamiliar and exciting, but it will soon become tedious and you may lose patience. Too bad. Keep going until every little grape is squashed and the tub contains nothing but juice and skins and seeds. I recommend putting the tub next to a counter so you can brace yourself as you dance in the tub à la *I Love Lucy*.

When you can no longer feel grapes popping under your feet, pour everything, including any muck (all the small twigs and smashed grape bits, including skin and pulp and seeds) into the bucket. Keep working in batches, repeating the steps until all your grapes are good and stomped.

Cover the bucket or cask with a towel or cloth and place the lid loosely on top. Store in a dry place at cool room temperature.

CONTINUES 🍸

After 2 or 3 days, remove the cover and get your (clean) hands in there (up to your armpits if you've gone with a cask). Give the grapes a good swirl, say hello to the seeds and the slippery skins, squish the pulp, and remove any larger stems you encounter. Replace the cover. Do this every day. It's important to keep stirring and squishing and jostling because the grape pulp will keep floating to the top, and if it's not stirred back down, it can grow mold.

Within another day or two, the mixture will begin bubbling and foaming and will give off a slightly funky, yeasty smell. You may wonder how this mess will ever turn into drinkable wine. Over the next few weeks, lift that lid every day. You'll be hit with a whiff of something that smells increasingly like . . . alcohol. Seeds and skins will float on the surface. Stir them back down, replace the lid, repeat daily.

Eventually, in 30 to 40 days, there will be fewer and fewer seeds floating on the surface until one day, it will be only a dark, shimmering pool with your own thirsty reflection gazing back at you (in other words, you can see the *moon shine* on the wine's surface). This is your cue that it's time to bottle the fruits of your labor. The grapes you have squished have fermented with the wild yeasts on your hands and feet, marking this particular moment of your life like a time capsule; for a whole month you have been intricately involved in the making of a batch of wine that is uniquely yours, uniquely tied to this moment in time.

To bottle the wine, work over your tarp, or your tablecloth, or any surface you want to be stained forever. (It will be.) Secure a large square of superfine cheesecloth over the lip of a clean bucket. A friend can hold the cheesecloth tight or you can secure it with a rubber band. Carefully strain what is now wine into the bucket. The gunk left in your cloth can actually be used to create distilled liqueur. (It will be strong, *really* strong, though—as in I still see pink elephants every now and again—so it wouldn't be responsible for me to share further details.)

Finally, pour the wine into clean bottles and cap them tightly. In my family, we usually pour the wine into empty 2-liter plastic soda bottles. We have never properly bottled the wine with a cork or anything official and it has always been fine. It's a little bit risky to wait too long to drink it, but we have gone as long as 10 years with a bottle that was shut tight. Regardless of how long you plan to keep your wine, store it in a cool, dark, dry place. When you open a bottle it will skunk easily, so always drink it within 24 hours of opening.

AN AMERICAN MOUSTACHE

MAKES 1 COCKTAIL

Jennifer Anderson, my recipe collaborator on this book, introduced me to Esteban Ordonez, a bar owner and cocktail savant. Born in Colombia to Spanish parents, he emigrated to New York at age ten and spent the summers of his youth helping at his grandfather's bar back in Spain. Always generous and endlessly creative, he agreed to develop this cocktail just for me. (I drove an hour to deliver the whey to him. It was time very well spent.)

This cocktail combines citrus and warm spices, plus a heady combination of orange flower water and almond (thanks to the orgeat syrup). Esteban's homage to these Iranian flavors meld beautifully with the whey

If you don't have a cinnamon stick, skip the garnish. Pre-ground cinnamon is less aromatic and won't give the same results.

11/2 ounces bourbon

1 ounce yogurt whey

3/4 ounce fresh lemon juice

1/2 ounce orgeat syrup, such as BG Reynolds

Cinnamon stick and lemon wheel, for garnish

Combine the bourbon, whey, lemon juice, and orgeat syrup in a cocktail shaker. Fill with ice and shake vigorously. Strain into an ice-filled large rocks glass or a double old-fashioned glass. Garnish with a few grates of cinnamon (use a Microplane), the cinnamon stick, and a lemon wheel.

WEATHERED WHEYFARER

MAKES 1 COCKTAIL

One of my favorite local haunts near The White Moustache factory in Red Hook, Brooklyn, was Fort Defiance, a cozy restaurant and bar that serves as a de facto living room for neighborhood denizens and a friendly destination for New Yorkers from all corners of the city. Fort Defiance's fiercely creative and talented bartenders have made it a haven for cocktail geeks from all over the world. Their weekly Tiki nights, dubbed "The Sunken Harbor Club," are always packed (and for good reason). Bartender Tyler Caffall took on the challenge of bringing the Tiki spirit to our whey and came up with this stellar creation. It calls for a few specialized ingredients admittedly outside the norm for the average home bar, but this drink is so good, it's worth letting your liquor cabinet branch out.

Tyler loves how yogurt whey gives cocktails a subtly tart flavor and silky body. Strega, a saffron-tinted, herbaceous Italian liqueur, gives the cocktail a sturdy, savory-bitter backbone, which offsets the sweetness of some of the other ingredients. The final spritz of absinthe and dusting of cinnamon enhance the aromas, flavoring every sip.

A bit of geek trivia for you: Tyler named this cocktail after a card from the game Magic: The Gathering—a pursuit near and dear to his heart. Know thy neighbor, love thy neighbor.

1½ ounces Denizen
  Aged White Rum

1 ounce yogurt whey

½ ounce Diplomatico Reserva Rum

½ ounce Strega Liqueur

½ ounce Hamilton Pimento Dram

½ ounce orgeat syrup

½ ounce fresh lemon juice

Dash absinthe (optional)

Paper umbrella, mint spring
  or pineapple frond, absinthe
  spray, and grated cinnamon
  stick, for garnish

Pour all the ingredients (except the garnish) into an ice-filled shaker. Shake for 20 seconds. Strain into a Tiki mug heaped with crushed ice.

Tuck a paper umbrella and mint sprig or pineapple frond into the glass. Mist the top with absinthe and grate cinnamon over the top. (A Microplane is ideal.) By dusting the mint and umbrella with absinthe and cinnamon, you'll get a whiff of the flavors with every sip. It's a pleasure for all your senses. Add a long straw and serve immediately.

ANCHORS A-WHEY PUNCH

MAKES 1 COCKTAIL

After a long day (or night) at the yogurt factory, hauling milk crates, scrubbing equipment, and whisking yogurt until we lose all feeling in our arms, a good, stiff drink is mighty welcome. I've found that using whey in cocktails contributes an alluring layer of flavor—a little bit tangy (but not as tart as lemon juice) and a little bit creamy (but not as thick or heavy as cream). Like the Weathered Wheyfarer (page 254), this drink is a shortcut interpretation of a Tiki cocktail. Whey adds one more note of complexity: to the fresh juices, exotic spices, and good rum bona fide Tiki drinks are known for.

1 ounce aged rum (such as Don Q Añejo or Appleton Estate V/X)

1 ounce white rum (such as Don Q Cristal or Cruzan Aged Light Rum)

3 ounces yogurt whey

3½ ounces passion fruit nectar (such as Alain Milliat Traditional Home-Style French Passion Fruit Nectar)

2 dashes aromatic bitters (such as Angostura)

1 lime wedge and a paper umbrella, for garnish

Fill a highball glass with ice. Pour in both rums, then the whey, passion fruit nectar, and bitters. Stir gently. Garnish with the lime and a paper umbrella. Serve.

WHEY DOWN SOUTH OF THE BORDER PINEAPPLE MARGARITAS

MAKES 2 QUARTS

The flavors in the Pineapple Probiotic Whey Tonic (page 247) were so good I boozed them up for this margarita. To get the overall sweetness right, I combined the elements in slightly different proportions, then added a kick of alcohol and a punch of heat. The drink comes together with almost no effort.

Make sure to use 100 percent pure, no-sugar-added pineapple juice. And don't skip the jalapeño. It doesn't just add a pleasant burn; the chile's essence and aroma buoy the whole concoction. (To soften its fire, halve the jalapeño lengthwise and remove the white membranes and seeds.)

NOTE: A batch of margaritas can be prepared a day ahead. If you like things spicy, add the jalapeño in advance, too.

2½ cups pineapple juice

3¾ cups yogurt whey

2 cups silver tequila

1 jalapeño, thinly sliced

Pineapple wedges, for garnish

In a 3-quart pitcher, combine the pineapple juice, whey, and tequila. Top off with ice cubes. If you haven't yet added the jalapeño, do so now. Serve in ice-filled glasses garnished with pineapple wedges.

YOGURT & WHEY

BLOODY MARY, TWO WHEYS

The origin of these drinks is a testament to how the bartending community of New York City has most warmly embraced whey into their culinary traditions. The White Moustache originally developed these whey-filled twists on the classic Bloody Mary for a beverage industry event. Bartenders, chefs, and executives of restaurant groups and social clubs would come to these events to sample new products and decide which ones to serve at their clubs or parties or big catering gigs. It was a party planners' party. The White Moustache was one of the only non-alcohol companies there, and we presented our wholesome whey as the next great mixer. Our whey fit right in and proved extremely versatile in these Bloody Marys and in our pitchers of Whey Down South of the Border Pineapple Margaritas (page 257), both of which we presented that night.

When prepping these cocktails, make the mixes a day ahead so the flavors can mingle. I like setting up a whole Bloody Mary station, with pitchers of the mixes, a bottle of vodka, and a garnish bar so guests can customize their skewers. (Don't skimp on garnishes—they're half the fun!).

If you've made the pickles on page 74, use some of that pickle brine here. Otherwise, open a jar of store-bought pickles and use the brine inside.

PICKLE MARY

MAKES 6 COCKTAILS

PICKLE MARY MIX

3 cups tomato juice

1½ cups yogurt whey

1½ cups pickle brine

2 tablespoons prepared
   horseradish

2 tablespoons hot sauce
   (such as Tabasco)

¾ teaspoon Worcestershire sauce

1 teaspoon freshly cracked
   black pepper

TO FINISH

9 ounces (1 cup plus 2 tablespoons) vodka

Cubes of smoked Gouda and salami, pickle slices or cornichons,
   and pitted olives, for garnish

Combine all the pickle Mary mix ingredients in a pitcher. Adjust the seasonings to taste.

Fill 6 tall glasses with ice. Divide the vodka among the glasses (about 3 tablespoons, or 1½ ounces per glass) and top each with 1 cup pickle Mary mix. Thread the garnishes onto long toothpicks or drink skewers. Prop one on the edge of each glass and serve.

BANGKOK MARY

MAKES 6 COCKTAILS

BANGKOK MARY MIX

4 cups tomato juice

2 cups yogurt whey

1 tablespoon Thai red curry paste

½ cup loosely packed
   fresh cilantro leaves

1 tablespoon fish sauce

¼ cup fresh lime juice

TO FINISH

9 ounces (1 cup plus 2 tablespoons) vodka

Lime wedges, cilantro sprigs, sugar snap peas, and
   ice-cold cooked shrimp (peeled), for garnish

Combine all the Bangkok Mary mix ingredients in a blender. Blend on low speed until the curry paste and cilantro are completely incorporated, about 2 minutes. (You'll still be able to see green flecks of cilantro, which is fine.) Taste for seasoning. Add more curry paste if you like it spicier, more fish sauce if you like it saltier, and more lime juice if you like it tangier. (The Bangkok Mary mix lasts for up to 3 days in an airtight container in the refrigerator if you're making in advance or storing leftovers.)

Fill 6 tall glasses with ice. Divide the vodka among the glasses (about 3 tablespoons or 1½ ounces per glass). Top off with 1 cup Bangkok Mary mix. Thread the garnishes onto long toothpicks or drink skewers. Prop one on the edge of each glass and serve.

THE SYMBOLIC GESTURE

MAKES 1 COCKTAIL

When I first met Doria Paci at the Coachella music festival, I was not yet a yogurt maker and she did not yet own a bar. I totally did not fit in at Coachella, dressed in my pencil skirt and dripping with social anxiety, but little did I know that five years later Doria would text me out of the blue that she had an idea for a new cocktail at the Counting Room in Williamsburg. She ordered some whey, then ordered some more. She kept ordering whey from me all summer, so clearly her customers were developing a taste for it as well. This intensely ginger cocktail is as special as the life circumstances surrounding how I met the bar owner who created it. Life is just funny that whey.

1½ ounces Averell Damson Plum Gin

½ ounce Dorothy Parker Gin

¾ ounce Amontillado sherry

½ ounce yogurt whey

½ ounce fresh lemon juice

¼ ounce ginger syrup

¼ ounce honey

Candied ginger, for garnish

Pour all the ingredients into an ice-filled cocktail shaker. Shake for 20 seconds. Strain into a glass. Garnish with candied ginger.

Acknowledgments & Apologies & Accusations

I'd like to thank God for giving me the strength to write this book. I'd also like to thank God for giving my friends, colleagues, and family the strength to stay with me during the course of writing this book. I have spent much of the last nine years in tears over these pages, in joy and pain over the existential crisis of examining the life that has led me to know all these foods. I could not have gotten through it without all the people listed below. I really wish I had been smart enough to keep a list from the beginning and I deeply apologize to anyone I left out—like I am still deeply sorry I forgot to invite Shirin Farahzadi to my wedding.

Speaking of weddings, Michael, darling, you are the heart in which I have finally found a home, and yet somehow I have nothing nice to say about you in the kitchen.

Jennifer Anderson, you are an indispensable part of this journey and infused these pages with adaptations of whey recipes and a love of Tiki drinks that brought out a lighter side of my work. I have missed your sense of humor in the last leg that I had to do alone. Lauren Tempera Brown, thank you for the inspiration to whey brine the turkey. Christopher Borunda, for the Shankleesh Labneh; Sohrab Irani, for the Kurdish Labneh; Elliot Peters, for the Ajo Blanco. Most other collaborators, I try to name right in the headnote.

Raina Robinson and Gabriella Stern, thank you for recipe testing the entire book at the factory in the early days, when the recipes were on Post-its on a door. Lindsay Silber, Marissa Grimes, and Allison Wightman, thank you for expanding your pantries to test recipes.

Kris Kurek, sharing a kitchen with you warms the cockles of me heart. When you taught me your meringue technique for the lemon meringue pie in this book, I couldn't tell if it was out of love for me or the meringue. You have taught me how to teach.

Niloufar Varahram, Ava Afsahari, Parvin Afshari, Khanoum Doktor Atosa Hormozyari, Vista Kushesh, and Natasha Torki, for being my West coast Zoroastrian support crew: your support and validation have been the most important for me. Siavash

Fooladian, if you are reading this, that means you still haven't tested the recipes you were assigned, and I will never forgive you.

I am so very lucky to cook alongside my parents, Parvin Jangi and Goshtasb Dashtaki. You kept the ways of our elders alive in a foreign land. I cannot remember a single time the kitchen was not full of love, laughter, bickering, and joy.

Nahid Dashtaki, you are the Anna to my Elsa, the Edith to my Lady Mary, the Pinky to my Brain. Thank you for proofreading only three pages in this book, but especially for keeping the factory at The White Moustache running—during a pandemic no less—to let me have so much space to work through the issues this book raised for me. I know you like to keep score: I owe you a few.

To all the customers of The White Moustache, who give us the encouragement and love to keep doing what we are doing, we don't take a single jar for granted.

Jason Hamlin, I got to steal your skills from the universe for a period of time, and you carried me over the finish line and breathed life into my tired soul right at the most important part. Thank you.

To the army of therapists who have gotten me here. Emily Stuart, I love you, even though you didn't let me off easy as this process unearthed me. You made me believe that I wouldn't die if I got the ceviche recipe wrong. Nora Danker, for helping me be a better collaborator when I just wanted to go it solo. Glenn, for you I am perhaps most thankful, and you have probably had it the hardest. My foul-mouthed spiritual and yoga teacher, Veesta Vafadari. And the writings of Sonya Renee Taylor, for creating the loving and freeing world where I could explore that some of the pain I was feeling was centered in white supremacy and my own internalized racism.

Cousin Farahnaz Rad, thank you for sending me the perfect tarreh and herbs for the photo shoot. And while I'm on the topic, I do owe a sincere apology to the FedEx customer service agent who was on the receiving end of my hysteria when we thought the tarreh was lost on the night before the photo shoot. To be fair, your driver was knocking on my door at the very moment you were telling me you had no idea where anything was. But I can see now you may not have intentionally been trying to sabotage me.

Firuzeh and Rostam Dastani, Farshad Rad, Sara and Seena Rad, for coming to the factory to be in the photo shoot. Cooking for you guys for real in our first COVID-era gathering was a comfort. Nicole Fiallo, Drew Kocal, and Tamina Daruvala, you are always game for a party; I love you all.

Sarah Cave and Victoria Granof, you two were part of my vision for this book from the proposal stages. You brought life into these pages and put together a photoshoot in the midst of a pandemic. Victoria, you were always the only one I could trust with cooking this food, with my family, making beauty with our chaos. Sarah Cave, birthday twin, you are extremely talented and super sexy when you are bossy on set. My best decision was to hand over the creative direction of this book to you and the team you inspired.

Chris Simpson, you and your team were so respectful to my vision and my space. Your photos take my breath away. It was the honor of a lifetime to share this space with you.

Keith O'Brien, you have been the most effortless design collaborator from the early days of The White Moustache. Thank you for making the desserts section, in particular, so delicious.

Roksana Pirouzmand, your illustrations were plucked from the same memories as mine in Yazd. I am so very lucky and proud to have your drawings live alongside my words. Your talent is from the heavens.

Betsy Hayley-Hershey, for shelter that made me believe I deserved something nice. To the staff at the Beekman Hotel, for the lovely notes and support as I put the final edits on the book.

Cheryl Sternman Rule, thank you for Lamaze breathing with me chapter by chapter to polish up my writing to the level it needed to be. What a summer to spend together.

Porochista Khakpour, your work has saved my life and my heart and now my book. Your eyes and encouragement on the early manuscript, as I agonized over whether I was exoticizing our culture, gave me the confidence and guidance to continue. I am your biggest fan.

To W. W. Norton, my publisher, I can't believe you let me get away with half the shit you let me get away with. I will forever be grateful for all the boundaries you let me push. Allison Chi, you took every outlandish request we all had and made it a reality. I think about your time and enthusiasm and unbridled talent as I look at every single page. Steve Attardo, for supporting us on art decisions; Lauren Abbate, for keeping us in check; Karen Wise, for copyediting; and Mo Crist, for keeping everything on track.

Jenni-Ferrari Adler, my agent—you are the only one, family and nonfamily—who has been with me on this book from day one. Thank you for always having my back and always telling me the truth very very quickly.

Melanie Tortoroli, when you inherited this book from Maria Guarnascelli I thought I got off easy, but thankfully you turned out to be as ruthless as this book deserved. I wrote this book with you by my side every step of the whey. You gave me grace and kindness over the last seven years as both this book and I morphed dramatically. You pushed me, you made this book special, you opened doors for me, and you let me write the aash-e-maast recipe exactly the way I wanted to. This is as much your book as it is mine. Now that this is all done, I am going to miss you the most.

Index

Photography Key

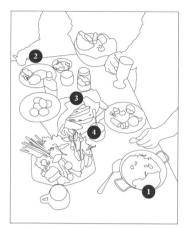

1. Sev (page 168) **2.** Whey-to-Start-the-Weekend Pancakes (page 174) **3.** Sour-Faux No-Knead Bread (page 182) **4.** Quince Preserves (page 195)

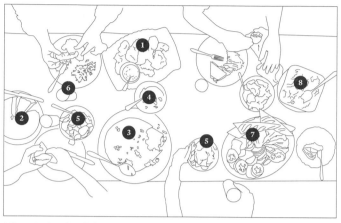

1. Yogurt-Marinated Fried Chicken with Saffron Honey (page 160) **2.** All the Whey Upside-Down Cake (page 222) **3.** Tachin (page 136) **4.** The White Moustache Yogurt (page 47) **5.** Chips and Yogurt (page 91) **6.** Cucumber Sekanjabin Sharbat (page 240) **7.** Fried Tongue Sandwiches with Labneh (page 157) **8.** Spinach Boorani (page 84)

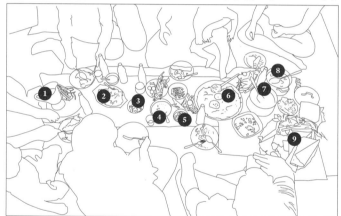

1. Doogh (page 235) **2.** Eggplant and Kashk (page 86) **3.** Torshi Makhloot (page 72) **4.** The White Moustache Yogurt (page 47) **5.** Torshi Sír (page 73) **6.** Persian Rice (page 124) **7.** Fesenjān (page 134) **8.** Ghormeh Sabzi (page 132) **9.** Kabab Koobideh (page 128)

1. Aash-e-Reshteh (page 101) with condiments **2.** Kashk Sauce (page 57) **3.** See-Rogh (page 178)

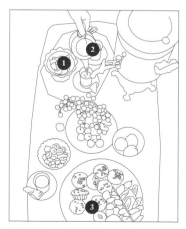

1. Nabaat (page 202) **2.** Tea (page 236) **3.** Cake Yazdi (page 220)

About the Author

Homa Dashtaki was born in Iran, on the eve of the Iranian Revolution, via a police-escorted ambulance after curfew. A practicing Zoroastrian, she immigrated to Orange County, California, in the 1980s and then to New York in the early 2000s. In 2011, Homa started The White Moustache with her father. What started as a quiet bonding activity with her community has turned into an advocacy effort in small food production. She is based in Brooklyn, with a strong connection to Southern California.

Editor: Melanie Tortoroli
Recipes: Homa Dashtaki and Jennifer Anderson
Creative Director: Sarah Cave
Illustrator: Roksana Pirouzmand
Photographer: Chris Simpson
Stylist: Victoria Granof
Designer and Art Director: Allison Chi
Desserts Section Design and Cover: Keith O'Brien

For information about permission to reproduce
selections from this book, write to Permissions,
W. W. Norton & Company, Inc., 500 Fifth Avenue,
New York, NY 10110

For information about special discounts for bulk
purchases, please contact W. W. Norton Special Sales at
specialsales@wwnorton.com or 800-233-4830

Manufacturing by ToppanLeefung
Book design by Allison Chi
Production manager: Lauren Abbate

ISBN 978-0-393-25453-2

W. W. Norton & Company, Inc.
500 Fifth Avenue, New York, N.Y. 10110
www.wwnorton.com

W. W. Norton & Company Ltd.
15 Carlisle Street, London W1D 3BS

1 2 3 4 5 6 7 8 9 0